KU-102-206

Books are to be returned on ~~
~~ date below~~

WITHDRAWN

LIVERPOOL JMU LIBRARY

3 1111 01026 0287

I.M. MARSH LIBRARY LIVERPOOL L17 6BD
TEL. 0151 231 5216/5299

WITHDRAWN

LEARNING TO DESIGN, DESIGNING TO LEARN

LEARNING TO DESIGN, DESIGNING TO LEARN: Using Technology to Transform the Curriculum

Edited by

Diane P. Balestri
Princeton University

Stephen C. Ehrmann
The Annenberg/CPB Project

David L. Ferguson
State University of New York–Stony Brook

Taylor & Francis
Washington • Philadelphia • London

USA	Publishing Office:	Taylor & Francis
		1101 Vermont Avenue, N.W., Suite 200
		Washington, DC 20005-3521
		Tel: (202) 289-2174
		Fax: (202) 289-3665
	Distribution Center:	Taylor & Francis
		1900 Frost Road, Suite 101
		Bristol, PA 19007-1598
		Tel: (215) 785-5800
		Fax: (215) 785-5515
UK		Taylor & Francis Ltd.
		4 John Street
		London WC1N 2ET, UK
		Tel: 071 405 2237
		Fax: 071 831 2035

LEARNING TO DESIGN, DESIGNING TO LEARN:
Using Technology to Transform the Curriculum

Copyright © 1992 by Taylor & Francis. All rights reserved. Printed in the United States of America. Except as permitted under the United States Copyright Act of 1976, no part of this publication may be reproduced or distributed in any form or by any means, or stored in a database or retrieval system, without the prior written permission of the publisher.

1 2 3 4 5 6 7 8 9 0   B R B R   9 8 7 6 5 4 3 2

This book was set in Times Roman by Hemisphere Publishing Corporation. The editors were Marilyn Davidson and Joyce Duncan; the production supervisor was Peggy M. Rote; and the typesetter was Phoebe Carter. Cover design by Michelle Fleitz.
Printing and binding by Braun-Brumfield, Inc.

A CIP catalog record for this book is available from the British Library.

⊗ *The paper in this publication meets the requirements of the ANSI standard Z39.48-1984(Permanence of Paper).*

Library of Congress Cataloging-in-Publication Data

Learning to design, designing to learn: using technology to transform
  the curriculum/edited by Diane P. Balestri, Stephen C. Ehrmann,
  David L. Ferguson.
    p.   cm.
  Includes bibliographical references and index.

    1. Computer-aided design—Study and teaching (Higher)   2. Computer-
assisted instruction.   I. Balestri, Diane Pelkus.   II. Ehrmann,
Stephen C.   III. Ferguson, David L., 1949–
TA174.L43   1992
371.3'34—dc20
                                                                   92-6905
                                                                       CIP

ISBN 0-8448-1706-6

Contents

II

DEVELOPING TOOLS FOR THE NOVICE DESIGNER

Contributors

DIANE P. BALESTRI, Princeton University, Princeton, New Jersey
PHYLLIS BLUMENFELD, University of Michigan, Ann Arbor, Michigan
KATHLEEN BRADE, University of Michigan, Ann Arbor, Michigan
JOHN N. CALLEY, University of Arizona, Fayetteville, Arizona
RAVINDER CHANDHOK, Carnegie-Mellon University, Pittsburgh, Pennsylvania
ANGELO COLLINS, Rutgers University, New Brunswick, New Jersey
STEPHEN C. EHRMANN, The Annenberg/CPB Project, Washington, D.C.
KEN EWING, University of Michigan, Ann Arbor, Michigan
DAVID L. FERGUSON, State University of New York, Stony Brook, New York
MARK GUZDIAL, University of Michigan, Ann Arbor, Michigan
IDIT HAREL, Massachusetts Institute of Technology, Cambridge, Massachussets
PETER B. HENDERSON, State University of New York, Stony Brook, New York
LUKE HOHMANN, University of Michigan, Ann Arbor, Michigan
JOHN R. JUNGK, Beloit College, Beloit, Wisconsin
YASMIN KAFAI, Harvard University, Cambridge, Massachussets
DAVID S. KAUFER, Carnegie-Mellon University, Pittsburgh, Pennsylvania
CAROLYN KIRKPATRICK, York College, City University of New York, New York, New York
KENNETH KOEDINGER, Carnegie-Mellon University, Pittsburgh, Pennsylvania
JAMES H. MORRIS, Carnegie-Mellon University, Pittsburgh, Pennsylvania
CHRISTINE M. NEUWIRTH, Carnegie-Mellon University, Pittsburgh, Pennsylvania
SEYMOUR PAPERT, Massachusetts Institute of Technology, Cambridge, Massachussets
NILS S. PETERSON, From the Heart Software, Monmouth, Oregon
ELLIOT SOLOWAY, University of Michigan, Ann Arbor, Michigan
JIM STEWART, University of Wisconsin, Madison, Wisconsin
MICHAEL J. STREIBEL, University of Wisconsin, Madison, Wisconsin
IRIS TABAK, University of Michigan, Ann Arbor, Michigan

Preface

The advent of relatively affordable computing and telecommunications has made possible a sequence of dramatic changes in colleges and schools:

1. the proliferation of computer labs that, when equipped with appropriate software and peripherals, can serve as design studios for a variety of disciplines, from engineering and English composition to biology and music
2. increased levels of designing by students in all these fields; and therefore
3. some important and long-awaited improvement in the basic shape of education.

We offer this collection of essays because we want to draw attention to the potential role that technology can play in helping schools and colleges transform teaching and learning through design-based curricula. In particular we hope to draw into this conversation many faculty members who already incorporate designing into their courses as well as those who devise the software that might ultimately be used in these new design studios.

BRIEF HISTORY

The observations and recommendations you will find in this book are based in practice rather than in theory. They are rooted in the experiences of a group of innovators, thrown together by circumstance some years ago, who began to recognize that they had much in common. These people were the seventy-plus members of the Fund for the Improvement of Postsecondary Education (FIPSE) Technology Study Group. All were directors of computer-related projects funded by the FIPSE between 1978 and 1988. They came from every kind of postsecondary institution, and represented many different disciplines. Most were faculty members, but others were experts in technology, and some were academic administrators and librarians. Of the editors, Ehrmann was the FIPSE program officer who started the study group in 1984. Balestri and Ferguson were project directors; Balestri was also the group's chair.

The study group had a diverse membership because of the way that FIPSE funds projects. Each year, the fund opens its doors to all comers, asking only that proposals be learner-centered, cost effective, and capable of far-reaching impact in the world of education beyond high school. Of the 2,000 preliminary proposals received each year, only the best 70 or so are ultimately funded. This intense annual competition among innovative ideas becomes, in effect, a way of detecting that year's most widely felt problems and most promising opportunities. The projects carried out by members of the Technology Study Group were representative of the most promising ideas for applying technology to learning during the decade when the personal computer was beginning to influence education.

During the meetings of the Technology Study Group, we began to notice that many of our projects were using software in similar or complementary ways. This realization was a surprise because, on the surface, the projects seemed quite different. Several offered new tools for students learning skills of academic writing. Several others provided simulated laboratory environments in which students could carry out scientific investigations. One helped architectural students as they learned to design energy-conserving buildings. Another devised a notation system that enabled students to learn about the structure of music through exercises in composition.

These projects shared the following: a similar understanding of the pedagogical problems to which they were responding, similar ways of using computers to support learning, and for those that reached implementation, similar achievements and problems when the software was put into use. Briefly stated, we all recognized that computers could be used as tools that students might use to do creative and constructive things, and to learn by so doing. Looking for a common term to describe what many of us were asking our students to do, we began to say that they were "designing." By that term we meant that they were using an iterative process to create complex products in response to somewhat open-ended instructions.

We also had discovered that the introduction of computers into the learning process dramatically changed not only what students were doing, but also the way they interacted with each other and, significantly, with their teachers. Because of these similarities, we found ourselves learning from one another's errors and accomplishments and looking for a larger understanding of what collectively we were beginning to achieve.

We were perhaps a little like the proverbial blind men encountering their first elephant, each touching a different part. The one discovering the trunk thought the elephant to be like a large snake; the one feeling the leg argued that the elephant was like a tree. In our "blindness" (that is, in our previous isolation from one another), we have invented very different pieces of software. But gradually we realized that our different inventions had features that overlapped and dovetailed in ways that suggested a more comprehensive picture of the role that software could play in making designing a central part of the learning experience.

To explore these issues further, we wrote and edited a double issue of the journal *Machine Mediated Learning* (II:1–2), in which we brought descriptions of several projects into one place and began to articulate their common themes. Our ideas gained increased visibility when the Digital Equipment Corporation bought copies for each participant in the 1987 EDUCOM annual conference. In 1990, the journal's publisher, Taylor and Francis, asked us if we would update and expand the work, turning it into a book. And here we are.

The effort has proven to be much more than an updating. Some of the original articles were dropped, and others (from authors not part of the study group) have been added. The remaining articles have been so thoroughly rethought and revised, based on years of intervening work, that they bear only a slight resemblance to their precursors.

Perhaps the most important single discovery of this phase of our effort was the realization that the issues faced by colleges are much the same as those faced by the schools: the potential importance of an expanded role for designing and composing by students, the kind of software that can be most useful for that purpose, and the challenges faced by teachers.

Our volume begins with an essay by Ehrmann and Balestri, who assert that designing by students can play three complementary and powerful roles in the curriculum. Through designing, students 1) develop designing skills for many later uses; 2) learn subject matter (thus, students write poetry in order to understand language, others' poetry, and the human situation); and 3) become engaged in the course as a whole.

With advantages as powerful as these, many teachers have wanted students to do as much designing as possible; however, several difficulties have impeded or blocked designing by students in almost every discipline. In recent years, advances in software and telecommunications have begun to offer capabilities that help faculty members overcome these barriers. This book describes a comprehensive model of the role that technology can play in making designing a more feasible and more powerful component of the curriculum.

The following chapters in this book describe the specific projects of individuals and teams. Taken together, they help to elaborate the elements of this general model.

TRANSFORMING THE CURRICULUM
BY USING PROFESSIONAL TOOLS

Where possible, teachers prefer to give their students the same software that professional designers use, such as word processors for composition, programming languages for computer science and mathematics. But providing professional tools to novices for the complex purposes of learning has its challenges as well as its rewards.

Carolyn Kirkpatrick starts our series of case studies with some sober reflections about her experiences teaching composition when her students first began to use word processors. Of special value are her observations about the collision that developed between her increased emphasis on the sequence and iteration of designing in the classroom and the challenges of assessment—both her own assessment of student work and her institution's standard methods of assessing student writing.

Idit Harel and Seymour Papert draw on the experiences of an urban school in Boston that has made extensive use of the programming language Logo. Their essay evaluates improvements in learning that resulted as fourth-graders used Logo to design instructional mathematics software for third-graders.

DEVELOPING TOOLS FOR THE NOVICE DESIGNER

Some faculty members have preferred the advantages of software specifically developed to help novices design. The development projects that lead to such software can be extensive and subject to much peril and redirection. The next two chapters recount the experiences of two teams that undertook to develop user-friendly tools that bear a resemblance to professional software for designing in different disciplines. The first, by Mark Guzdial, Elliot Soloway, and their colleagues, is entitled "The Future of Computer-Assisted Design: Technological Support for Kids Building Artifacts." In the second, David Kaufer, Christine Neuwirth, Ravinder Chandhok, and James Morris recount the fascinating and unpredictable evolution of a development project for software to improve academic writing.

LEARNING TO THINK LIKE A DESIGNER

Other developers have taken a different tack, creating computer-based environments that give students various kinds of feedback and support for learning how to design. Two chapters describe microworlds that integrate tools and simulations for the novice designer. John Jungck, Nils Peterson, and John Calley offer a laboratory for science experiments called the Genetics Construction Kit. Peter Henderson and David Ferguson have developed an environment in which students learn how to design algorithms for computer programming. The last chapter describes an expert tutor called MENDEL, developed by Michael Streibel and his colleagues to help students learn to use the Genetics Construction Kit effectively.

NEXT STEPS

We hope that faculty members who read this text will gain a richer sense of the learning possibilities that can open up when the curriculum is enriched by technology-supported design activities; we expect that they will also discover some of the obstacles and pitfalls that will come their way as they try to implement this new kind of curriculum. We hope that software developers will see features that they might build into their own software and gain insights into how software might be used.

Beyond these immediate lessons, however, this book should convey two important messages. First, it is worth looking over the high walls of discipline and educational level that ordinarily separate us. There is an extraordinary amount for a college writing teacher to learn from the developer of software for an elementary mathematics class, for instance. And biologists have much to offer computer programmers. It is our loss that we so seldom look for such learning.

Finally, we think these essays convey a promise that education can become what we have always wanted education to be: an activity dominated less by the talking head of the lecturer, and powered more by students able to spend time working on the challenging, creative, complex, reflective activities we have called designing.

1

Learning to Design, Designing to Learn: A More Creative Role for Technology

Stephen C. Ehrmann
The Annenberg/CPB Project, Washington, D.C.

Diane P. Balestri
Princeton University, Princeton, NJ

Abstract Designing in one of its many guises (composing, modeling, researching, etc.) can be found in virtually every discipline. Designing has three kinds of value: (1) educating students for later work as designers, (2) helping students understand the ideas underlying designs and their functioning, and (3) engaging students more fully in all their studies. An environment that can support novices as they design and learn to design requires four elements: an open-ended environment, ample opportunities for practice, channels for communication, and support for developing expertise. Extensive designing by students has been more valued than achieved in most fields, but recently technology has been used to overcome the difficulties and better support teaching in each of these four areas. In the process the door has been opened to a larger, more effective role for designing in the curriculum. Examples of successful implementations suggest new features for software used in the support of designing by novices.

Across the curriculum, in college and in schools, faculty members are asking their students to do more designing:

• A first-year engineering student empties a box of balsa, dowels, and rubber bands and wonders how to create a cart that will automatically follow a "figure-eight" course without veering or breaking down.
• In a music theory class, a student improvises a tune and then transforms it into a chorale, an aria, and a twelve-tone invention.
• A junior in biochemistry devises an experimental lab procedure to purify an enzyme.
• Sophomores in an urban studies course create a video documentary that analyzes the shocks and strains of migration in a nearby neighborhood.
• In an art studio, young art historians practice classical techniques of Renaissance painting.

This chapter is derived from a previous article by these authors (Ehrmann and Balestri, 1987), which in turn owed a great debt to the work and discussions of the Fund for the Improvement of Postsecondary Education (FIPSE) Technology Study Group. Many of the projects cited in the present article were carried out by members of the Study Group, and their ideas have been invaluable in the evolution of our own thinking about the role that technologies can play in enlarging and shaping the role that designing can play in the college and school curriculum.

- Grade-school poets wrestle with their first pieces, reading them to one another and then revising.

In constructing this list, we have purposely aggregated activities that usually have other titles—constructing, modeling, composing, investigating, writing—and called them all *designing*. In our view, designing is both a skill and a learning process, not limited to a few traditional design disciplines (architecture, engineering, etc.) but potentially common to all.

To support designing in the curriculum, faculty members in many different disciplines are turning to applications of technology. We examine a number of those experiments in this chapter. As we shall see, there is no single standard or teaching method for applying technology to the tasks of designing. In fact, there is quite an extraordinary variety of useful ways for technology to support design-based learning. However, we argue that underneath these apparent differences, there are common themes and strategies that seem to be working. We even hope to show how faculty members in different disciplines can enrich their own teaching by adopting ideas and methods that have been successful in other fields (FIPSE Technology Study Group, 1988). As we focus on these common strategies for teaching and learning, we are also suggesting that those who develop technology-based materials for designing face common challenges and possibilities, despite differences in the discipline, educational level, or teaching style for which their materials are intended.

WHAT IS DESIGNING?

To understand the common characteristics of designing across the curriculum, let's look again at the students we have described above. Not one is sitting passively in a chair and absorbing the wisdom of others. Instead, all are using complex and highly personal processes of analysis and synthesis, replete with trial and error, as they work to create a product. They are also attending to such subtle issues as the expectations of their intended audience and an internal sense of satisfaction or closure. They are being challenged to ask thought-provoking questions: "What is my goal?" "Are my ideas and materials the most efficient for the task?" "Is my creation beautiful?" "Does it work?" Because they are novices, these students also need a special kind of guidance that informs them without dictating what they should create.

Designing by these students crosses a spectrum of activities and outcomes. To begin with, the goals or products of these young designers vary considerably. Our engineering student, for example, has been given limited materials and a well-defined set of parameters for her construction: Her product, to be successful, must perform in a determined way. Our students in the writing workshop, on the other hand, may set their own parameters, redrafting their criteria as often as they redraft their products. Their work emphasizes the importance of novelty, optimization, and integrity. These differences in the products or outcomes of designing are not restricted by field: In another assignment, the engineer might design an innovative solution to a problem of her own choosing, and our poets might be required to fit their words into the rhythm and rhyme scheme of a sonnet.

One may observe a similar range in the processes of designers, particularly in the extent of interplay between initial plan and final product. At one end of the spectrum are linear methods of designing that involve careful planning and analysis, strategic drafts prepared for scheduled critiques, and a predetermined deadline. These organized designing styles are particularly suited to well-specified or large products, to projects in which the resources are preset, and to projects being designed by a team. Our sophomores may have delegated aspects of their video project in a similar manner. At the other end of the spectrum are design processes that barely seem to qualify as "processes" at all: They stress improvisation, with much recursion and revision of the initial plan and minimal "look-ahead" at each stage of synthesis. These apparently more serendipitous designing styles usually work best when the product, time frame, and resources are not strictly defined in advance of the designing work. Such, for instance, might be the experience of the music student who explores aspects of theory by improvising variations on an original theme. However, we stress that designing usually includes elements of planning and experimentation, patient analysis, and fortuitous synthesis.

To summarize, designing is:

- *constructive*, that is, aimed at producing a material product that meets some set of more or less defined specifications;
- *creative*, that is, requiring a novel response to an open-ended problem or situation;
- *sustained, sequential, and recursive*, including a healthy proportion of discovery by trial and error; and
- *subject to analysis* from several important perspectives, including feasibility, aesthetics, and economics.

THREE ARGUMENTS
FOR GIVING DESIGNING A MAJOR ROLE
IN THE CURRICULUM

There are at least three reasons why faculty members make a commitment to designing in preprofessional, professional, and general curricula.

(1) Through designing, students acquire skills they can use to design things later in work and in life. They develop mastery of tools and processes, for instance, laboratory procedures for chemists, writing strategies for lawyers and journalists, and construction principles for civil engineers. Designing skills are not only of value to preprofessional and professional students. When students learn writing, artistic, and other designing skills in general education courses, they are developing habits and practices for use in later life. We call this educational goal *learning to design*.

(2) Designing helps students understand ideas and the world. Students in a literature class may write their own poetry to gain a concrete understanding of language and expression. When the same students read their poems to an audience, their understanding of human nature may also be enriched through the ensuing critiques and conversations. We call this educational goal *designing to learn*.

(3) Faculty members ask students to design because designing energizes them and engages them more fully in the other elements of the course. This energy comes from at least two sources: the empowerment that students can feel when

they create something personal and meaningful, and the pleasures of working on a team. We refer to this goal as *engagement*.

With so many of the national reports of the 1980s focused on engagement, active learning, and hands-on inquiry, one would expect to see many opportunities for designing in colleges and schools today. It is unfortunate that designing plays much less of a role in the curriculum than faculty members might desire as the ideal. There are some long-standing reasons for this gap, which we enumerate below. We also suggest that here is an educational problem that technology is particularly well-suited to help us solve. In the remainder of this chapter, we recommend four steps that faculty members can take to increase the role of designing in the curriculum:

(1) Describe the physical teaching facilities and curricula that best support novice designer-learners in their fields;
(2) Identify the barriers that have prevented the creation of such design-oriented facilities and curricula;
(3) Capitalize on specific capabilities of technology to ameliorate some of those problems and thus enlarge the role of designing in the curriculum; and
(4) Recognize and tackle problems that result when the role of designing is enlarged.

A TEACHING ENVIRONMENT THAT SUPPORTS THE NOVICE DESIGNER-LEARNER

First, let's consider the general conditions that optimize designing in the curriculum, without any particular attention to technology. Whatever the faculty member's goals for a particular course—learning to design, designing to learn, or engagement—novice designers require teaching and learning arrangements that incorporate four elements:

(1) An open-ended design studio in which students can frame and work on meaningful design problems;
(2) A pedagogy that demands and supports plenty of practice;
(3) A means for students to communicate with others about their designs and designing process; and
(4) Strategies to help them master the recognized skills and values of designing in the discipline without forcing mechanical imitation.

An Open-ended Design Studio

Most students are not accustomed to open-ended learning environments. Their learning activities are usually quite focused and bounded, mapped out by syllabi, chapter headings, learning objectives, lectures, drills, problem sets, and examinations. In contrast, courses that incorporate designing cannot be so well-bounded because the designers must have the freedom to make choices among realistic options. Thus, designing requires both physical and curricular spaces that pose a series of invitations or challenges to students and then offer the means for them to respond to those possibilities in creative and therefore unpredictable ways.

Across the disciplines, the physical spaces used for designing have many names: laboratory, studio, library, theater, or "the field." The space might be nothing more than a blank page, a pen, and a table; it might be the "virtual" space of a computer environment. We have chosen the term *design studio* to refer to any or all of these spaces. A good design studio is equipped with appropriate tools: sketch pads and pencils, workbenches and mallets, lab tables and test tubes, or reference catalogs and writing implements. It also contains a vast array of raw materials (far greater than students can imagine using at first): texts, paints, chemicals, wires, or software libraries. A designer's materials often include archives and mental images as well: prototypes and classic examples, past designs the student has collected and critiqued, diaries, journals, or notebooks.

This resource-rich environment is truly open-ended only if students are given the freedom to explore it. Its potential is wasted if the curriculum brought to it is fixed and every assignment has a uniform and predetermined answer. Thus, we must expand our concept of a design studio to include the curriculum as well as the space. Here and later in this chapter, when we say that "the design studio supports . . . [a learning activity]," we mean not only that the physical capabilities for doing that activity are available but also that the curriculum encourages students' designing. In both of these senses, the design studio must support open-ended assignments. For beginners, the faculty member may pose a specific problem for which there are many appropriate solutions. Later assignments may require students to identify a problem as well as to develop one or more designs for solving it.

Practice, Practice, Practice

Learning to design requires continual practice. The design studio we have just described as a space and a curriculum must therefore meet several conditions not required of a traditional classroom. The design studio must be highly accessible and offer ample time for practice in both class and homework sessions and across the term. The time consumed by practice will often reduce the time available for traditional instruction (lectures and textbook readings, for instance, that cover a large number of small topics). If the practice is to be productive, the design studio should also foster experimentation—trial, error, and fresh trial without substantial penalty. If the studio is to encourage the unexpected and the original, the experimenting novice must not be unduly inhibited by restrictions based on cost or time.

What do we intend students to *do* when they are practicing in the design studio? Most students assume they know what *practice* means. Their childhood hours on the athletic field or at the piano were filled with repetitive drills that disciplined muscle and mind to perform in predictable ways. Thus, for them, practice implies routine and monotony, even boredom. Although it is true that novice designers must often solidify their basic skills through repetition, practice in designing also takes many other forms. Students may doodle, brainstorm, sketch, or scribble freely. These unstructured, largely nonrepetitive experiments may lead rapidly to a single plan or, more likely, they may suggest multiple alternatives to be explored. Students also practice by examining a canonical problem or a partial solution from several different perspectives or by representing a problem in several different ways: in words, numbers, pictures, or graphs. As they practice, students can also learn to keep and analyze records of their work. Perhaps most important, practice should imply that the student will "do it again, thoughtfully"—go back to a draft, think it through again, and revise it (FIPSE Technology Study Group, 1988).

Opportunities for Interaction with Others

Although it is possible to design in isolation, most designers interact with many others: partners, contractors, producers, manufacturers, clients, audiences, critics, judges, interpreters, and consumers. As important as this interaction is for the professional, it is even more important for the novice.

. A curriculum rich in designing should create opportunities for student designers to learn both from expert designers and from peers. Advice or hints offered when the process of designing is not yielding results can provide a fresh perspective and a new start. Feedback on early drafts or partial solutions can offer an important mid-course corrective. This feedback should include review both from an expert's perspective and from the intended audience for the finished design. Too often, however, the product of students' work is never tested on anyone other than the faculty member. Creating situations in which students' designs can actually be tested with a legitimate audience (other students may be the appropriate audience) can also increase students' motivation to design products that work.

Advice and criticism are only two forms of help interaction. A third is collaboration with other student designers on a joint piece of work. As they decide how to proceed with a complex project and specify the elements of the completed product together, students become more conscious of what they are learning and of what tactics will and will not work. From such interactions, they may discover their own strengths and limitations as designers. Along the way, students are also learning the interpersonal skills of working on a team.

Learning to Design like Experts

Practice, even coupled with helpful interactions and feedback, is not enough to turn a novice into an skilled designer. Past designers have accumulated substantial knowledge through trial and error, talent, and research, and no novice, no matter how talented, can recreate the rich cognitive framework of the field simply by a few successful exercises in designing. Therefore, along with practice and interaction, the design studio should introduce students to the vocabulary, conventions, methods, classic designs, and typical pitfalls of a field. Especially when they are learning to design, students need to develop a critical understanding of this heritage. Some expert knowledge can be conveyed through lectures, textbooks, and other readings, research, examples, and demonstrations. Nevertheless, other expertise must be somehow acquired in direct conjunction with practice.

The most difficult decision in creating the curriculum for a design studio is how to help students internalize relevant expertise: by assignments in imitation of exemplary designs of the past? by lecture and reading? by design critiques from practitioners? Where in the process of designing is the expertise of other designers most likely to be understood and used by the novice? Is expert designing even an appropriate model? Some research in expert behavior suggests that an expert model is extremely cumbersome to import wholesale into an environment for student designing and may, in fact, not be particularly relevant to novices' behavior (see Chapter 5).

Certain strategies can be practical and helpful, however. For example, by following an established design process (perhaps simplified for the novice designer), students can test the value of a traditional approach in their own designing. The design studio should make available examples of complete designs that have successfully solved problems similar to those that students are tackling, so that students can practice adapting elements of those solutions and ideas into their own designs. A design curriculum can also offer students the knowledge of experts through tutorial materials that focus on particular stages or problems in the design process.

BARRIERS TO A LARGER ROLE
FOR DESIGNING

Readers with experience in helping students design may now be objecting, "It's not that easy." They are quite correct. Designing as a strategy for teaching and learning is challenging to implement, even in disciplines such as engineering, composition, and the fine arts, in which laboratories and design projects are standard features of the curriculum. Designing has been even more difficult to incorporate into curricula in which learning has been based on texts and lectures.

The barriers to designing can be expressed as three complaints:

(1) "Extensive designing by students requires more resources and more time than we are willing to commit."
(2) "Faculty members and students are not prepared to work effectively in a design studio."
(3) "Designing skills can neither be taught nor assessed."

Scarce Resources and Time

The tools and resources required for designing are often costly and scarce. In institutions where these tools and resources are available, they may be reserved for graduate students and faculty members. In some fields, furthermore, the tools and resources for designers are either too difficult or too dangerous for novice designers to use at all.

Designing is also time-consuming. This fact can be disconcerting and disruptive for both teacher and student. Faculty members who try to incorporate significant designing for their students quickly realize that other elements of their curriculum may have to be unexpectedly curtailed or abandoned as design problems multiply. Students may need to first develop rudimentary, and then more complex, skills with their tools, for instance. Once having climbed that learning curve, students will discover that they need quite a lot of free time for practice—probably more time than they previously spent gathering and memorizing information from textbooks. The need for time quickly conflicts with limits imposed by the nature of the design tools or materials. If equipment is expensive or scarce, undergraduate use of it may be limited to a few hours per semester, not enough time for practice, exploration, and real learning. Sometimes the design problem simply turns out to be unexpectedly rewarding, and the faculty member may have to decide whether to cut other activities to accommodate it.

The need for frequent interaction in the design studio is time-consuming as well. In many departments, faculty may lack the time to observe, coach, and assess their students as they work through a series of drafts and problems. This lack of time may stem from the demands of heavy teaching loads or of professional research. In addition, in many educational institutions faculty members' and students' available time may not coincide. The course period is short, and in the evenings or on weekends when the student is designing, neither the teacher nor the student may be at the educational institution. These same barriers of distance and scheduling also make it difficult for students to design and learn in teams.

Unprepared Faculty Members and Students

Traditionally, a novice learned design skills as an apprentice to a master teacher or craftsman. This one-on-one interaction provided the apprentice with both models of expert practice and continual criticism of his or her work.

Such a model requires that the teacher be a master designer. However, in the modern lecture-based classroom the teacher is almost never perceived by students as a practitioner. Moreover, as the realms of knowledge expand, it is increasingly likely that faculty members will, in fact, lack designing experience with at least some of the problems students could tackle in a design studio. Academics tend to value knowledge that is explicit, replicable, and publishable. A significant fraction of design knowledge fails to meet those criteria, and so in some fields designers are not sought out for faculty appointment. In many fields, especially in the schools, there is such a great disparity between salaries paid to expert designers and those paid to educators that only a few institutions are able to attract any practicing designers at all.

Even faculty members who are expert designers may have to adjust traditional teaching strategies and syllabi to accommodate more extensive designing by students. They must assess the relative value of coverage against the opportunity to increase their students' depth of designing skill—a difficult call to make. They must learn to encourage students' experimentation and withhold early judgment of student errors. They may find themselves taking new responsibility for creating and even maintaining the physical environment in which their students are designing. They must manage both individualized and collaborative learning situations in which they exert very little control over the short-term outcomes. In short, they will have to devise new ways of recreating the productive relationship between master and apprentices.

From the students' perspective, the open-ended nature of designing can be particularly intimidating or even incomprehensible if they have been accustomed to a traditional curriculum weighted toward analysis and right answers. In designing, the starting places are usually vague and the goals may not be evident. Although some students are stimulated by the challenge of more independent learning, others are bewildered by the many choices they must face when they are asked to design. Not all students are psychologically ready to make an intellectual commitment to one line of work when other legitimate paths are also possible (Perry, 1981).

Can Designing Be Taught or Assessed?

The complex nature of expertise in designing makes it difficult for faculty members to teach designing as either a skill or a learning strategy. The knowledge and skill of an experienced designer cannot be simply articulated as a set of rules or as an explicit, universal "theory of design." In fact, as Polanyi (1967) argued, a good deal of that knowledge and skill cannot be put into words at all. Expert designers appear to synthesize the following:

(1) Explicit knowledge of tools, materials, and phenomena derived from generations of research or criticism;

(2) Empirical knowledge drawn from their own and others' successes and failures (Petroski, 1985); and

(3) A personal, tacit knowledge (sometimes called intuition or judgment) that enables experienced designers to identify patterns and create strategies without being able to say exactly how they do it.

Answers to questions such as: "How did he write that symphony?" or "Why did she make the bridge look that way?" cannot be fully communicated in lectures. It is this disorderly, often tacit, character of design knowledge that makes it so difficult to convey as a body of expertise, and that makes teaching a balancing act, constantly skirting the dangers of saying too much and saying too little.

To complicate matters further, student achievement in a design-based course cannot be measured by the number of right and wrong answers. In fact, the usual student question, "What will be on the test?" becomes largely irrelevant. Assessment of students' design work involves making complex judgments, and assigning grades becomes problematic for several reasons:

• It can be difficult for a faculty member to observe, assess, and provide helpful feedback to students on a regular basis when most of their work for the term is continually "in process"—both as an emerging expertise (which is itself a very complex kind of knowledge) and as emerging products in many intermediate stages.

• Assessment becomes harder when the process of designing enters into the calculation of the final grade in a course (see Chapter 2). Should a poor second draft be penalized, when the fifth draft is superb? when most students did only two drafts? when the student had conferences with the faculty member after two of the drafts? If the poor initial draft lowers the final grade (or the faculty member's help fails to raise it), what will be students' future willingness to make mistakes and expose them?

• When students work in teams, the faculty member will have to devise an equitable scheme for assessing both the collaborative achievement and the individual contributions.

USING TECHNOLOGY
TO TRANSFORM THE ROLE OF DESIGNING
IN THE CURRICULUM

To increase and enrich designing in the curriculum, therefore, we must find ways to create design studios for many disciplines that meet our criteria for open-ended environments and at the same time help institutions and faculty members lower the other barriers to effective designing that we have identified.

We believe that technology can help significantly in both of these areas. In the following sections we ask: How well does an electronic studio implement the model for designing we have outlined above? Can it provide the necessary tools and resources, the opportunities for extensive practice, ready communication with others, and access to expertise? We draw on examples of current projects and implementations in a number of different disciplines to illustrate our view that the idea of an electronic design studio is generalizable to many fields. Furthermore, we ask: How effectively can this electronic design studio help to solve other problems related to increasing designing in the curriculum?

We are directing what follows both to faculty members teaching today and to developers of the software that design studios will use tomorrow. We are aware that software in one field (e.g., music) may offer a particular feature that software in other disciplines (architecture or chemical engineering) may not yet offer. This gap may be frustrating for the teacher, but we hope it poses a useful challenge to developers of future software for novice designers in those other disciplines.

The Electronic Design Studio

The computer and its peripherals bring several distinctive strengths to the creation of more fertile studio environments, including tools for designing, enhanced ability to analyze and test designs quickly, and flexibility.

Tools for Designing

The design tools in an electronic studio may be identical to the computer-based tools that professionals in a given field use for designing (e.g., CAD packages), or they may be reduced versions that are safer, simpler for a novice to use, or less expensive and therefore more accessible. Some composition classes may use full-featured word-processing packages, for instance, whereas others may ease the students' learning burden by starting with simpler and less expensive word-processing programs. Bank Street Writer has been frequently used by schools for this purpose. Parallel versions of tools for professionals and novices exist in fields as different as music composition and molecular modeling.

Analysis of Problems and Designs

The electronic design studio also provides tools for analysis of problems and draft designs. For instance, a program for composing in French, called "Systeme D' ", offers in addition to a simple word processor, a host of reference data bases for the novice (Noblitt, Sola, and Pet, 1990). In computer science, Elliot Soloway's analytic tools for computer programming help students to decompose their draft programs (Guzdial and Soloway, 1992). For students of architecture, G. Z. Brown's "Energy Scheming" (1987) is a computer-aided design program equipped with tools for quick analysis of draft designs of buildings, including the ability to gauge the amount of energy lost through windows of a given size.

One of the most potent analytic tools for a design is the ability to create alternate visual representations of a design's structure. Word processors, for example, make it easy to display compositions as outlines or, in some cases, as tree structures, sequences of title sentences, and other reduced forms that enable the designer to detect and revise the structure of an essay or report. In a similar manner, some music programs permit several visual representations of the same composition (Balzano, 1987).

Simulations for Testing Designs

Designs must also be tested: Do they accomplish their purpose? In some fields, such as creative writing, the drafts are themselves evolving versions of the final product. However, in other fields, such as music and engineering, draft designs are usually models created in a symbolic medium (notes or lines on paper). Novices in these fields have often found it impossible to imagine exactly how their designs would function. Today, music editors play back sounds as they are entered in notation, which enables composers to hear their designs as they progress. In a similar manner, some CAD programs permit the designer to visualize the simulated motion of a machine that, as yet, has no physical existence.

In many fields, software developers have created *microworlds*, integrated, computer-based environments that support open-ended design activities in a particular discipline. Microworlds combine materials (frequently simulated versions of materials) with tools for planning, drafting, analyzing, and testing many designs. For example, James Hoburg of Carnegie-Mellon University has designed software that enables students to create simulated electrical devices such as phonograph needles and electric blankets; students then observe on the computer screen a simulation of the normally invisible electromagnetic fields generated by their designs (Hoburg, 1987). Students designing in this microworld are both learning to design and designing to learn: They practice creating more efficient needles and blankets. They can also discover qualities of electromagnetic fields by creating and modifying them through their designs. John Jungck and John Calley have built a Genetics Construction Kit (see Chapter 6) that provides students with a simulated laboratory for breeding and crossbreeding generation after generation of fruit flies. Here too, students are learning to design experiments while inducing principles of classical genetics.

Practice, Practice, Practice

The electronic design studio offers many features that enable students to practice and develop their design skills efficiently and effectively. For the most part, drill-and-practice software does not support this kind of learning very well because it tends to constrain students' choices and emphasizes right answers. Practice in designing requires an environment that supports trial-and-error and unforeseen conclusions. In contrast with the drill-and-practice model, the electronic design studio supports practice by extending students' options and transforming practice into an exercise in progression and innovation.

The Importance of Power

The powerful tools available in the electronic design studio promote extensive practice of the kind we envision. Traditional versions of tools for designing, such as a hand calculator or a drafting table, may allow novices only one or two attempts at a design for each assignment; more may simply be too time-consuming. In contrast, the electronic studio offers tools to manage or eliminate tedious tasks that in the past have distracted attention from the central object of an assignment. Students can perform extensive calculations very quickly, for instance, and easily recopy an entire design to experiment with a single modification.

This ease should not be considered a luxury. When the mechanics of calculating, synthesizing, or reorganizing design elements are complex, difficult, or time-consuming, they can overwhelm the novice designer and put a premium on finding an adequate solution at the first attempt. On the other hand, when students are able to see the preliminary results of their work quickly and are able to modify it simply and often, they are more likely to persist in their efforts.

By using computer-based tools to create and critique many versions of a single design, the novice designer focuses on the significant educational aspects of designing: the iterative process of play and discovery, of decomposing and structuring, of revising and refining. As we have argued elsewhere (FIPSE Technology Study Group, 1988), this ability to "do it again, thoughtfully" is one of the most important contributions of computing to the curriculum because so much important learning stems from rethinking one's initial trials and ideas.

Doodles

Professionals in some fields were originally drawn to computer-based tools for applying an elegant finish to their products: perfectly straight lines and perfectly formatted texts. But equally useful are tools that help designers to practice the earliest phases of developing a design idea: to play, to improvise, and to create doodles that can then be progressively organized, analyzed, and refined.

Software for writing offers an especially wide range of such tools, including "prewriting" packages that aid improvising by encouraging the student writer to brainstorm by jotting notes in sidebars, outlines, diagrams, or tree structures that branch from left to right rather than from top to bottom (Joyce, 1988). Visual thinkers may use their word processor or drawing package to create tables or sketches to help them play with inchoate new ideas that do not yet fit the discipline of an outline.

Several music composition programs take the idea of an outliner a step further by providing the student with a way of playing directly with musical patterns and developing them into larger and more complex structures. Sometimes the manipulation is done with a keyboard, sometimes with classical notation, and sometimes with new notational schemes that permit the student to focus more closely on particular aspects of the music than standard notation permits. For example Gerald Balzano's program "Streaming" (1987) includes notations that enable students to improvise by modifying and combining pitch, timbre, volume, and rhythm patterns. Some of these programs for doodling keep a record of the designer's process, records that can be reactivated and modified at any time.

A third example, drawn from architecture, shows how appropriate software can enable the designer to move smoothly from doodling into analysis of the emergent design. Brown and Novitski's program "Energy Scheming" offers a paint facility that allows the student to create free-form sketches and scrawls. Later, the student can apply software-based tools of mathematical analysis to the sketches that will estimate the potential energy efficiency of the design. For example, the student might scrawl a picture of a house and then easily calculate the heat transfer through the windows as they were roughly sketched (Brown and Novitski, 1987). This ability to test even a preliminary plan against specifications could be implemented in other fields in which sketching and analysis play interactive roles in the designing process.

Alternate Representations and Visualization

Sometimes we understand a problem or see a better solution only when we gain a completely new perspective on it. Software developers in many fields have been experimenting with ways to provide designers with several views of a design and its performance. Often these alternate views are vivid visualizations of what might otherwise be an abstract verbal or numerical representation. Commercial spreadsheets turn tables of data into charts and graphs and so help the person interpreting the data to see what is more and less significant. In a similar manner, computer software can represent musical scores with traditional notation and sound, as we noted above, but also with symbols that describe pitch, timbre, and volume. Software for writing computer programs can draw pictures that represent the unfolding consequences of implementing an algorithm as the algorithm is being coded (see Chapter 7). These views help the designer to uncover weaknesses in the design (or to perceive hidden strengths) earlier in the process and also promote frequent revision.

The appropriate kind of representation can help the novice designer differentiate among the hierarchical levels of his or her design. For writing, outliners now available with many commercial word-processing programs can hide or reveal levels of detail, making it easier for writers to focus on the overall structure of a piece or on the relationships between major and subordinated topics. The Isolated Heart Laboratory (Peterson and Campbell, 1985) enables the novice designer of simulated physiological experiments to shift the view from a model of the whole cardiopulmonary system to a display of its most minute operations (e.g., simulation of blood movement through capillaries). By allowing students to move hierarchically and to change parameters at different levels, Peterson and Campbell's simulation offers deeper insight into the often nonintuitive relationship between behavior at the macro and micro levels, and a deeper understanding of ideas of hierarchy and system dynamics. Design tools in other disciplines could offer similar hierarchical shifts in perspective on a complex design.

Opportunities for Interaction with Others

Learning to design is partly a social process. Novices learn in important ways through their interaction with mentors and peers. Although some faculty still fear that computers isolate students from one another, in fact the electronic design studio usually seems to do the opposite—fostering richer interaction with the faculty members and other students. Hardware and software help to accomplish this task by enabling new forms of conversation and communication.

Red Ink and Beyond: New Possibilities for Annotation

Written comments on finished projects are the most common way in which students interact with instructors about their work. Whether a hastily scrawled grade or a sea of thoughtful but demoralizing red ink, such comments judge but rarely improve the students' work. Nevertheless, written comments are often potentially valuable for the designer, particularly when they point to places in a draft that need revision.

Developers of software for composition instruction have been particularly interested in the problem of how to link comments to specific points in a draft text without distorting or obscuring the whole (Davis, Kaplan, and Martin, 1989). Some annotation programs enable comments to be hidden and selectively revealed or incorporated into the draft; others provide electronic versions of the margin for linked comments (see Chapter 5). Developers of commercial word processors have also introduced a variety of modes for rendering comments alternately invisible and visible, and for integrating into the authoritative version of a text those suggestions that have been accepted by the author. When annotated documents of this sort are available over a network, the comments can become an ongoing asynchronous conversation between the author and the reader or critic—a strategy particularly suited to promoting the design process.

The problem of unobtrusive annotation is not limited to writing. Brown and Novitski's program "Energy Scheming" offers an electronic version of one classic medium of architectural communication: tracing paper. It is common practice for critics of an architectural drawing to cover the original drawing with tracing paper, on which they place their comments and alternatives. Each new set of proposed additions appears on a different sheet of paper. Brown and Novitski offer the critic (or the designer) electronic overlays that can be flipped in and out. Some commercial drawing packages today enable a designer to create a drawing in several layers and then to hide or display those layers. When the layers are displayed, they appear as part of the drawing; the designer can also copy all or part of the overlay elements and paste them into the original design.

Recording the Process of Designing

A faculty member may find it useful to see not only the student's draft designs but also a reconstruction of the process by which they were created. For composition, some developers have created keystroke recording systems so that the author and others can observe a text in creation. The data from these systems can be complex, however, and have been more often used for research purposes than for instruction. More commonly available and more useful is commercial software that compares two successive drafts and creates a "redline" copy showing the net changes made between the two. Novice designers in other fields might also profit from this ability to document changes in a draft after the fact; it would help both the collaborator and the critic to see and understand the changes the designer has been making.

Communication across Gaps of Space and Time

Face-to-face exchanges between student and critic are not always easy to arrange, even on residential campuses; such conversations are often next to impossible when students are part-time and commuting. The electronic design studio can help solve this problem by supporting two-way communication that bridges gaps of space and time among the student, collaborators, and critics. Electronic mail and file transfer can provide a good way for students to share work and ideas with one another and with their teachers. Such asynchronous conversations are convenient when schedules do not dovetail, and they can be surprisingly fast-paced as deadlines approach. They also provide a record of the conversations, which students can refer to later. Finally, many faculty members have observed that students can be more thoughtful in the exchange when they have minutes or hours to consider their reply rather than only a second or two, as in a classroom (Ehrmann, 1990).

As students are busy at work, there are moments when instantaneous conversation is advantageous to help solve a particular problem. Several programs make it possible for two callers to talk on one phone line while seeing and manipulating one another's screen displays at the same time. Their shared visual space, similar to the "tracing paper" in the Brown and Novitski architectural software described above, provides a substantial aid to collaborative work.

Learning to Design like Experts

As we have argued, it is not always easy to incorporate *expertise* in designing into the curriculum. The student using only the software capabilities described above would have only limited ways of learning how past masters perceived, created, and analyzed; however, the electronic design studio can also include some software and curricular materials developed to help the student acquire expertise.

"Friendly" Microworlds and Tool Boxes

Novices lack the trained perception to see the forest amid the trees. Thus, some software can help develop expertise incrementally by first reducing the cognitive complexity of a design task to more manageable proportions. For example, the microworlds for engineers and biologists described above provide students with a simpler, simulated designing environment that shapes their assignments around skills and concepts they are prepared to learn. This kind of software can also hide levels of difficulty or power that can be accessed later as students mature through practice.

The tools of designing may also be simplified for the novice. The word processor used to write this chapter has a feature called *short menus* that eliminates many of the options that might otherwise confuse a novice. In computer science, Henderson and Ferguson use a simplified, English-like version of a professional programming language in their software for learning to design algorithms. This "pseudocode" makes it easier for the novice to focus on strategic issues—on the process of developing the ideas that will shape the computer program—rather than becoming preoccupied with the complexities of a new language (Chapter 2).

A Library of Plans for Improvisation

The challenge of helping novice designers think more strategically, "from the top down" as experts often do, has been met in other ways, too. Elliot Soloway's software for teaching programming offers the novice programmer a library of plans that are short, functional segments of computer programs that students can adapt and incorporate into their own work. Such segments may include functions that might be too difficult for novices to program efficiently or that require a distracting amount of detailed work. Students focus instead on developing overall plans and choosing the right functions to implement them (see Chapter 4). As students mature and create more plans of their own, their work can be added to the library, which then contains an increasingly rich and diverse set of plans on which they can draw. Some music synthesizers similarly enable users to borrow from and add to a library of elementary musical structures.

On-line Tutorials, Drills, and Hypermedia Resources. Expert assistance can go beyond providing collections of sample designs and structure for the design process. Many pieces of instructional software also consist of or include tutorials to which students can refer when they get stuck or want to go further on their own than the class has traveled.

A particularly impressive example of this sort may be found in the Comprehensive United Learning Environment (CUPLE), currently being developed by faculty around the country under the aegis of the American Association of Physics Teachers (Wilson and Redish, 1992). CUPLE offers an extensive set of tools for creating simulated experiments in physics and comparing the results with input from actual laboratory versions of the same experiments. It also includes a hypermedia resource of instructional and reference material that incorporates text, dynamic graphics, and videodisc images. In the midst of an experiment, students can immediately review old ideas or learn needed new material.

The Promise of Expert Tutors. Novice designers working on open-ended assignments require individual attention as they pursue unique problems at different work paces and with different styles of attack. As the class proceeds, it becomes increasingly difficult for faculty members to provide either timely didactic instruction or coaching for every student. Because of this diversity, there has long been interest in using computer-based expert systems to provide individualized tutoring. However, real progress in creating expert tutors has been slow, relative to early predictions. The more complex the expertise, the more difficult it is to represent that knowledge adequately in a system that is, by nature, rule-based. For supporting open-ended and partially intuitive processes such as designing, expert tutors may never play more than a limited role.

The expert model has even been brought into question as a model for novices, with some evidence that experts may perceive and design in ways qualitatively different from those possible for novices. Working in the relatively unstructured field of writing, for instance, Kaufer and his colleagues have all but abandoned the effort to create design tools that are explicitly based on an expert model (Chapter 5). The promise of expert tutors is greater in disciplines in which the design tasks are relatively well-structured. Streibel and his colleagues, for instance, have built a tutor for students learning to design research projects in Mendelian genetics (see Chapter 8).

THE THREE BARRIERS, RECONSIDERED

At the beginning of this chapter we established four criteria for a studio that supports significant designing in the curriculum: (1) an open-ended environment, (2) ample opportunities for practice, (3) channels for communication, and (4) support for developing expertise. We have shown how an electronic design studio that incorporates a variety of information technologies can strengthen the teaching and learning of design in many disciplines. However, we had previously cited three complaints that represent barriers to extensive designing by students: scarce resources, unprepared faculty and students, and the nature of designing, which does not lend itself to efficient teaching or assessment. To what extent are these barriers overcome with the introduction of technology-based strategies?

Scarce Resources

"Extensive designing by students requires more resources and more time than we are willing to commit."

As we have seen, the electronic design studio is particularly good at providing tools and resources that support extensive practice. The electronic design studio can also make tools more accessible to students by providing them at convenient times and places. But it is not a complete or simple solution to the problems of time and resources. For instance, whereas the design studio can usually decrease the time it takes for a student to create a particular draft or design, it does not change the fact that courses that emphasize designing will generally have less time available for covering content.

Furthermore, relative to more didactic courses, courses involving extensive designing will almost always be more expensive. Relative to design courses that do not use electronic technology, however, the use of information technology does not necessarily either increase or decrease costs. For example, computer-based simulations may be considerably less expensive than the real-world tools they simulate. Even more important, a single computer lab, stocked with a variety of software, may serve as a design studio for a variety of different courses in different disciplines.

Nevertheless, in many institutions, computers and telecommunications linkages are themselves still a relatively scarce resource for student use, as is the technological support for maintaining them, improving their software, and helping faculty members and students to use them. For this reason, and also for pedagogical reasons related to a particular course or discipline, faculty members will still need to make careful decisions about how and when to incorporate an electronic design studio into the syllabus of a course. We have mentioned the role that simulations play in the electronic design studio, for instance. But simulations are always simplifications of the real world and, in that sense, are always distortions. Students at some point will need to develop an appreciation of the distinction between simulations and the messiness of reality. Faculty members will then have to choose a simulation that offers the best learning options for students and know when to assign a different kind of hands-on experience—a wet lab or field work, for instance.

Another question these faculty members will face is when to use professional design software and when to use instructional software designed specifically for use by novice designers.

Professional design tools have many advantages for instruction, aside from their power. Students see the relevance of such tools to their work after graduation. Faculty members, confident that this software (or something very similar) will be available for several years to come, can take the time to integrate it into their curricula. Distributors, hoping to accustom future users to their products, are increasingly offering affordable versions of their professional software for educational use. However, a commercial design tool is not always suitable or sufficient for students. It may have more features than novices need, for example, so it may be intimidating or simply too time-consuming to learn. Second, relative to instructional design tools, commercial tools are less likely to provide the support functions that are important for novices. Other pieces of software providing instructional functions may not be easy to integrate into the environment that runs the commercial product. Third, despite discounts, commercial software for designing is likely to be expensive.

In contrast, instructional software is designed with specific teaching functions in mind. It may fill just a few functions or, occasionally, it may provide and integrate many of the functions outlined in this chapter. Instructional software can be more affordable than professional tools, particularly if distributed through non-profit channels.

However, instructional software presents its own problems. If the instructional software only serves one or two functions, then several purchases may be required and students will have to be trained in the use of each piece. Second, instructional software may lack flexibility, having been tailored to suit only one style of instruction or one style of learning. Finally, because it usually has a much smaller and less lucrative market than professional tools and has been subjected to less testing, instructional software, may have more bugs, or be less robust, less transportable, and shorter-lived than professional software.

These difficulties have been severe and, as a result, most programs use commercial software where they can and instructional software where they must.

Unprepared Faculty and Students

"Faculty members and students are not prepared to work effectively in a design studio."

The addition of designing to a course will always reorganize the interactions between faculty and their students. The electronic design studio supports those new interactions by providing methods of communication that are supportive and non-threatening. The open-ended environment can be provocative for faculty members and students alike, an occasion for inspiration and the bending of the imagination to new learning.

Nevertheless, faculty members and students are too often inadequately prepared for design work. Nothing in the technology alters the initial responsibility of the institution to provide appropriately qualified faculty and a curriculum that engages its students. Even qualified faculty will need to rethink their roles as teachers in and out of the classroom. For example, in choosing to place their students in an environment as challenging in so many ways as the electronic design studio, they have committed themselves to becoming much more attentive to what their students are doing on a day-to-day basis. As a faculty member we know once put it, "I feel as though I'm now responsible for organizing their beer-time."

Happily, however, students who design are more likely to educate the faculty members than are students sitting in a lecture hall and taking notes. Faculty can learn from student errors as well as student achievements, and, if the studio allows students to undertake projects in areas thus far unfamiliar to the faculty member, that can be a learning experience for all.

Teaching and Assessment

"Designing skills can neither be taught nor assessed."

Although the electronic design studio does not, and cannot, reduce designing to an exact science, we have shown how such studios can help create the conditions in which students can acquire appropriate, personal expertise as designers. We have also shown how, in a variety of ways, the electronic design studio enriches and enlarges the dimensions of assessment: through feedback from simulated designs, through new ways to annotate student work, and through communications channels that enable interaction between students and distant critics.

Table 1

Pedagogical model	Software that offers/supports:
(1) Novices need an open-ended environment for problem-framing and designing.	(a) tools for designing (b) tools for analysis (c) simulations for testing designs
(2) Novices need to practice by creating and editing many drafts and many designs.	(d) ability to create and edit designs quickly and easily (e) feeding doodling easily into designing (f) alternative representations of the problem, the design, and the design's functioning, especially visually and at different hierarchical levels
(3) Students need to work with design partners, coach-critics, and the people grading the work.	(g) comments linked to features of the design without obscuring the design (h) ability to re-create the process by which the design was created (i) ability to communicate with coach-critics and designing partners across time and space
(4) Students need to learn from experts.	(j) microworlds and flexible designs that help students learn to see what matters (k) access to expert plans that the novice can adapt (l) On-line tutorials (m) On-line coaching provided by expert systems

SUMMARY

Designing varies, not only by field but by task. As we have argued, however, there are important common features in the kinds of instructional environments that faculty in virtually every discipline seem to want, and there are parallel roles that technology can play in creating such an environment in each discipline (Table 1).

We draw three conclusions from this inquiry:

(1) Designing will widen its role more quickly and efficiently if faculty members (and developers of instructional software) compare practices across disciplines. They will discover stimulating and suggestive parallels in their work. In the process, they will also discover ways to bridge gaps and overcome difficulties.

(2) The result of this kind of comparison, and of the fuller use of technology to support designing, ought to be a curriculum that can more successfully reach the three instructional goals we have associated with student designing: learning to design, designing to learn, and student engagement.

(3) Such a result can be attained if institutions seek to reduce three barriers to successful education in designing by meeting the following goals: investing resources intelligently, providing appropriately prepared faculty and students, and fostering skills and values that cannot be developed by reliance on lectures and multiple-choice tests.

REFERENCES

Balzano, Gerald, "Restructuring the curriculum for design: Music, mathematics and psychology," *Machine-Mediated Learning*, 2(1–2):83–109, 1987.

Brown, G. Z., and Barbara-Jo Novitski, "Combining the technical and artistic: A software model for teaching about energy conservation in the architectural design process," *Machine-Mediated Learning*, 2(1–2):161–172, 1987.

Davis, Stuart, Nancy Kaplan, and Joseph Martin, *How to do things with prose*, New York: McGraw-Hill, 1989.

Ehrmann, Stephen C., "Reaching students, reaching resources: Using technologies to open the college," *Academic Computing*, 4(7):10–14, 32–34, 1990.

Ehrmann, Stephen C., and Diane Balestri, "Learning to design, designing to learn: A more creative role for technology," *Machine-Mediated Learning*, 2(1–2):9–33, 1987.

FIPSE Technology Study Group, *Ivory towers, silicon basements: Learner-centered computing in postsecondary education*, McKinney, TX: Academic Computing, 1988.

Hoburg, James, "Personal computer based education tools for visualization of applied electroquasistatic and magnetoquasistatic phenomena," *Journal of Electrostatics*, 19:165–169, 1987.

Joyce, Michael, "Siren shapes: Exploratory and constructive hypertext," *Academic Computing* 3(4):10–14, 37–42, 1988.

Noblitt, James, D. F. Sola, and W. J. A. Pet, *Systeme-D: Writing Assistant for French*, Boston, MA: Heinle & Heinle, 1990.

Perry, William, "Cognitive and ethical growth: The making of meaning," in Arthur Chickering et al. (eds.), *The Modern American College*, San Francisco: Jossey-Bass, 1981.

Peterson, Nils S., and Kenneth B. Campbell, "Teaching cardiovascular integrations with computer laboratories," *The Physiologist*, 28:159–169, 1985.

Petroski, Henry, *To engineer is human: The role of failure in successful design*, New York: St. Martin's Press, 1985.

Polanyi, Michael, *The tacit dimension*, Garden City, NY: Doubleday, 1967.

Schön, Donald A., *The reflective practitioner: How professionals think in action*, New York: Basic Books, 1983.

Simon, Herbert A., *The sciences of the artificial* (2d ed., rev. and enl.), Cambridge, MA: MIT Press, 1981.

Wilson, Jack M., and Edward F. Redish, The Comprehensive Unified Physics Learning Environment, Part I: Background and System Operations, *Computers and Physics*, 6(2), March–April, 1992.

I

TRANSFORMING
THE CURRICULUM
BY USING
PROFESSIONAL TOOLS

2

Computer-Mediated Writing Instruction: Reflections on Early Experiences

Carolyn Kirkpatrick
Department of English
York College/City University of New York

Abstract *This chapter builds on an earlier report on the first semesters in which word processing was used to implement* process pedagogy *in a developmental writing course. Students found the new technology congenial and instructors achieved their goal of integrating multiple-stage assignments into their classes. At the same time, instructors found that managing computer technology was difficult, and the computer's impact on instruction was more unsettling than expected: Word processing encouraged student collaboration. It also created a chaotic class atmosphere, forced more individualized instruction, and compelled instructors to reexamine basic assumptions about grading, assessment, and even the nature of writing competency. From the vantage point of six years of experience, confirmed by the reports of other investigators, the author concludes that the computer acts as a catalyst, impelling changes in the entire instructional system that are pedagogically wholesome but taxing for the instruction. Moreover, there is, as yet, limited institutional support for such changes, which are nevertheless irreversible.*

In 1985, a colleague and I undertook an investigation of the uses of word processing for instruction in our developmental writing classes. This chapter grows out of an earlier report on the first three semesters of using word processing extensively with basic writing students. In embarking on this experiment we had asked, "Will the students be able to handle word processing? Will it improve their writing?" It had not occurred to us to ask, "How will this new technology affect *us*?" Our earlier report was ambivalent. Students loved the computer, and we had no wish to abandon our experiment; however, adopting computer technology was changing our teaching in ways we had not expected. When we started this project, my colleague and I thought of word processing as an interesting new tool as a means of reaching our instructional goals, ends that we believed we understood reasonably well. However, the use of word processing altered almost immediately—and uncomfortably—our perceptions of the ends themselves: our view of our subject matter, our methods of teaching it, and our ways of evaluating what was learned.

The earlier report of work pursued in collaboration with my colleague Mary Epes appeared in a special issue of *Machine-Mediated Learning*, 2(1–2):35–45, 1987. Our experimentation had been supported by a Title III grant that encouraged faculty exploration of computer applications (U.S. Department of Education, Title III Grant #G008202239, 1982–88, York College/CUNY, Dr. Che-Tsao Huang, Director). This expanded essay has profited from the critical reading of Syva Meyers and Cornelia Kittler Reid.

Continued work with word processing since then (and the corroborative experience of other investigators) has only strengthened our earlier conclusions. Surprisingly few problems arise in orienting students to the computer and getting them to use it as a writing tool; however, the computer has acted as an unexpectedly powerful catalyst on instruction itself. The results are more far-reaching and exciting than we had anticipated, but they also exacted a greater toll on the teacher and have altered conventional patterns of instruction in ways that are highly desirable, yet difficult to assimilate and support.

INITIAL EXPERIENCES OF IMPLEMENTATION

My colleague and I had used word processing for several years for our own professional activities. We were not software developers or even "computer people" on our campus, but we were interested in pedagogical innovation, having long been advocates and authors of self-teaching methods and materials. When our college began a Title III project focused on instructional applications of computer technology, we asked to participate to explore the use of word processing at the basic writing level. In our setting, a small four-year college within the City University of New York (CUNY) system, most basic writing students are minority-group members, many of them new immigrants from varied language backgrounds and many of them older than traditional college age. Most have had little practice in expressing their ideas on paper and they control written English with difficulty, committing errors in nearly every sentence.

Of course, we had expected that adopting a new technology for instruction would present practical problems, and we tried to prepare ourselves by attending conference sessions and workshops and talking with people who were already using computers to teach writing. In 1985, articles about using the computer in composition were beginning to appear in the professional journals, but little had been written with direct reference to basic writing; we learned most from the ground-breaking work of our CUNY colleagues at LaGuardia Community College (reported in Arkin and Gallagher, 1984).[1] Guided by their good advice, we were careful both in our choice of a word-processing program and in our instruction to keep the focus on writing, not the technology of word processing itself.

As it turned out, getting students started was not difficult; they were able to learn the basics of the program and of computer and printer operation within two to three hours.[2] Virtually without exception (and regardless of their attitudes toward writing), students have been delighted to acquire this new skill. They throw themselves into mastery of the computer with absorption and commitment. Probably fewer of our students can type than would be the case for traditional college freshmen; yet lack of typing ability is not a problem. It is the students who type *least* well who have the most to gain from using word processing, and they recognize the advantages at once.

What basic writers gain when they write on the computer is, immediately and obviously, a large leap in legibility and control over format. The first person to benefit is the writer, who can see much more clearly what he or she has written. In my first semester working with word processing, I thought I saw a "miracle effect" on correctness. Certain errors, notably those of punctuation and capitalization, proved to be artifacts of handwriting, and disappeared. The miracle has turned out to be more limited than I had hoped; nevertheless, handwritten papers always improve when they are entered into the word processor. Students have told us that they can see their errors more easily, both on screen and in print, and this seems to be true (though the number of serious mistakes that survive in version after version of hard copy is still startling).

Orienting students to the computer was not a problem, but nothing we had heard or read suggested how difficult it is to conduct classes in a computer lab. Small technical problems are common in a room full of machines being used by students unfamiliar with the system's crotchets: Files get lost, printers won't print (or print incorrectly), and inexplicable error messages appear on the screen. The effect of these interruptions, frustrating enough for an individual user, is amplified in group work. Of course, the lab staff has been helpful and solves most problems quickly, but the sense of conducting class at the edge of a precipice has remained a constant.

We had underestimated the practical problems posed by this new technology; we had not even thought about the difficulties of learning to work with the human dimension. Contrary to a fear sometimes voiced, using computers does not isolate user and machine, at least not in the setting of a computer lab. For students, that is good, encouraging collaboration in ways that have often been described.[3] For the teacher, the lack of privacy in the computer lab can be a trial. In our lab setting, we often teach under the eye of casual observers and have had to learn not to mind. There was an early phase when the lab staff tried to fill empty stations with drop-in users, in the interest of using resources efficiently. Even with a screen dividing the room, this practice was impossibly distracting and was quickly abandoned. But it is inevitable that lab time must be scheduled and computer resources allocated in advance; an idea for one's class that formerly could be carried out on the spur of the moment now requires planning and coordination. Thus we have found ourselves involved in new interactions with colleagues and support staff— negotiations that have taken a toll on our energies.

More disconcerting is that teacher–student interactions changed in the lab. Sitting at an active computer, it turned out, is not at all like sitting at a desk; the machines are enormously seductive of students' attention, so much so that it is nearly impossible to get students to focus on anything else. The effect I am describing is a strong one, now often reported in the literature with references to "an improved classroom culture" or students' "new independence" (the phrases are from Hawisher, 1988, but the observations are ubiquitous). Computers foster small-group collaboration (read: compelling side conversations about work in progress) and intense focus on the task at hand (read: unwillingness to stop for group instruction—or even for instructions).

The chaotic lab atmosphere worried us at first; we finally accepted and worked around it. We now seldom try to use the computer lab as a classroom but rather schedule some hours in a conventional classroom and others in the lab, using the class hours for group instruction and the lab hours for workshop-style activities comprising about one-third of the course. In these workshop sessions, the dynamic quality of the computer (apparently not an effect of novelty) continues to intensify individual involvement with work in progress but, at the same time, actively prevents whole-group activities.

A networked lab will soon be part of our local resources and may provide a way to channel this dynamic engagement into group activities, though some observers warn that the energy may be dammed, not channelled (e.g., Moran, 1990). No doubt these matters need more exploration. In any case, the tendency of the computer to subvert and supplant conventional patterns of classroom interaction is a common discovery, and one that can be difficult for the teacher to cope with.

To sum up the immediate, practical experiences of implementation, we found that adopting the computer subjects teachers, especially those with limited technical expertise, to a great deal of frustration. In addition, the computer lab is a social setting that carries frustrations of its own. Especially unsettling is the tendency of the computer to disrupt conventional patterns of classroom interaction. Nevertheless, word processing is, even in its simplest applications, a powerful tool for developmental writing students—one that they can use easily and find highly congenial.

THE WORD PROCESSOR
AND THE PROCESS APPROACH

In the past two decades there has been a major change in the teaching of writing, away from the traditional assign-and-grade cycle, which focused on written products, to what is called the *process approach*—a change in thinking and practice so substantial that it is often referred to as a *paradigm shift* (Hairston, 1982; Young, 1978). The process movement in teaching writing has been allied with the growth of writing programs in colleges across the country and the development of composition as an area of academic interest. Attention to process was sparked by observational studies of the activities that writers engage in as they work. Emig (1971) was the pioneer for this kind of investigation; Perl (1979) is perhaps the best known of researchers who have focused on college students at the basic writing level. Following the findings of these investigators, writing theorists and teachers (the line is often impossible to draw) have transformed discussions of writing instruction at every educational level, calling for a pedagogy that actively guides students through the stages of producing a piece of writing.

My colleague and I were excited by this new way of viewing writing instruction and were convinced that it was sound, but we had found it difficult to apply to teaching our basic writing students: hence, our experiment with using the computer to implement "process." What we meant was not complicated nor deeply theoretical. We simply hoped that working with word processing would help our basic writing students to do the things we had, with little success, been exhorting them to do: to spend time on prewriting activities, then draft an essay, receive responses to that draft, revise for content, and, finally, to edit systematically for correctness.

Some may question whether I am discussing here the effect of the computer or the effect of process pedagogy. I cannot make the distinction. Before using word processing, I would have said that, in some serious sense, basic writers could not revise. Whenever we had assigned revision of a paper, students would copy it over with minimal changes. They felt that papers were better because they were neater; their *ideas*, once committed to paper, were fixed, almost never reordered or elaborated.

As is widely recognized (and has been widely discussed), the word processor is most essentially a tool for revision. Our experience confirmed its value. With this new tool, students have been able to revise and improve the organization and development of their writing. In fact, they have tended to catch on quickly.

The word processor assists revision directly. Basic writers typically produce short, skimpy essays stated in generalizations. On the word processor, the inherent structure of such undeveloped writings can be highlighted by moving the cursor to the appropriate places and inserting paragraph breaks. (These are often breaks between single sentences.) Students can then expand and develop their ideas into fuller paragraphs, inserting details, explanations, and examples. Students with the opposite difficulty, who write entirely in specifics, can be coached to formulate and then insert the organizing statements that a reader expects at key points. In our basic writing courses, we teach students only the essentials of entering, saving, editing, and printing text. However, increasingly, some students come to us already adept at word processing, and the capacities of the word processor can be exploited further with them (as for students in more advanced courses) as options for revision are tried, printed out, and compared. For example, using the block move function, a student can compare alternative organizational strategies for a comparison essay to see which is more effective.

The success of students' revisions exceeded our expectations. Of course, the ability to revise does not arise spontaneously. Teachers must redesign their approach to assignments, and that was (as I have noted) the focus of work with my colleague. We devised multiple-stage writing assignments, building in *revision for content and organization* and *editing for correctness* as steps to be carried out in the writing of any paper. Each paper was handed in at least three times, and at different stages we gave different feedback. For example, at the draft stage we refrained from comment on anything but ideas and organization, to force attention to these.

Our report of success may be questioned in view of early formal investigations that produced the disappointing finding that use of word processing resulted in revisions in surface features such as spelling and word choice, not in ordering or development of content.[4] To one who works with basic writers, the explanation for those results seems obvious: The word processor does help students revise, but writers can make only those changes that they are aware are needed. One can scarcely expect the word processor to supply reader awareness—that is the business of instruction and practice. When this awareness is cultivated, however, the word processor makes it possible to act on it. And that is what is new.

Increasingly, researchers in computers and writing have reached the same conclusion, that the effect of word processing on writing quality can be assessed only in relation to the crucial role of instruction.[5] Nevertheless, others have found, as we did, that it offers surprisingly great benefits for students at the basic writing level (Hawisher, 1986, 1988). If pressed to offer a technical explanation, I would speculate that using the word processor overcomes basic writers' weakness in encoding skills and thus liberates their attention for developing and ordering their ideas. In any case, with advice and feedback on the successive drafts that the word processor makes possible, students have been able to revise and develop the content of their writing—sometimes very impressively.

THE SURPRISES

When it came to students' relationship with this new technology, the surprises attendant on the adoption of word processing were happy ones. However, with them came unforeseen consequences for instruction.

To start with the one we first encountered: You may have noticed my reference above to successive drafts, in the plural. We had begun our work with the idea that each paper would be submitted three times, as a draft, then as a revised paper (with focus at these two stages on developing ideas and revising for content), and only then as a final copy (with focus on editing for correctness). I soon found myself encouraging students to write Draft B and Draft C, and even Drafts D and E, if necessary. It became impossible to enforce deadlines that the entire class met with regularity. If the word processor makes it possible to keep revising, then the teacher in me wants to urge a student to keep at it until the writing is "done," has reached a satisfying shape. But who decides when a paper is finished, and on the basis of what criteria? The decision demands negotiation between teacher and student. Without its having been our intention, instruction has become substantially individualized since we adopted word processing.

Actually, we were pleased that use of the computer promoted individualized as well as process-centered instruction, but such instruction can only be labor-intensive for the teacher. I did not mind reading and rereading students' essays; it was enjoyable to see how they developed from one version to the next. However, it was and is hard to keep up with the constant flow of writings; I did and do mind the increased burden of record keeping that became necessary to keep students on track. (Remember that these are underprepared students, many of whom have trouble completing assignments and meeting deadlines, even when they are uniform for the whole group.)

Another difficulty cut deeper: the unanticipated problems for evaluation that arose with our adoption of word processing. By this I do not mean the kind of comparison-group evaluation that might seek to answer the question "Can students write better on the word processor?" I consider such questions wrong-headed, or at least premature, because students are writing in such a different way that the variables cannot be isolated. What I mean is that I myself could not evaluate this new kind of writing.

We had imagined that, in the interest of drawing conclusions about the success of our experiment, we would keep students' assignments the same as they had been in previous classes that did not use the computer. This proved impossible. Computer-mediated papers took more time to accomplish and became lengthier than conventional papers written by basic writers, and students wrote fewer of them. To complicate the matter, although the number of formal papers has decreased, the amount of written work performed has *increased*, as we have come to assign a variety of response writings, letters, and short writing-to-learn activities. (The focus of this chapter does not permit elaboration, but the incremental approach to writing I am describing here not only promotes the production of more unshaped writing as raw material for formal papers, but has also raised our awareness of the instructional value of *writings* as distinct from fully organized papers.)

To my mind, students indisputably do write better papers by using word processing. Their essays are longer and, after revising, are more detailed, logically developed, and interesting. As noted above, some students write dramatically more correctly on the word processor. More usually, the teacher has the disorienting experience of seeing a paper riddled with errors—all in neat print—at the draft stage. Even so, as the paper goes through successive processes of revision and editing, the errors are corrected. Any paper that goes through multiple drafts and critiques is likely to become a good paper. The question is, what grade should the student get, and at what point, and judged by what standards?

At the end or my first semester of using word processing, I discovered that I was giving every student who passed at least a B. Students either did not finish the course or they had completed several successful essays. However, as a colleague was quick to point out the following semester, my grades did not predict what a student would be able to do in her class, no longer using the word processor and faced with more difficult writing tasks. I was forced to reflect on how much coaching that student had received along the way, from me and often from fellow students as well.

Increased collaboration has been, as noted, a spontaneous outgrowth of work on the computer, one that we have abetted wherever possible. Because the teacher is constantly busy in the lab, students turn to one another for help; at first, for help in operating the system, but then, scarcely noticing the difference, for help with work in progress. There is a public quality to writing displayed on the screen that, rather than making the writer feel exposed (as I have heard colleagues worry that it might), does the reverse and invites writers to talk about their work objectively. Others have noted this effect: "Writing displayed on a monitor is more public and creates a new social context and therefore a different classroom environment" (Gay, 1991; see also Kantrov, 1991).

I agreed with my critical colleague that a grade ought to reflect what a student can accomplish independently, especially the grade in a developmental course, where one's primary concern is to cultivate basic competencies. On the other hand, I valued this increased collaboration, and I have found that the coaching and demonstration urged by the literature of process—even outright modeling of various strategies, such as transitions, on a particular essay—is especially helpful to students.

To recapitulate: We had seen in the word processor a tool to shape instruction, not just a writing instrument. Nevertheless, we were surprised that the effects were so powerful and so unsettling. The writing process was facilitated, but it also *changed*, and instruction changed with it. Work became more collaborative for many; it became more individualized for all. Although the new methods of instruction we were devising imposed new burdens, the process of discovery was exhilarating. That exhilaration was offset in turn by erosion of confidence in the validity of our assessment of students' work and uncertainty about the place of our course in the larger instructional system. In particular, our accustomed ways of grading, based on the formal written product, no longer seemed appropriate.

A NEW VIEW OF WRITING PROCESSES

Paradoxically, one reason why we suddenly had less confidence about grading was that we had begun to know much more about each student's writing abilities and performance. A powerful quality of word processing (and, as Ehrmann and Balestri suggest in the previous chapter, a defining quality of designing) is the ability to repeat with controlled variations. One can ask students to revise their work by making changes in one dimension at a time. This selective focus enhances students' chances of success by raising to awareness what was not apparent to them before. It also enables the teacher to see more precisely what students understand (or control) and what they do not.

For example, after students have revised and edited their papers to what they consider a final version, I mark their writing for errors—just mark it, without correcting or identifying exactly what is wrong. The students' last task is to edit their essays one more time, analyzing and correcting the errors to produce a polished final copy. The mistakes they make in translating a marked essay into a corrected copy are fascinating to observe, especially for what they reveal about student writers' tenuous relationship to their own meaning. It is not uncommon for students to give up immediately on a sentence marked only for mispunctuation and toss the whole idea out. Alternatively, they may take an error completely out of context, changing, for example, *the childs behavior* (marked for its lack of the possessive apostrophe) to *the children behavior*, even though the writer himself plainly knows that he intended *child* to be singular. I had always been aware that students had difficulty deciphering their instructors' comments and corrections. I had not been forced to realize how great the difficulty is, and for how many.

Similarly, in matters of content development, comparing performances on successive drafts has revealed that students vary widely in their ability to rethink their own work, to profit from editorial suggestions, to turn messy ideas into organized papers, or to develop and elaborate their generalizations. These are now revealed as distinct and isolatable skills, formerly only dimly visible, not called upon (because students generally wrote one-time-only efforts), or confounded with one another in my mind.

Confronted by the discovery that writing is not a unitary ability, how shall we teach it? How do different skills interact in the process of writing? In what order? Which ought to be most highly valued or rewarded? In the word processor we possess the lens by which we can begin to explore. Just as introduction of the microscope and telescope revealed worlds formerly invisible, so comparison of computer writing to handwriting on a variety of tasks, and comparison of computer-mediated writing from one version to another, promise continuing insights.

A NEW VIEW OF ASSESSMENT

In this course, besides the papers I have described, written on the word processor, students also write by hand a number of impromptu in-class assignments to prepare them for CUNY's university-wide Writing Assessment Test, an essay on a set topic, written within 50 minutes and judged holistically. Those who fail this assessment test typically do so because of problems with correctness; and in my college, if students do not pass the test, they cannot pass the course. We had naively hoped, in the early days of our experiment, that students' gains with the word processor would translate back into their handwritten work. However, very soon it became apparent that they would not.

When my colleague and I began our experiment, I was a proponent of CUNY's essay assessment. It has substantial virtues; not least is keeping both students and teachers aware that the goal of writing instruction (however process-oriented) is a written product, one that will be judged by well agreed-on standards. Certainly writing quickly, sensibly, and correctly is not too much to require of a college graduate. Furthermore, CUNY's essay test is as reliable as can reasonably be expected; I have confidence in the consistency of our scoring. However, I have been forced by my work with word processing to realize that such a test does not measure what I, at least, had been assuming it did measure: some general level of writing development.

I now face the problem of students whose written work for class is satisfactory or better, but who cannot pass this examination or who pass with an atypically weak performance. Working with the word processor, basic writers can edit for correctness to an acceptable level if they are taught to approach the task systematically. This ability does not mean that they can write correctly under pressure. Even worse is the effect of a timed test on content development: It flattens out students' performance and can even favor weaker students over stronger. Those with skimpy ideas express them more readily and in conventional structures. Risk takers and serious thinkers are penalized.

Evaluation remains a problem, with respect to both the course grade and the university's assessment test. I now question the validity of the test we administer, or at least its use as an exit instrument. Instruction and assessment of progress should be intimately connected. If we are to adopt process-oriented instruction, we must find process-oriented means of evaluation.

Within my own courses, I have found a partial solution in portfolio evaluation at the end of the term. The portfolio contains a variety of written work, including letters of self-assessment and previous drafts of formal essays, as well as the final copy. My expectations have become higher for essays written and revised on the word processor. I am increasingly alert to what a student adds to my own suggestions and I try to reward independent solutions.

Nevertheless, to pass the course, students must pass the assessment test, and each semester a few otherwise capable students do not. Even in the case of those who do pass, I must keep reminding myself not to take the often disappointing results on the timed test too seriously. Recent discussions of portfolio evaluation suggest that such a multiple-sample procedure may also answer the difficulties I have raised here about outside assessment, though I suspect that the approach will remain too cumbersome and expensive to be feasible for large-scale testing.

REFLECTIONS ON COSTS

When I wrote my earlier account, I was not sure how much to credit the positive surprises my colleague and I had experienced. Since then, there has emerged a wealth of similar natural-history observations of computer experimentation; these reports affirm (with surprising consistency) the computer's power to effect increased interaction in the classroom, promote a more intense engagement with learning, and support new styles of assignment. The phrases "new classroom environment" and "committed learning" begin to seem very familiar, even as we struggle to define them. Increasingly, the reports, like the chapters in this collection, bear witness to the computer's peculiar power as a catalyst that fosters, almost compels, wider changes in instruction itself.[6]

My second theme had been the cost of such changes. I reported that for us, the experiences I had related had been "exhilarating, but also unsettling, even painful," and I was unsure if those pains would prove transitory. Ehrmann and Balestri wrote that the added burden of teaching in new ways "can be a strain until the faculty member learns the needed skills" (1987:27), then they cited my account. I smiled wryly at their confidence, by no means certain that the needed skills would develop.

Those drawn to innovation are not easily discouraged, however, and the computer's advantages for students were clear. We continued to work with word processing, extending its use to writing courses at other levels. Now, from the vantage point of elapsed time and wider experience, the negative surprises my colleague and I encountered fall into several categories, some remaining more problematic than others.

First were those associated with implementation of computer technology. Ours has been a straightforward application, involving no software development; word processing has been used in a writing class under the control of a single teacher. Even so, the frustrations have been considerable. Efforts to move beyond our circumscribed use of the computer (to use a large-screen projector, for instance) broke down, literally. A colleague had to abandon an effort to network her writing class in the third week of the term. The technology itself is still a formidable obstacle for anyone who is not a computer natural or who is unwilling to put in long hours of learning with no guarantee of success. Accounts of educational computer applications seldom dwell on practical difficulties, but teachers who plan to experiment should be cautious in their first efforts; our experience has reaffirmed a personal commitment to minimum feasible technology.

A second category of practical difficulty was the greater burden on the instructor of a more interactive, individualized approach to instruction. This, too, is a real cost, one that not every teacher might be willing to accept. Record keeping is more complicated, and teaching has become more taxing. Interacting over individual work in progress demands a mindfulness that grading a stack of essays on a set topic does not, and it is hard to keep up with reading and responding to students' drafts. On the other hand, we have been learning some effective coaching techniques, and the fact that the interactive process is more enjoyable and interesting offsets, for me at least, the increased demands. A strong incentive for continued close attention to students' work in progress is my fascination with what it reveals about writing processes and writing development.

More difficult to cope with, in retrospect, was the psychological cost, the slipping away of one's sense of control. It started with the chaotic lab atmosphere, continued in our shifting view of the writing process, and came to a head in the problem of grading. Here, I am happy to say that the effect *was* largely transitory. The adjustment demanded a certain resilience, but one learns what to expect in the lab, gets used to students' new productions, once again develops a sense of what will emerge at various junctures, just as one painfully gained such experience in one's first days of teaching. The portfolio approach to grading does not work perfectly yet, but it feels like a move in the right direction. The unpredictable demands of this new kind of instruction came as a shock to us; teachers who know what to anticipate may adapt more quickly.

Most intractable are the difficulties that have arisen from a lack of fit between the course and the larger instructional system, one sign of which is my continuing conflict over the university-mandated writing assessment test. Measured by this test, the new approaches cannot be shown to result in better performance. I do not want to overstate the problem; students who succeed in my terms usually pass the outside test with at least an acceptable score. To do so they need practice with impromptu writing, however, and this creates a tension. Students like the longer computer assignments but, understandably, focus on the concrete skills and tasks that will help them pass the assessment, tasks that reinforce the limited, one-shot view of writing I am trying to wean them from.

Furthermore, as the very presence of the test signifies, the new view of writing is one that colleagues do not generally share. Extended experience has strengthened our earlier judgment that to be efficacious (especially with underprepared students), this kind of practice-with-feedback should continue over several semesters or, better yet, a student's entire college career. That is not likely to happen soon; the larger system of a publicly funded college is conservative for many reasons, and it is much easier to change one's own teaching than to bring about change in a program or a curriculum.

Not least of the impediments to change is budgetary. Unless there are outside grants, computer exploration (like most work on teaching improvement) must be supported by individual faculty members' energies. Such work largely remains outside the professional reward system, and changes are likely to be restricted to the classes of those who are drawn to innovation in spite of the difficulties. This lack of support creates a further personal cost: the frustration of rising expectations. Having assimilated the experiences of word processing, I am eager to experiment with networking and other computer-mediated approaches now being discussed in the literature. However, the public budget is shrinking, class sizes are increasing, and I find myself cutting back on teacher-intensive practices in self-defense.

Even so, that is cutting back, not giving up; I would not think of it. And so, these reflections return me to the peculiar power of the computer to impel a kind of learning that leads to irreversible changes. Students may not immediately go on to another class based on the process approach to writing, but many of them (probably most) do continue to use the word processor, with its built-in impetus to revision and editing. Faculty members who want to use the computer for their own purposes are willing to invest enormous amounts of time and energy, despite the frustrations they encounter. Many come to extend use of the computer to their classes and so open themselves to some version of the effects described here. I think it is significant that, despite the pains of implementation, I know of no teacher who has engaged in word processing with basic writing students who has gone back to old ways of instruction.

REFERENCES

Arkin, Marian, and Brian Gallagher, "Word processing and the basic writer," *Connecticut English Journal*, 15(2):60–66, 1984.

Bernhardt, Stephen A., and Patricia G. Wojahn, "Computers and writing instruction," in Michael G. Moran and Martin J. Jacobi (eds.), *Research in basic writing: A bibliographic sourcebook*, 165–190, Westport, CT: Greenwood Press, 1990.

Bridwell-Bowles, Lillian, "Designing research on computer-assisted writing," *Computers and Composition*, 7(1):79–91, 1989.

Cohen, Michael E., "In search of the writeon," in Lisa Gerrard (ed.), *Writing at century's end: Essays on computer-assisted composition*, 116–121, New York: Random House, 1987.

Collier, Richard M., "The word processor and revision strategies," *College Composition and Communication*, 34:149–155, 1983.

Erhmann, Stephen C., and Diane Balestri, "Learning to design, designing to learn: A more creative role for technology," *Machine-Mediated Learning*, 2(1–2):9–33, 1987.

Emig, Janet, *The composing processes of twelfth graders*. NCTE Research Report No. 13. Urbana, IL: NCTE, 1971.

Gay, Pamela, "Questions and issues in basic writing & computing," *Computers and Composition*, 8(3):63–81, 1991.

Gerrard, Lisa (ed.), *Writing at century's end: Essays on computer-assisted composition*. New York: Random House, 1987.

Hairston, Maxine, "The winds of change: Thomas Kuhn and the revolution in the teaching of writing," *College Composition and Communication*, 33:76–88, 1982.

Hawisher, Gail, "Studies in word processing," *Computers and Composition*, 4(1):6–31, 1986.

Hawisher, Gail, "Research update: Writing and word processing," *Computers and Composition*, 5(2):7–27, 1988.

Kantrov, Ilene, "Keeping promises and avoiding pitfalls: Where teaching needs to augment word processing," *Computers and Composition*, 8(2):63–77, 1991.

Kirkpatrick, Carolyn, "Implementing computer-mediated writing: Some early lessons," *Machine-Mediated Learning*, 2(1–2):35–45, 1987.

Moran, Charles, "The computer writing room: Authority and control," *Computers and Composition*, 7(2):61–69, 1990.

Nichols, Randall G., "Word processing and basic writers," *Journal of Basic Writing*, 5(2):81–97, 1986.

Perl, Sondra, "The composing processes of unskilled college writers," *Research in the teaching of English*, 13:317–336, 1979.

Rodrigues, Dawn, and Raymond Rodrigues, *Teaching writing with a word processor, grades K–13*. Urbana, IL: NCTE, 1986.

Rodrigues, Dawn, and Raymond Rodrigues, "How word processing is changing our teaching: New technologies, new approaches, new challenges," *Computers and Composition*, 7(1):13–25, 1989.

Thoms, John C., "Observations on a new remedial language arts course," in Lisa Gerrard (ed.), *Writing at century's end: Essays on computer-assisted composition*, New York: Random House, 1987.

Young, Richard E., "Paradigms and problems: Needed research in rhetorical invention," in Charles R. Cooper and Lee Odell (eds.), *Research on composing: Points of departure*, 29–47, Urbana, IL: NCTE, 1978.

NOTES

1. Those starting now with word processing for instruction can consult many sources; in particular, they should be aware of the lively range of articles in the journal *Computers and Composition* (Department of Humanities, Michigan Technological University, Houghton, MI 49931) and the concise practical wisdom of the Rodrigues and Rodrigues monograph *Teaching Writing with a Word Processor* (1986).

2. At first we used Bank Street Writer and later switched to Professional Write, both on IBM microcomputers.

3. Hawisher (1986, 1988), Bernhardt and Wojahn (1990), and Gay (1991) provide thoughtful analyses of the growing body of reports and studies of word processing for writing instruction.

4. Collier (1983) is still often cited; see also Nichols (1986) and a review of the inconclusive results of studies of word processing in Bernhardt and Wojahn (1990).

5. Cohen (1987), Bridwell-Bowles (1989), and Gay (1991) offer interesting discussions.

6. See, for example, Thoms (1987) and other essays in Gerrard (1987), and Rodrigues and Rodrigues (1989).

3

Software Design as a Learning Environment

Idit Harel and Seymour Papert
Massachusetts Institute of Technology, Cambridge, MA

Abstract *This article describes a learning research called the Instructional Software Design Project (ISDP) and offers a constructionist vision of the use of computers in education. In a Logo-based learning environment in a Boston inner-city public school, a fourth-grade class was engaged during one semester in the design and production of educational software to teach fractions. Quantitative and qualitative research techniques were used to assess their learning of mathematics, programming, and design, and their performance was compared with that of two control classes. All three classes followed the regular mathematics curriculum, including a two-month unit on fractions. Pre- and post-tests were administered to the experimental and control groups. The evaluation revealed greater mastery of both Logo and fractions as well as acquisition of greater metacognitive skills by the experimental class than by either control class. Selected results from several case studies as well as an overall evaluation are presented and discussed. By using ISDP as a model project, a constructionist vision of using technology in learning is elaborated. The ISDP approach of using Logo programming as a tool for reformulating knowledge is compared with other ways of learning and using Logo, in particular, the learning of programming per se in isolation from a content domain. Finally, ISDP is presented as a way of simultaneously learning programming and other content areas; the claim is made that learning these together results in better learning than if either were learned in isolation from the other.*

CHILDREN AS SOFTWARE DESIGNERS

This chapter has a double intention: It adds to the description and discussion of an experiment that formed the centerpiece of Harel's doctoral dissertation (Harel, 1988), and it uses the discussion of this particular experiment to situate a general theoretical framework (developed over the years by Papert and his colleagues) within which the experiment was conceived. The experiment is referred to here as the Instructional Software Design Project (ISDP), and the theoretical framework as *constructionism* (e.g., Papert, 1990).

The ISDP experiment involved studying a class of fourth-grade students. Each student worked for approximately four hours per week over a period of 15 weeks on designing and implementing instructional software dealing with fractions. A

The research reported here was conducted at Project Headlight's Model School of the Future during 1987–1988 as part of Idit Harel's Ph.D. thesis at MIT's Media Laboratory; and was supported by the IBM Corporation (Grant # OSP95952), the National Science Foundation (Grant # 851031-0195), the McArthur Foundation (Grant # 874304), the LEGO Systems A/S, and Apple Computer Inc. The preparation of this chapter was supported by the National Science Foundation (Grant # MDR 8751190) and Nintendo Inc., Japan. The ideas expressed here do not necessarily reflect the positions of the supporting agencies.

This chapter first appeared as an article in the journal *Interactive Learning Environments*, Vol. 1(1), 1990. Reprinted with permission from Ablex. Another version of this paper appeared as a chapter of the same name in the book *Constructionism*. Norwood, NJ: Ablex, 1991.

narrow description of our intention in doing this is that we wished to turn the tables by giving the learner the active position of the teacher/explainer rather than the passive recipient of knowledge, and the position of designer/producer rather than consumer of software. This idea is in line with constructionism's use of building, constructing, or knowledge-representing as central metaphors for a new elaboration of the old idea of learning by doing rather than by being told *(Constructionism* rather than *Instructionism).*

The usual passive view of integrating computers into education supports instructionism and technocentrism (Papert, 1987). ISDP, like all projects at Papert's Epistemology and Learning Group, attempted to change this approach by giving children the control over their learning with computers. Children were the agents of thinking and learning—not the computer. Our view is: Computers cannot produce "good" learning, but children can do "good" learning with computers.

> *Does wood produce good houses? If I built a house out of wood and it fell down, would this show that wood doesn't produce good houses? . . . [Q]uestions ignore people and elements that only people can introduce: skill, design, aesthetics . . . (Papert, 1987:24).*

It ought to be equally obvious that people are the agents when it comes to thinking and learning, not computers. People use computers to do things. If we were to say anything meaningful about the thinking and learning involved, then we should look at what people are doing with computers and not at what "the computer" is allegedly doing to them. For in reality, there is no such thing as "the computer" in general—only specific uses of computers in specific contexts. With a passive view of education, we open the door to technocentrism when we speak about the computer as an "educational tool". It should not be an "educational" tool, but just a tool. Like other tools, it allows us to do things we couldn't do before, or more usually, to do some things that we could do before better.

Building on the computer (or with the computer) a piece of instructional software about fractions is discussed here as a privileged way for children to engage with fractions by constructing something personal. In this, it may overlap educational techniques that use materials such as Cuisenaire rods, fraction bars, or pattern blocks. However, constructing software goes far beyond the physical manipulations involved in using such materials. To the adage "you learn better by doing," constructionism adds the rider, "and best of all by thinking and talking about what you do." Without denying the importance of teaching, it locates the important directions of educational innovation, less in developing better methods of teaching than in developing "better things to do and more powerful ways to think about what you are doing" (e.g., Papert, 1971a, 1971b). The key research question is to determine what kinds of things are "better." In this chapter we focus on attributes such as *appropriability* (some things lend themselves better than others to being made one's own); *evocativeness* (some materials are more apt than others to precipitate personal thought); and *integration* (some materials are better carriers of multiple meanings and multiple concepts).

We see several trends in contemporary educational discussion such as *situated learning,* and *apprenticeship learning* (e.g., Brown, Collins, and Duguid, 1989; Collins and Brown, 1987; Suchman, 1987), as being convergent with our approach but different in other respects. Two features are discussed here as giving specificity to constructionism in relation to this essentially synergistic body of literature. The first is our emphasis on developing new kinds of activities in which children can exercise their doing, learning, and thinking (e.g., turtle geometry, and ISDP). The second is our special emphasis on project activity that is self-directed by the student within a cultural and social context that offers support and help in particularly unobtrusive ways. ISDP provides us with insights into the unique ways in which constructing instructional software generates and supports personal reflection and social interaction favorable to learning.

In elaborating the constructionist vision we take the time to dissipate misunderstandings by contrasting it with derivatives of Papert's early work that radically miss its epistemological essence. In particular, we emphasize the fact that ISDP has little to do with the idea that learning Logo is, in itself, either easy or beneficial.

WHAT WAS ISDP?

Context

ISDP was conducted as part of a larger project to study the uses of computers in elementary schools. Project Headlight, as it is called, is based in an inner-city public school, the Hennigan School, in Boston. Only one third of Hennigan students, with children from first through fifth grades, participate in Headlight. (The experimental ISDP class and control class C1, which did daily programming in Logo, were both part of Project Headlight. Control class C2 was not.) As at many Boston public schools, the majority of the student population at Hennigan is Black or Hispanic and, in most ways, the school is quite conventionally structured. A major purpose of Headlight was to gain understanding of how a computer culture could grow in such a setting. One feature that is not typical in Hennigan is its building, which dates from the early seventies when there was a fad for "open architecture." When we first saw the school its architectural features were virtually unused, but we viewed them as an opportunity to reinforce our open-ended educational philosophy through the design of the space. We saw the physical environment as a very important factor in shaping a learning culture. These open spaces allowed us to (a) bring the technology closer (physically and conceptually) to students and teachers; (b) integrate the computer activities with the regular classroom activities; (c) facilitate movement and action around the computers; and (d) reinforce communication and information-sharing regarding computer-based activities across grade levels and among teachers.

In Headlight there is no long hallway leading into one classroom called the "computer lab" where children take their weekly "computer literacy class." Rather, there are two large open areas (the *pods*) housing four large circles with 100 computers, and each pod is surrounded by six classrooms. At Headlight, children use computers at least one hour a day, for working on their different computer projects, as an integral part of their homeroom learning activities. In Headlight there is virtually no use of "ready-to-use software" and little emphasis on learning *about* computers and programming as ends in themselves. The students learn programming but it is a means to different ends, which we conceptualize as entering a new learning culture—developing new ways of learning and thinking.

Our vision focuses on using technology to support excellence in teaching, in learning, and in thinking with computers—technology as a medium for expression.

We particularly eschew naive views of the computer as replacing (in the guise of improving) some of the functions of the teacher. Headlight students are encouraged to tackle exceptionally complex problems and work on very large-scale projects in a culture where they have a great responsibility for their own learning. They are able to work individually and collaboratively in a variety of styles in which the differences are reflected in gender, ethnicity, cognitive development, and in the individual personality of the teachers as well as in the personality of the learners (see also Goldman Segall, 1989a, 1989b; Harel, 1986, 1988, 1989a–1989e; Motherwell, 1988; Resnick, 1989; Resnick, Ocko, and Papert, 1988; Sachter, 1989; Turkle and Papert, 1990).

ISDP Procedures

During the period of the ISDP project, one of the pods in Headlight was turned into a software-design studio, where 17 fourth-grade students worked on constructing personally designed pieces of instructional software; the only requirement was that they should "explain something about fractions" to some intended audience. Before they started their software design work, the students were interviewed individually and were tested on fractions and Logo programming. Presenting herself as a researcher and a helper, Harel explained to the students that they were not being graded but were involved in a new kind of activity that she wanted to observe, evaluate, and report on for the benefit of others. Students were encouraged to think of themselves as collaborators in the project and its data collection.

ISDP was open-ended but somewhat more structured than the other Headlight projects. It included a series of activities that all the experimental students performed. Each working day, before going to the computer, the students spent 5 to 7 minutes writing their plans and drawing their designs in their personal designer's notebooks; then, they worked at their individual computers for approximately 45 to 55 minutes. They implemented their plans and designs, created new, ones, and revised old ones. When they wished, students were allowed to work with friends, help each other, or walk around to see what other students were doing. At the end of each daily ISDP period, students saved their Logo files on a diskette. In their designer's notebooks, they then wrote about the problems and changes of the day (related to Logo, fractions, instructional design, teaching, etc.) and sometimes added designs for the next day. The students had full freedom to choose which concepts they wanted to teach (within the domain of fractions), how to design their screens, what the sequence of their lesson should be, and what instructional games, quizzes, and tests to include, it any. In short, the period was open-ended in terms of what the students chose to design, teach, and program. The only two requirements were that (a) they write in their designer's notebooks before and after each working session; and (b) they spend a specific amount of time at the computer each day. The purpose of this second requirement, regarding time limitations, was to allow the project to fit into the schedule of the class and of the school. This requirement also made it possible to estimate and draw generalizations about what students could accomplish in a project of this kind, within time periods that could fit into the regular schedule of any class or school in the future.

Several focus sessions about software design, Logo programming, and fraction representation were conducted in the classroom during the project. In the first session, Harel briefly introduced and discussed with the students the concept of instructional design and educational software. Together—the children, teacher, and Harel—we defined the meaning and purpose of instructional software and briefly discussed a few pieces of software with which the students were familiar. Harel showed the students her own designs, plans, flowcharts, and screens from various projects she had worked on in the past. She also passed among the students the book *Programmers At Work* (Lammers, 1986) and asked them to look at notes, pieces of programs, and designs by real hardware or software designers and programmers, such as the people who had designed the Macintosh, PacMan, Lotus 1-2-3, and others. In this first session the students also received their personal diskettes and their designer's notebooks (see Appendix), and we discussed the ways in which they could and should be used during the project.

Other focus sessions encouraged the students to express themselves on issues such as the difficulties of specific concepts and on how they might be explained, represented, or taught. For example, in two of these discussions, we hung two posters, one on each side of the blackboard. On one poster we wrote, "What is difficult about fractions?" and on the other, "What screens and representations could be designed for explaining these difficult concepts?" We asked the students to generate ideas for both posters simultaneously. Other discussions focused on specific Logo programming skills. For example, in some of these short sessions about programming, the teacher, the researcher, or one of the students could stand next to one of the computers that were in the classroom or in the computer pod, in front of the whole class or a group of students, and explain how to use REPEAT, IFELSE, variables, and so on. The students could take notes on such concepts and programming techniques in their notebooks or go directly to their computers and write a procedure that included that new programming technique or concept.

In addition, the fourth-grade students/designers worked with third graders from another Headlight class, who visited the ISDP class once a month, for the purpose of trying out ("evaluating") the students' pieces of software as they were developed. The fourth graders gave the third graders "demos," and then, different pairs of children were engaged in discussing different aspects of the software projects: Some were teaching/learning fractions; some were teaching/learning Logo programming; some discussed design issues; and so forth. A great deal of teaching/learning through socializing went on during these sessions. However, the actual teaching was not as important as the fourth graders' feeling that they were working on a real product that could be used and enjoyed by real people. It reinforced the "thinking about explaining things to others" during their product development, and it placed them in the role of epistemologists.

The teacher and the researcher (Harel) collaborated and actively participated in all the children's software design and programming sessions during the project: walked around among the students, sat next to them, looked at their programs, helped them when asked to, and discussed with them their designs, programming, and problems in a friendly and informal way. In general, there were no specific plans for the project's sequence or for our presentations and focus discussions; rather, they were initiated by the teacher or by the researcher as needed, at times when they were relevant to the children's work or problems, or according to the children's requests.

To summarize, the children's daily activities resulted in seventeen different pieces of instructional software about fractions—one product for each child in the experiment—and seventeen personal portfolios consisting of the plans and designs they wrote down for each day's work and the pieces of Logo code they had programmed as well as their written reflections at the end of each session on the problems and changes they had dealt with that day.

To our pleasure, we observed that students worked with great intensity and involvement, over a period of four months, on a subject that more often elicits groans or yawns than excitement—namely, fractions. What seemed to make fractions interesting to these students was that they could work with them in a context that mobilized creativity, personal knowledge, and a sense of doing something more important than just getting a correct answer.

ISDP Atmosphere

Procedures as described in the above section could be carried out in very different atmospheres but would then, from our point of view, constitute radically different projects. It is therefore appropriate to devote some space here to capture the particular ambience of this project.

The ISDP environment was marked by the deep involvement of all participants. There were interactions and reciprocal relations among the students, teacher researcher, members of the Massachusetts Institute of Technology (MIT) staff, and sometimes visitors—all of whom walked around the computer area, talked together, helped each other, expressed their feelings on various subjects and issues, brainstormed together, or worked on different programming projects individually and collaboratively. Knowledge of Logo programming, design, and mathematics was communicated by those involved. Children, much like the adults in this area, could walk around and observe the various computer screens created by their peers or look and compare the different plans and designs in their notebooks.

Young students were developing knowledge and ideas without workbooks or worksheets, working within a different kind of a structure. They became software designers, and were representing knowledge, building models, and teaching concepts on their computer screens. They were thinking about their own thinking and other people's thinking—simultaneously—to facilitate their own learning. The following description illustrates the atmosphere of this noisy, flexible, and productive learning environment.

Debbie is swinging her legs while sitting at her computer and programming in an apparently joyful way. To her right, Naomi is busy programming letters in different colors and sizes. To her left, Michaela is engaged in programming and debugging a screen that shows a mathematical word-problem involving fractions, comparing thirds and halves by using a representation of measuring cups that are filled with different amounts of orange juice and water. She is very involved with her design, typing with one hand on the keyboard while her other hand is moving and touching the figures on her computer screen. A few computers away, the teacher is trying out Tommy's program, giving him feedback on one of his explanations about "what mixed fractions are." In the background, Charlie is walking around the other computer circle, holding his designer's notebook in one hand, and chewing on the pencil that is in his mouth. He suddenly stops next to Sharifa's computer. He chats with her for a moment, presses a key or two on her keyboard, and observes Sharifa's designs as they appear on her computer screen. After looking at her Logo code, moving the cursor up and down on the screen, he calls out, "Hey, Paul! Come see Sharifa's fractions clock!" The noise and movement around

Michaela and Debbie do not seem to bother them at all at this moment. Now, Naomi, who sits next to Debbie, has just completed the title screen for her software, which reads: "Welcome To My Fractions Project! by Naomi." She is stretching her arms while moving her head to the left and to the right, looking around to see what is new in her friends' programs. She then stretches toward Debbie's computer and asks her to show her what she is doing.

Debbie shows Naomi her programming code. "It's a long one," she says, running the cursor down the screen, very proud of the 47 lines of code she has programmed for her "house" procedure. She then gets out of the programming editor to run her program, which impresses Naomi, who moves her chair even closer to Debbie's computer. In a quiet and slow voice, pointing to the pictures on her screen, Debbie explains to Naomi: "This is my house scene. All these shapes [on the screen] are one-half. In the house, the roof has halves, the door has two halves. And I will add to this scene two wooden wagons and a sun. I'll divide them into halves too. . . . The halves [the shaded parts] are on different sides [of the objects]. You can use fractions on anything, no matter what you use. . . . Do you like the colors?" Their conversation goes on and on (Figure 1).

The idea of representing halves on the different sides of the objects, the objects being "regular human things" in a real-life situation, is Debbie's. In her final version of the teaching screen, there is an explanatory text next to the pictures on the screen, which says: "This is a house. Almost every shape is 1/2! I am trying to say that you can use fractions almost every day of your life!" Debbie is the only child in her class who has designed such a screen. She is very clear about why she designed it: to teach other children that fractions are more than strange numbers on school worksheets. As she discovered, fractions can be all around us: they describe objects, experiences, and concepts in everyday life. Debbie has painted half of each object a different color, and left the other half blank. The house half is painted in light blue, the roof half in orange, the sun half in yellow, the door half in red, and the wagon half in red. While Debbie is working on this, the only advice

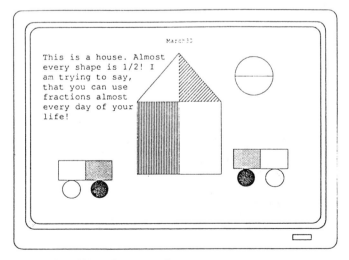

Figure 1 Debbie's "house scene."

she asks of her friend Naomi is about the colors: "Do you like the colors?" Naomi, who has adopted a different design strategy for her software, tells her: "It's nicer if all the halves are in the same color." They negotiate it for a minute or two but Debbie does not agree: "No. It will be boring." Naomi and Debbie continue to work on their projects with the computer keyboards on their laps.

EVALUATION OF ISDP

The evaluation of ISDP was designed to examine how students who learned fractions and Logo through the ISDP differed from students who learned fractions and Logo through other pedagogical methods. Three fourth-grade classes from the same inner-city public school in Boston were selected for this evaluation. One class, from Project Headlight ($n = 17$), was involved in the ISDP (experimental class). Control Class 1, or C1 ($n = 18$), studied fractions only in their regular math curriculum and programmed in Logo as part of Project Headlight. Control Class 2, or C2 ($n = 16$), studied fractions in their regular math curriculum, was not part of Headlight, and programmed only once a week in the school's computer laboratory.

Experimental Design

In January 1987, all three classes were pre-tested on specific skills and concepts in fractions and Logo. Thereafter, one of the classes participated in the four-months ISDP experiment. All 51 pupils were then tested again in June on their knowledge of fractions and of Logo (see Figure 2).

Using the set of pre-tests, it was established that no significant differences existed between the experimental and the control children's knowledge of fractions and Logo before the experiment began (Harel, 1988, 1989e). Four months after

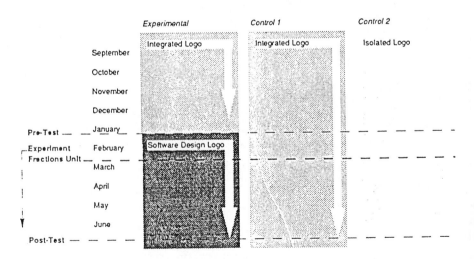

Figure 2 Experimental design and procedure.

the pre-tests, by using a similar set of post-tests, the ways in which these students differed in their knowledge and understanding of fractions and Logo were investigated in detail. In addition, during the project the researcher and the teacher conducted careful observations and interviews with the experimental students and assessed (by the use of case study methods and videotaping) the development of the students in the ISDP.

Many research questions could have been raised concerning the ISDP experiment because it involved many variables within a complex pedagogical situation. However, for the purpose of this study, the objectives and questions were narrowed down to two main sets of assessments:

(1) An assessment of the experimental children's knowledge of basic fraction concepts; and

(2) An assessment of the experimental children's knowledge of Logo programming concepts and skills.

The experimental treatment integrated the experimental children's learning of fractions and Logo with the designing and programming of instructional software. Because the experimental students and the C1 class had equivalent, though differently styled, exposure to Logo (i.e., both classes were part of Project Headlight), it was an open question whether participation in ISDP would result in greater Logo knowledge, but one naturally expected both of these groups to exceed class C2 in this area. With respect to fractions learning, the experimental group had additional (but not formal) exposure to fractions concepts through ISDP, so that improved performance of the experimental class was expected in this area as well. However, the assessment sought to determine whether this was in fact true and, if so, what the nature of the improvement was. As will be seen in the next sections, the assessment uncovered some surprising results, more finely textured than these general surmises.

Within the fractions domain, emphasis was placed on children's ability to translate between various modes of fractional representations. This aspect has been shown to be a crucial part of rational-number knowledge and particularly difficult for young children (e.g., Behr, Lesh, Post, and Silver, 1983; and others; Lesh and Landau, 1983). However, standard school tests were also used, which concentrated on students' use of algorithms. In Logo, the evaluation investigated the children's knowledge, use, and understanding of programming commands, instructions, and operations. More specifically, it assessed whether the students from the experimental class knew and understood more programming commands and operations (such as REPEAT, IFELSE, SETPOS, variables, and inputs in their projects), and became better at these skills, than the students in the two control classes. The evaluation also investigated whether the experimental students could understand, implement, debug, transform, optimize, and modify someone else's programming code better than the students from the control classes. Finally, the evaluation assessed whether the experimental students were able to construct Logo routines for someone else's design or picture and were better at this than the students in the two control classes.

Given the breadth of the learning experience and the mixed methodology of the assessments—including the extensive case studies of several students (i.e., examination of the children's progress, designer's notebooks, finished products, and interviews with participants during and following completion of the project) as well as the more formal pre- and post-tests—it was possible to trace in detail the microgenesis of Logo and fractions skills and concepts, exploring different approaches taken by the experimental students with different personal and learning styles (e.g., Debbie's case in Harel, 1988:76–245; and the Appendix in Harel's article in *Journal of Mathematical Behavior,* 1990a), as well as to draw inferences concerning their acquisition of metacognitive skills. The experimental design of ISDP and the analysis of its results we present here raise methodological issues for education research. Most acutely, these concern the question of what kinds of rigor are appropriate.

A simplistic position would maintain that the highest standard of rigor is always required. However, we argued elsewhere (e.g., Papert, 1987) that this can sometimes result in an analog of the complementarity principle in physics, stronger formal rigor sometimes being obtained only at the cost of thinner results. Thus, Harel (1988) adopted different kinds of rigor for different aspects of her work, and we do likewise in this chapter.

The first Results section demonstrates with statistical rigor that learning took place: The ISDP subjects learned quantitatively measurable skills in the programming and in standard school domains. The section that follows illustrates some aspects of the in-depth investigations into what and how they learned, going beyond test scores to obtain qualitative insights into the changes that occurred in students' thinking about fractions, and the dynamic of the process that led to those changes. Finally, a discussion section follows, in which we discuss why the students learned what they learned.

RESULTS

Quantitative Results from ISDP

The thinnest and most formally rigorous part of the analysis shows that the subjects in the experiment did improve in their ability to perform on standardized quantitative tests of performance in their work with fractions (as presented in the following subsection). Here, the solidity of the results derives from the existence of a large established body of data on how students perform in such mathematics tests (e.g., Behr et al., 1983; Lesh and Landau, 1983). We also present some quantitative data to show that the ISDP subjects did learn much more about Logo programming than the subjects in the two control groups (as presented in the subsection about Logo results).

Results from the Fractions Post-tests of the Three Classes

All the teaching of fractions, for all the three classes, was conducted for two months, during regular math lessons only and following the city-wide curriculum and traditional teaching methods (see Figure 2). The experimental class was not provided with any additional formal instruction on fractions, although we note that the representations of fractions in the context of instructional design was discussed in a few informal focus sessions. More information about the characteristics of the pupils, teachers, and their math curriculum is available in Harel (1988) and Harel (1991).

The post-test included 65 multiple-choice questions. Out of these, 60 were

Table 1   Average percentage correct of pre- and
            post-tests on fractions knowledge

Treatment	Fraction knowledge	
	Pre-test (%)	Post-test (%)
Experimental class	52	74
Control Class 1	54	66
Control Class 2	47	56

taken from the Rational Number Project (RN Project; Lesh and Landau, 1983:309–336). The remaining 5 were designed by the researcher and included word problems and construction of representations. Of the 60 RN Project questions, 43 were given to the students in the pre-test and then again in the post-test. As examples, Table 1 shows the children's average percentages of correct answers on the fractions pre- and post-tests; Table 2 shows the table of results for the two-way analysis of variance (ANOVA) with repeated measures for the fractions pre- and post-test scores; and Figure 3 shows the interaction diagram of the two main variables. In general, the difference in pre- and post-test scores of the students from the experimental class was almost twice as great as that achieved by the students from class C1, and two-and-a-half times as great as that of class C2.

RESULTS FROM THE MORE DIFFICULT QUESTIONS ON THE FRACTIONS TEST

We gave specific attention to the analysis of the more difficult translation modes between rational-number representations that the students had to carry out in the test. Some of these translations were the most difficult for students of all ages in previous studies, and were equally so for all students in this study's pre-tests. In the post-tests, however, these translation modes were still relatively difficult for the control students, but dramatically less so for the experimental students. Consider an example: Lesh and Landau considered Question 50 to be so complex that it was not given at all to the fourth graders in the RN Project, only to sixth-, seventh-, and eighth-grade students (Lesh and Landau, 1983:326). To answer this

Table 2   Two-way repeated measures analysis of variance

Source	df	F statistics
A (groups)	2	15.31**
Subjects between samples	48	
Within subjects	50	
B (pre–post)	1	110.99**
A × B	2	8.29**
B × subjects	48	
Between subjects	51	
Total	101	

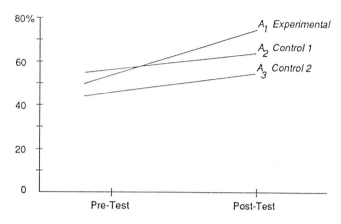

Figure 3   Interaction diagram of the two main variables in the analysis of the pre- and post-test scores.

question, the students had to translate a pictorial representation into a written (verbal) representation of a fraction.

Question 50 presented students with a polygonal region representation, with a numerator that was higher than 1, a denominator, a representation of a rational number lower than 1, in a discrete object that included a perceptual distraction (i.e., one part was "outside" the triangle area). To choose one of the options, the students had to (1) translate the given picture into symbols or words (two fifths are shaded in), (2) read the question again and realize that the question referred to the denominator of the shaded fraction, and (3) find the correct answer, which was b. Option a is confusing because it is written like a spoken symbol and includes relevant numbers—five and thirds. Option b is confusing because it does not mention *fifths,* but rather *five* (the denominator is five). Table 3 shows the scores in their percentage of correct answers for Question 50.

The ISDP students scored twice as high on Question 50 as did the control students, and twice as high as the sixth to eighth graders from the RN Project. The chi-square analysis shows that the differences of frequencies are highly significant.

Perhaps there is some transfer from Logo programming experience at work here. Decomposing a given picture into its geometrical components is a common

Table 3   Contingency table statistics, comparing performance of the study sample with the performance of the background sample (Lesh and Landau, 1983, average of grades 6–8)[1]

Class	% correct in study sample	% correct in background sample
Experimental class	66	33
Controls 1 and 2 (avg.)	29	33

[1]χ^2 = 33.49.

Figure 4 Question 50. What is the denominator of the fraction that tells us what part of the picture . . . is shaded?
a. five-thirds   b. five   c. three   d. two   e. not given

process in Logo programming and a skill that students usually acquire in their ongoing programming experiences. What Lesh and Landau (1983) and Behr et al. (1983) consider as a "perceptual distraction" (i.e., the one little triangle that was outside the big triangle area) was probably not a distraction at all for the students who looked at the picture with "Logo eyes" and decomposed it into its five geometrical components.

Another example is Question 42. It involved a translation of pictorial into symbolic representation (see Figure 5). This question was the 13th most difficult of the 18 asked in this subset. It was the 44th most difficult in the whole set of 60 questions given in the RN Project to students from fourth through eighth grades (Lesh and Landau, 1983:323). It included a discrete object representation in which the represented rational number was less than one; moreover, parts of this object were not congruent and were visually distracting. Table 4 shows the scores (given as percentage of correct answers) on this question according to the children's division into math groups (see Harel, 1988, for the detailed description of the math groups).

As seen in Table 4, none of the high-math experimental students made any mistakes. The medium-math experimental students scored like the high-math students in the two control classes. The experimental class as a whole scored 100% better on this subset than the students in the RN Project, and 14% better and 27% better than Class C1 and Class C2, respectively. Table 5 shows that the chi-square analysis of differences of frequencies is highly significant.

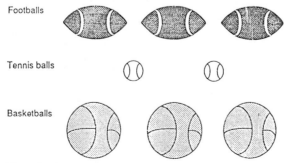

Figure 5 Question 42. What fraction of the balls are tennis balls?
a. 2/8   b. 3/2   c. 2/6   d. 6/2   e. not given

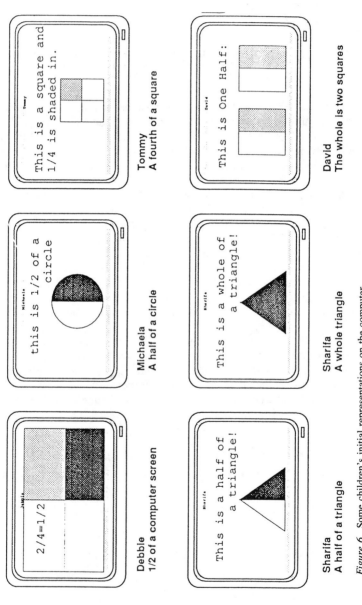

Debbie
1/2 of a computer screen

Michaela
A half of a circle

Tommy
A fourth of a square

Sharifa
A half of a triangle

Sharifa
A whole triangle

David
The whole is two squares

Figure 6 Some children's initial representations on the computer.

48

Table 4 Percentage of subjects responding correctly to question 42, by treatment and mathematical ability

Treatment	Mathematical ability		
	Low (%)	Medium (%)	High (%)
Experimental class	50	72	100
Control Class 1	40	68	72
Control Class 2	20	50	72

In addition, all the pupils were tested in math, as part of their end-of-year public school series of "referenced tests." This mathematics test included 40 multiple-choice questions. The average number of incorrect answers was 5.06 incorrect answers per child in the experimental class, 6.27 per child in Class C1, and 9.45 per child in Class C2.

Of the 40 questions, 6 were specifically on fractions ordering and equivalence, 4 on decimals, 4 on measurements of distance and time that required the use of fractions, and 1 on understanding geometrical shapes (i.e., this was the subject of 15 questions directly related to rational-number concepts, their representations, and computation). The average number of incorrect answers to this subset of 15 rational-number questions was 1.60 per child in the experimental class, 3.16 per child in Class C1, and 4.62 per child in Class C2.

Several conclusions can be drawn from analyzing these results. The first is that the experimental students, in general, did much better on the entire conventional school test than the two control classes. The second conclusion is related to the children's incorrect answers in the rational-number concepts subset of this test. In the experimental class, only 29% of the incorrect answers in the whole test (40 questions) were incorrect answers about rational-number concepts. However, in both Class C1 and Class C2, approximately 50% of the incorrect answers were on rational-number concepts (51% and 48%, respectively). This shows the superiority of the experimental class on rational-number knowledge in particular, as measured by this standard test.

The third conclusion is related to "transfer." By subtracting the average of incorrect answers on the fractions subset from the average of incorrect answers on the whole test, we can examine the children's average of incorrect answers to all the non-fractions questions: For the experimental class, $5.06 - 1.60 =$ an average of 3.46 incorrect answers per child on non-fractions questions; for Class C1, $6.27 - 3.16 = 3.11$; and for Class C2, $9.15 - 4.62 = 4.83$. The differences

Table 5 Contingency table statistics, comparing performance of the study sample with the performance of the background sample (Lesh and Landau, 1983, grade 4)

Class	% Correct of study sample	% Correct of background sample
Experimental class	74	36
Controls 1 and 2 (avg.)	53.5	36

[1]$\chi^2 = 42.62$.
Results from standard Boston public schools math tests.

between the experimental class and Class C1 are not significant here, but the differences between these two classes and Class C2 are. This finding is interesting because it might be that the experience of Project Headlight students (experimental class and Class C1) with Logo programming contributed to their general mathematical ability.

SAMPLE RESULTS
FROM THE LOGO POST-TESTS

In the pencil-and-paper Logo Test the students were asked: "Please list all the Logo instructions and commands that you know and use—in column A; then write an explanation and give an example for each one—in column B." The results for this question were divided into two major groups of findings. The first are simple findings that relate to how many instructions and commands each child actually listed. The second findings relate to the children's understanding of the meaning and functions of these commands and instructions in the Logo language, that is, how many Logo commands, operations, function keys, control keys, and so on, they listed and explained in the post-test. The experimental students listed 25.6 on average, whereas the two control classes did not do nearly as well (C1 = 12.0; C2 = 8.3; χ^2 = 10.8426). The students were also evaluated on the quality of their definitions and examples for each of the items they had listed. In Class C1 no one was evaluated as *very good,* whereas in the experimental class, three students who wrote over 40 commands and instructions, and four who wrote over 30, and gave very good examples and definitions of each, were evaluated as *very good.* No one was evaluated *low* or *very low* in the experimental class. However, four students in Class C2 were evaluated as *Low* because they listed fewer than five commands and instructions and did not provide examples or definitions for all or most of those.

We also tested the children's ability to analyze a given programming code and execute it on paper. A long, linear Logo code composed of short strips of Logo primitives was given to the students, and they were asked to draw the graphics. This task required that students read the given linear code, comprehend it, understand its flow of control, build a mental model of what the computer would do when each of the lines in this program was executed, and draw the picture accordingly, step by step.

Many researchers in the field of programming distinguish between writing a linear program and a modular program. We consider a linear program as one that emphasizes the generating of effects without any consideration and understanding of the inner structure of the code (e.g., Carver, 1987; Papert, 1980; Papert, Watt, diSessa, and Weir, 1979; several researchers in Pea and Sheingold, 1987; Soloway, 1984; and others). On the other hand, a modular program emphasizes elegant and efficient programming and is accompanied, they claim, by a higher level of understanding of programming in general and of the programming language characteristics in particular. Our results show that students who had written linear as well as modular programs during their process of learning to program were better able to understand and correctly execute this confusing linear program. The students in C2, who only knew how to write linear programs, were not able to solve this problem accurately, unlike many of the ISDP students. We should note that ISDP

Table 6 Results from the debugging task

Class	Number of bugs found and fixed	Identify and fix bugs in computer program	Identify and fix bugs in paper program	Average time for solving tasks 1 and 2
Experimental	16—all bugs	17 children—yes	17 children—yes	15 min
(n = 17)	1—one bug	100% succeeded	100% succeeded	per child
Control 1	9—all bugs	13 children—yes	8 children—yes	35 min
(n = 18)	4—one bug	5 children—no	10 children—no	per child
	5—none	70% succeeded	44% succeeded	
Control 2	2—all bugs	6 children—yes	2 children—yes	55 min
(n = 16)	4—one bug	10 children—no	14 children—no	per child
	10—none	37% succeeded	12% succeeded	

students often introduced structure (i.e., subprocedures and functional naming) into their programs only after a long period of purely linear programming, and only when they themselves decided it was necessary; it was not imposed on them from the outside. They learned to introduce structure, modularity, and elegant coding when they themselves realized the need for it in maintaining their long programs, in adding new parts to them, or in re-using (instead of re-writing) certain subprocedures in several places in their programs.

Another interesting aspect of these results came to view in the *number of trials* category. Many of the ISDP students tried more than once to draw the picture on paper, and finally found the right solution; whereas the students in the control classes who had gotten it wrong in their first trial were apparently not motivated or determined to try again or to find the right solution. Many of them simply wrote "I don't know how to do it," and went on to the next task on the test. Finally, we mention that on a debugging task given to the students on the computer, the ISDP students were faster at identifying the bugs, locating them, and then re-evaluating the program to create an output that corresponded perfectly with the original goal given to them. The data in Table 6 show the results for Tasks 1 and 2 on the computer, which required that the students run a given bugged program, analyze the features of the resultant graphics, identify the discrepancies between them and the desired graphics, enter the Logo code on the computer, locate the different bugs causing the discrepancies, fix the program on the computer, and add the corrections on the program that were written on the paper. Table 6 speaks for itself. The superiority of the ISDP students over the other pupils is clear, as is that of Class C1 over Class C2. Table 7 shows a chi-square analysis of these results.

Table 7 Contingency table analysis, comparing the number of bugs found in the debugging task between the experimental and control classes

Bugs found	Experimental class (%)	Control 1 class (%)	Control 2 class (%)
2	94	50	13
1	6	22	25
0	0	28	62

In addition to the above quantitative results, we made a number of qualitative observations about the children's debugging strategies. For example, the first thing that all the ISDP students did was to change the HT (hide turtle) command at the very beginning of the procedure, to ST (show turtle) so that they could follow the turtle as it executed the code. On the other hand, the first strategy that most of the students in Class C2 and many in Class C1 used was to copy the program given to them on paper (in subtask 2) into the Logo Command Center and execute it line by line. This strategy worked well until they reached the REPEAT statements, which were written on more than one line. Then, the students got confused because the program still did not work, though they were sure that they had located a bug. Instead of trying a new strategy, these students then erased everything and started to copy the procedure into the computer in "direct mode" again, which resulted in the same thing happening again, and so on.

In Tasks 3 and 4 on the computer, the students were asked to optimize the code given to them in Tasks 1 and 2 and make it clearer and shorter. To solve these subtasks, the students had to cease operating on the individual command level and start thinking in a procedural mode, using repeats, procedures, and inputs. To summarize these results, the experimental students were more flexible and attempted to explore a greater variety of ways for producing the same Logo drawings. They understood and reached a more modular level of code, and many of them tried to use repeats, subprocedures, and variables. The experimental students also performed significantly better than the control students on the three other items of this test, covering use of inputs, modification of procedures according to specific requests, and prediction of results of short but confusing graphics programs (see Harel, 1988, 1989b, 1989d).

It is interesting that all the ISDP students, who had already performed much better than the control students in the similar pencil-and-paper tasks, performed even better when using the computer. Moreover, the students from Class C2 got more confused at the computer and performed less well than they had on the pencil-and-paper task. Class C1 was somewhere in between: The high-math students, like those from the ISDP class, performed much better at the computer, and the medium and low-math students performed similarly to those from Class C2—far less successfully than they had in the pencil-and-paper task.

Similar trends were found in the results of the Logo post-tests and in the fractions post-test: The ISDP students consistently scored higher than the other two classes, but Class C1 usually scored higher than Class C2. In addition, the high-math students from Class C1 made up a special group. They were never as good as the high-math ISDP students, but most of the time they were as good as the medium-math ISDP students. Their scores in the fractions test were often higher than those of the students from the RN Project and stood out from those of the other control students. What does this mean? It seems as though only the high-math students in Class C1 strongly benefited from Project Headlight experience with respect to the pictorial-to-symbolic translation of fractions. This was probably due to their programming expertise, which contributed to their ability to translate picture representations into written ones, and vice versa. This phenomenon requires further investigation. It is an interesting one because it suggests a correlation between the children's level of understanding and involvement in Logo programming and their ability to understand different representational systems.

QUALITATIVE RESULTS ABOUT WHAT
AND HOW THE STUDENTS LEARNED

Denser descriptions than "getting better at" fractions or Logo in the school's terms were derived from an analysis of a large body of qualitative data derived in three ways: formal interviews, preservation of students' work, and observations of process. The fifty-one students in the experimental and control groups were interviewed before and after the ISDP experience. The ISDP students' work was preserved in designer's notebooks and in computer files showing the state of their software projects at the end of each day. In addition to direct daily observations by the researcher and teacher, videotapes made in two modes gave many opportunities for microanalysis of behaviors: In one mode, the video camera was carried by an observer and directed at interesting events; in the other, it was placed in one position on a tripod for an entire session and simply allowed to run. These sources of data allowed us to see subjects discovering new ways of talking about fractions and relating to fractions spatially and kinesthetically as well as linguistically and conceptually (e.g., Harel and Papert, 1991).

The interpretative nature of such conclusions required rigor that is different in kind from statistical analysis that checks whether or not the probability of the differences in scores could be due to chance. However, it is the richness of observation obtained from so many different sources that yielded a coherent sense of the development of individual subjects as well as of shared developmental trends, and this gave us confidence in our conclusions that we could not have obtained by any other means. To appreciate this coherence in full, it is necessary to refer to finer textured case studies published elsewhere (Harel, 1988, 1990a). Here we focus on four issues, which we label as development of concept, appropriation of project, rhythm of work, and cognitive awareness and control.

Development of Concept

Under the rubric of development of concept, we analyze the movement from rigidity, particularity, and isolatedness toward flexibility, generality, and connectedness. In the initial interviews, questions such as "What is a fraction?" or "When you close your eyes and think about fractions what images do you have?" or "Can you give me an example of a fraction?" revealed several aspects of particularity. There was particularity in the use of particular rational numbers (usually one half or one fourth) as prototypes. Most striking was that there was particularity of restriction to the spatial: A fraction is part of something, and "something" means something physical or geometrical. Of course, children from an early age use fraction words linguistically to refer to parts of other kinds of entities, such as time ("half an hour" or "I am eight-and-three-quarters") and money ("a quarter"). However, in the interviews they very seldom seemed to connect such usages to a general notion of a fraction. When specifically prompted to look for fractions in a real calendar or clock, subjects gave answers referring to the squares on the calender or shape on the clock face. One student even referred to the pattern strap-watch-strap as analogous to the numerator, the slash, and the denominator in the school representation of fractions! Furthermore, even within the spatial there was a high degree of particularity in choosing examples that happened to coincide with those one expects to meet in schoolbooks: "A fraction is half a pie" or "A fraction is like an apple or an orange divided in the middle." When asked to draw a fraction, most commonly they would draw a circle or a square, divide it vertically (not necessarily equally), and shade some parts. In some cases the degree of rigidity of the particularity bordered on the bizarre. For example, Debbie was committed to the idea that a fraction is the right, shaded part of a circle divided by a vertical diameter. When asked whether the unshaded part of the circle is a fraction, she said, "No, It's not a fraction. It's nothing." Such tendencies were also seen in the choice and modes of representation of fractions in the very first examples of computer screens made in the experimental students' software projects. All this changed dramatically in the course of the project. The content of the software as well as the post-interviews revealed a widening diversity of kinds of examples and representations among the ISDP students. Even more significantly, there was often a conscious—indeed, one might well say philosophical—recognition of the achievement of greater generality. In Figures 7a through 7f, we show a few examples of some children's further representations. Although it is difficult to capture the colorfulness and playfulness of those animations in this static black-and-white medium, the children's general ideas, and their diversity and complexity, are captured here.

Consider Debbie again. After a whole month of explaining about fractions—by creating a representation showing a half of her computer screen, and different geometrical shapes divided into halves and fourths—Debbie discovered something. Her discovery was expressed in her choosing to teach an idea of a different, more philosophical nature than how to cut a shape into thirds or how to add a third and a half. She chose to explain that "There are fractions everywhere . . . you can put fractions on anything." To teach this idea, Debbie designed a representation of a "house, a sun, and two wooden wagons" (see Figure 1). She worked very hard on

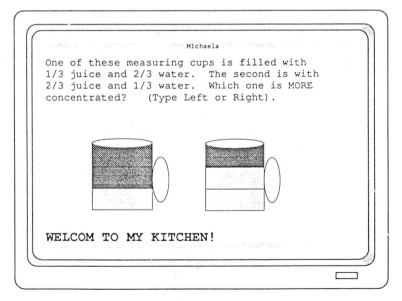

Figure 7a Michaela's "kitchen scene."

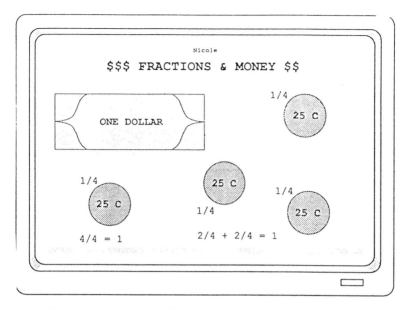

Figure 7b Nicole's "money scene."

implementing this representation by using some quite complex Logo programming codes (see Harel, 1988:118–140, for a detailed description of her lengthy and complex programming process and her work on this particular screen).

Debbie was not alone. A few weeks later, Tommy's house appeared, and then Paul's. The idea that it is important to teach others that "fractions are everywhere" and that one could "find fractions in regular human things" was spreading around the design studio.

Michaela and Sharifa, who used Debbie's software and received her full set of explanations about it, also chose to teach the same principle, but in another way. Sharifa selected to represent fractions by using a clock, teaching her users that "Half an hour is a half of ONE hour!" Her enthusiasm in announcing to the world that "half of an hour is a fraction too!" (and her use of exclamation points) is evidence for the philosophical importance of the breakthrough as she experienced it. Michaela chose to teach this principle through using a representation of "two measuring cups filled with different quantities of orange juice, water, or flour— depends on the fraction . . ." Later she confessed, "I found so many fractions in my kitchen . . . I told my mom about it too . . ."

These observations are consistent with the ways in which ethnographers such as Scribner and Lave (1984) have demonstrated the separation of school knowledge of mathematics from practical, everyday knowledge. However, we note something further that has a disquieting as well as an educationally hopeful aspect. The disconnection seems to be well-entrenched within both the practical, everyday side and on the school side, as shown for example by the fact that Sharifa had to discover a connection between "half an hour" and "half an apple." On the other hand, she did make the discovery and did so without explicit or directive prompting by adults. In a similar vein, we see clear evidence that many students do not

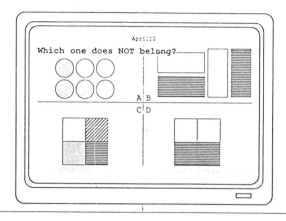

If the user typed C, the computer answered...   If the user typed A, B, or D, the computer answered...

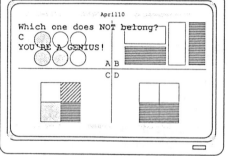

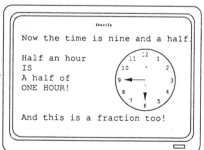

And the program continued to the next screen...   The question was printed again and again, until the
                                                       user found the right answer. Then, the program
                                                       continued to the next screen...

Figure 7c   Example of one child's representation of fractions.

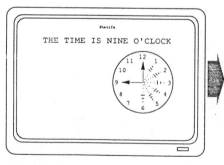

Figure 7d   Sharifa's "clock scene."

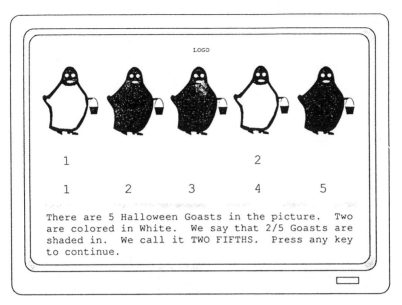

Figure 7e Example of one child's representation of fractions.

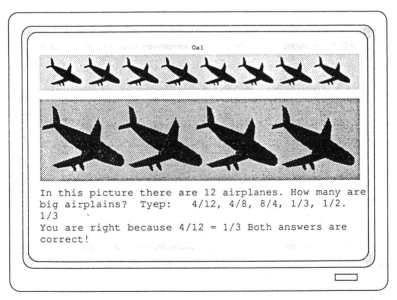

Figure 7f Pay attention to the options Oai gave to his users (4/12, 4/8, 8/4, 1/3, 1/2). He probably had an idea of what could be their problems with understanding this representation. He programmed it so both the answers 4/12 and 1/3 would receive the same feedback ("you are right . . ."). He also had an explanation for the users for why their answers were incorrect.

see "a quarter" as related to either the $1/4$ in their school worksheets or the "25%
off" in a store's sale pricing.

Our conjecture is that "disconnection of knowledge" must not be seen primarily as a limitation of "schoolish" knowledge but rather as a universal characteris-
tic of how knowledge develops, first as "knowledge in parts" (to use Andrea
diSessa's phrase) and then by the unifying effect of control mechanisms such as
those described by Lawler in *Computer Experience and Cognitive Development*
(1985), by Minsky in *Society of Mind* (1986), and by Papert in *Mindstorms* (1980).

Appropriation of the Project

Our second rubric, appropriation of the project, refers to observations about a
shift from a reluctant, impersonal, and mechanical mode of working to a growing
personal engagement, assertive individuality, and creativity. Debbie's case once
more illustrates this process. Her initial response to the project was globally very
negative. She simply did not want to develop software about fractions. In the
culture we tried to maintain, she was allowed to hold back but gradually began to
succumb to generalized social pressures. Thus, by the end of the second week, she
was beginning to put fractions on her computer screen. Nevertheless, what she put
up was still a direct reflection of the stereotyped model of fractions she had derived from math class. However, a new process was also beginning. We would say
that she was "working through" her ideas (and no doubt her feelings, too) about
fractions. It took her approximately a month to achieve her breakthrough. Now
she had an individual philosophical position that she pursued with something of a
missionary zeal. She had given herself the task of leading the rest of the world to
her discovery.

Time Frame and Rhythm of Work

This category appears to be an essential element of the process of appropriation. Switching in and out of projects in the fragmented time of the regular school
simply does not provide the conditions for personal appropriation and expression
of personal intellectual style. Observations in the ISDP also show the importance
of pace in the student's rhythm of daily work and in the radical differences in
individual style of work, action, and thought. Analysis of videotapes set up to run
continuously at fixed places show a pattern of work in striking contrast with the
regular school notion of "efficient time on task." In the videos, we do see periods
of intense concentration, but we also see periods in which students' attention is
elsewhere: sometimes looking at a neighbor's work, sometimes engaged in play,
chatting, and interactions that have no discernible connection with the project. Is
this an "inefficient" use of time? Although we did not measure this with any rigor,
it appears to us that the rhythms of work adopted by the individual students have
an integrity that contributes to getting the job done and especially to getting it done
creatively. And in making this assertion we feel supported by such ethnographic
studies as Bruno Latour's (1987) description of the ways in which engineers and
scientists at work mix "serious" talk about the problems in hand with intrusions
from everyday life and personal concerns.

Metacognitive Awareness

In this rubric, we describe in what ways ISDP encouraged children's meta-cognitive awareness (i.e., children's thinking about their own thinking), their cognitive control (i.e., planning, self-management, and thinking about these processes), and their meta-conceptual thinking (i.e., children's thinking about their own knowledge and understanding of concepts). Through the project the students developed problem-finding skills. For four months, students involved themselves in discovering problems they wished to solve. No one specified the problems for them; rather, they were the ones in charge of deciding, for example, what was difficult about fractions, what screens to design to explain fractions, what Logo procedures to create and how, and so on. Students also developed an awareness of the skills and processes needed to solve the various problems they posed. The designer's notebooks, as another example, required that children design and think about their screens on paper. Their initial drawings and plans demonstrated that they were not very aware of either the programming or the fractions knowledge and skills needed to accomplish their designs; however, as the project progressed they rarely came up with a design they could not manage in Logo. They also had to be aware of their target users' knowledge of fractions so that they could make the representations they had created on the computer comprehensible to them. Not only did children become aware of strategies to solve a problem at hand, they also learned to activate them. The Logo post-tests, for example, showed that the experimental children were able to optimize, modularize, and debug Logo procedures better and faster within given time constraints.

Over the course of the project, children developed the ability to discard inefficient designs, plans, and solutions and to search for better alternatives. In other words, they developed cognitive flexibility. During the project they learned to adjust their cognitive efforts to match the difficulty of the problem. They would often begin to implement their designs in Logo, but when they realized that too much effort was needed to accomplish a simple or "unimportant" design, they stopped working on it and moved on to a screen that was more crucial for their software or decided to redesign the screen that was giving them problems. As a result, the ISDP students were not rigid in their solution processes in the Logo post-tests and did not stop working on difficult problems (unlike many of the control children who simply answered "I don't know"), but kept trying until they found the solution.

Another thing they learned was how to control distractions and anxiety. In this project (and in Project Headlight in general), children worked in an open area next to their classroom. Different children worked on different problems, with other children, teachers, and visitors often walking around. Children learned to keep their attention focused on the problems they were working on and to resist being distracted by external stimulation. They also learned to control their anxiety when a problem was difficult. Post-tests showed that Project Headlight children (both ISDP and C1) did better in avoiding anxiety, focusing efficiently on the problems given to them, and not letting external interference distract them from their thinking and writing.

The community supported a practice of continual evaluation: Children evaluated their own and each other's performance every day when they ran their software and made entries in their designer's notebooks and when they looked at other

I.M. MARSH LIBRARY LIVERPOOL L17 6BD
TEL. 0151 231 5216/5299

children's software—sometimes making suggestions or borrowing ideas. They were constantly relating their current performance and implementation phases to the general goals of the task and making appropriate changes if the result was too slow or unclear.

The students learned to monitor their solution processes. Because they were in charge of their own learning and production, they knew that when they had a problem or difficulty, they could look first to themselves for a solution. They developed self-reliance and faith in their thinking.

Finally, the students became articulate not only about general planning and specific design tasks but about the subject domain as well. They talked, thought about, and actually related to fractions, both during their involvement in the project and in the interviews and tests that took place afterwards. From their point of view, it was having to teach and explain fractions to someone else that caused them to embrace it so thoroughly because, as they said, "How can you teach it if you don't know it yourself?" Much like professional educational-software producers—who gain deeper understanding of the topics involved in their software by thinking of ways to build explanations and graphical representations for their future software users—the experimental children, through teaching and explaining, also gained an awareness of what fractions were or of what they knew and did not know about fractions. To give some examples of students' metacognitive expressions, here are four related quotes from the post-interviews.

Andy: "It's supposed to be for littler kids, right? But to program it so they can understand it, you have to be sure that you know what you are talking about. 'Cause the teacher has to know more . . . You don't know how the other kid will react to it and all of that . . . It was really hard to get it so they will like it . . . Always to think about and imagine that you are small, right? and how would you like it?!"

Naomi: "It is hard to teach. You have to have a pretty good understanding of something, so you'll be able to explain it well to others . . . and a lot of times it's really hard to understand what's happening with these fractions . . ."

Debbie: "You have to show them fractions and explain, little by little. To program the scenes, so they will learn how to do fractions, and what they did wrong . . . then, someone can listen to you, to the computer, I mean, and understand."

Paul: "It's hard to tell someone else that doesn't know about fractions how to do these things. So I program this software for them, to help them understand it . . . But I have to think a lot about what I really know and how to show it on the computer, and how to explain it. And at the end, how to test them about it."

DISCUSSION: WHY DID THEY LEARN?

The simplest description of the ISDP reads like a "treatment" type of experiment: These subjects did something particular (made instructional software) for so many hours (close to 70 hours of work). In fact, the situation is vastly more complex than anything that could be sensibly described as "changing one variable while keeping everything else constant" because there were too many particulars involved. To make their pieces of software, the students used particular computers (IBM PC jrs.) and a particular programming language (LogoWriter). The project included focus sessions in which the specific content of fractions was discussed in a particular way—informally and compared with school classes, briefly. The project took place in a particular part of the school with a particular "computer culture." Moreover, during the ISDP the culture developed further in a particular way, with particular customs of interaction, attention, mutual help, secrecy, humor, and so on. The students and their teacher were aware of having a unique relationship with the research staff. They reacted in particular ways to the presence of video cameras, question-askers, and notetakers.

One can raise innumerable conjectures about the real source of their learning about fractions, for example. Did the simple fact of spending some 70 hours programming representations in Logo contribute to the results? Was the moral climate in the project largely responsible? Or the fact that the teacher felt she was part of something important or simply different? Some such conjectures, or aspects of such conjectures, we can, and do, try to check by studying control groups. But there are far too many of them to treat in a rigorous way. What can be said with some certainty is that we created a total learning environment in which some impressive learning took place. Teasing out the contributions of particular aspects of the environment is not a reasonable goal for any single well-defined experiment. Understanding will come through a process of gradual accumulation of many projects and of a great deal of theory building (e.g., Jackson, 1990; Kafai and Harel, 1990; Resnick, 1989). What we can do here is to share our own intuitions and, as part of the larger scientific enterprise, to formulate and discuss some conjectures concerning these intuitions.

In the following sections we speculate that improvement in performance might be affected by factors related to (a) the affective side of cognition and learning; (b) the children's process of personal appropriation of knowledge; (c) the children's use of LogoWriter; (d) the children's constructive involvement with the deep structure of fractions knowledge (namely, construction of multiple representations); (e) the "integrated learning" principle; (f) the "learning-by-teaching" principle; or (g) the power of design as a learning activity. However, the main point we would like to make here is that each one of these conjectures, when considered alone, would only give very partial information about why ISDP took the form and yielded the results that it did. Only by considering them together, and by speculating about their interrelations, can we take a step toward understanding the holistic character of constructionism in general and of ISDP in particular.

The Effects of Affect

From certain instructionist points of view (e.g., Papert, 1990), one could see a paradox in the results obtained here. Here are a few examples from the ISDP students' test scores: Debbie scored 51% correct on the fractions pre-test and 84% on the post-test (33% difference); Casey scored 55% on the pre-test and 83% on the post-test (28% difference); Rachel, 55% on pre-test and 87% on post-test (32% difference); and Oai, 55% on pre-test and 97% on post-test (42% difference). Debbie's, Oai's, Casey's, and other children's ability to work with fractions improved considerably from working on a project that was entirely self-directed, gave them no feedback in the form of marking responses right or wrong, and gave them very little guidance or information about fractions. How could worrying about whether "fractions are everywhere," to take Debbie's concern as an example, lead to greater ability to do school problems in manipulating fractions? The obvious explanation, which nevertheless has more than a little truth, is that the students developed a better attitude toward fractions, perhaps even came to like fractions. We recall that Debbie was initially reluctant to have anything to do with such stuff but ended up with enthusiastic missionary zeal. One does not need any complex theory of affectivity to conjecture that she might therefore be more likely to engage her mind with fractions both in the regular math class, so that she would learn more of what she wanted to teach, and in test situations, so that she would score higher.

Pursuing the idea that Debbie changed her relationship with fractions leads into an area where the line between the affective and the cognitive becomes hard to maintain. We see something happening that is analogous to the development of a greater intimacy in relationships with people. Debbie becomes willing to take more risks, and allow herself to be more vulnerable, in her dealings with fractions. As long as fractions knowledge was teacher's knowledge regurgitated, she was emotionally safe; the risk of poor grades is less threatening than the risk of exposing one's own ideas.

Our view of people such as Debbie is strongly colored by the sense that when they allow themselves to tap into personal knowledge, they allow knowledge about fractions to become connected with the personal sides of themselves. We conjecture that improvement in performance is related to the extent to which the students respond to a problem about fractions by "digging around" in their own stocks of knowledge as opposed to trying to follow set procedures. We note that this point could be formulated in Scribner's language by saying that their thinking about fractions shifts from scholastic intelligence, characterized by rigid, inflexible, externally imposed methods, to practical intelligence characterized by the use of multiple, flexible, and personal methods.

The Importance of Situatedness

The idea, though not the word, is an important theme in the development of Logo-based constructionism (Papert 1980, 1984a, 1984b, 1987). In this spirit, we attribute the fluency with which our students work with fractions to the fact that this knowledge is situated in computational microworlds, much as Jean Lave's weight-watchers benefit from the supportive consequences of the fact that fractions are situated in the microworld of the kitchen. A similar example is how Michaela was able to grasp fractions' significance in the context of using cooking tools for representing fractions. An even more striking example is provided by Sharifa, who got a grasp on the fractional nature of time through support from an overlap between the way the clock face represents fractions as angles and the way in which the Logo turtle (which, by then, was familiar to her) does something very similar. In that sense, our observations are consistent with those of Lucy Suchman, Jean Lave, and John Seeley Brown about situated knowledge. Like these researchers, we are strongly committed to the idea that no piece of knowledge stands and grows by itself. Its meaning and its efficacy depend on its being situated in a relation to supporting structures. However, we attach more weight than we think those writers do to the *Society of Mind* metaphor (e.g., Lawler, 1985; Minsky, 1986; Papert, 1980) that would allow the situating of knowledge in internalized, mental environments to act in much the same way as when it is situated in external, physical environments. Looking at the performance of Sharifa from this point of view we would say that her work with the computer enabled her to bring together in her thinking mutually supportive internal microworlds, in this particular case, microworlds of clock-time and of simple fractions.

The Contribution of Logo

There is a body of literature that addresses the question whether programming in general or Logo in particular can induce cognitive effects and, if so, to what extent. In this sense, Logo would be seen as a causal factor in the improvement of fractions knowledge or cognitive skills seen in our study.

However, Papert (1987) has used the term *technocentrism* to warn against simplistic forms of this question. In different contexts the import of the phrase "learning Logo" can differ so greatly that the question borders on meaningless. Nevertheless, in the particular context of the ISD Project, in which Logo was not isolated from a total context and the students programmed intensively and extensively, one can meaningfully begin to ask how various features of Logo contributed to the success of the children's work. At least one important contribution of Logo in this study was *indirect*, having less to do with acquiring cognitive skills than with mastering a subject domain; learning how to program and using Logo enabled these students to become more involved in thinking about fractions knowledge.

Nevertheless, we do think that Logo, because of its structure (or ISDP, because of the unique way it used the structure of Logo), had direct effects. Sharifa's ability to see the analogy between the clock and the turtle is one example of these effects. Our conjecture here, stated in its most general form, is that the structure of Logo brings students into direct and concrete contact with issues of representation—in the case of ISDP, representation of the specific object of study, fractions—and more generally, with the representation of objects, projects, structures, and processes in terms of subprocedures, LogoWriter pages, and other computational structures.

It is relevant to note that much of what the ISDP students did could, in principle, be done by other methods, such as using pencil-and-paper to draw representations or using physical manipulatives of various kinds (for representation construction). This might seem to make the contribution of Logo quite incidental. However, in practice, we find it implausible that traditional media could equal the ease with which Logo allows students to save and connect concepts and their different representations, and especially how it allows them to develop and modify such representations over long periods of time. Even more important, working in Logo on one's own machine, in a culture where that is what everybody else is doing, reinforces the learner's contact with his or her personal knowledge that is expressed in a real product—a piece of software—that can be used and re-used by oneself or others, changed, modified, and can grow with the knowledge of the learner and of the culture. Logo facilitated this ongoing personal engagement and gradual change of knowledge; at the same time, it also facilitated the sharing of the knowledge with other members of the design studio, and it allowed learners to continue and build on their and others' ideas and comments very easily. Logo facilitated communications about the processes and acts of cognition and learning.

Of course, we do not maintain that only Logo could do this. Surely, many new media will develop that can do it better. However, looking carefully at the features of Logo that contribute here, and the ways it was used in the ISDP context, will be of use in guiding such developments (e.g., Harel and Papert, 1990). Pursuing such issues requires much further research. However, the research that will elucidate them is not well-guided by the kind of questions that have often been posed in the literature, such as "Does Logo have a certain cognitive effect?" but rather "Can Logo be used to amplify and support a certain direction of children's intellectual development, or a certain change in a learning culture?"

The Deep Structure of Rational-Number Knowledge

Whereas most school work touches only on the surface structure of rational-number knowledge, we believe ISDP puts students in touch with the deep structure.

Elementary-school children's processes as well as difficulties in learning fractions and understanding their representations have been well documented. Unlike whole numbers, the meaning of which students largely come to grasp informally and intuitively out of school, learning the rational-number system is confined almost exclusively to school. Because rational-number concepts and algorithms are so difficult for so many pupils, they figure prominently in school curricula from the second grade on, mainly in the form of algorithmic tasks and the working out of specific well-defined mathematical problems. Even so, several national assessments have found that children's performance on fraction ordering and computation was low and accompanied by little understanding (see the discussion of this topic in Harel, 1988, 1989b, 1990a, 1991). This is particularly unfortunate because fractions are ideal tools for learning about number systems and representational systems in mathematics. We see the understanding of the rational-number representational system as a privileged piece of knowledge among the other pieces of rational-number knowledge. Representations form part of the deep structure of rational-number knowledge, whereas algorithms put students in touch with only the surface structure (e.g., Janvier, 1987; Lesh and Landau, 1983).

Logo can be a direct route to this encounter with the deep structure, enabling students to explore the concept of fractions through various on-screen representations of their own devising. In ISDP, this process was catalyzed by setting students the task of creating good pedagogical aids for other students, in the course of which they thought to create fractions representations in such forms as money, food, or clocks, as well as geometric shapes, and to accompany them with symbolic or verbal explanations they thought would be helpful to their target audience.

By becoming designers of instructional software, the students gained distance and perspective in two senses. In the first place, they were dealing not with the representations themselves but with a Logo representation of the representations. Moving between representations was subordinated to programming good examples of representations. Second, the students programmed not for themselves, but for others. They had to step outside and think about other children's reactions. The depth and creativity of such an experience contrasts with the rote, superficial quality of what typically occurs when a student is put through the paces of an externally conceived sequence of learning.

In summary, ISDP recast fractions learning in essentially three ways:

(1) It emphasized more involvement with the deep structure (representations) over the surface structure (algorithms) of rational-number knowledge;

(2) It made fractions learning simultaneously incidental and instrumental to a larger intellectual and social goal, that is, having students think about and explain what they think and learn in an interactive lesson for younger children; and

(3) It encouraged both personal expression and social communication of rational-number knowledge and ideas.

The "Integrated Learning" Principle: Learning More Can Be Easier Than Learning Less

It must be admitted that there are certain problems with integrating instructional software design activity into a school's curriculum. Software design is a time-consuming and complex enterprise for a teacher to handle, and it is not yet clear how it can fit into the average class schedule. In addition, at the present time it is not very clear which school subjects would lend themselves best to this process of learning (e.g., Jackson, 1990; Kafai and Harel, 1990).

Knowledge about computation (such as programming) and the sciences of information (involving control over one's own processing, metacognition, and information construction) has a special character in this respect because it has a reflexive synergistic quality—it facilitates other knowledge. In ISDP, the learning of fractions and the learning of the complex skills (programming, design, etc.) encompassed in the phrase *software design* did not compete for time; rather, we maintain that each took place more effectively than would have been the case had they been taught separately.

The reflexive quality of information science offers a solution to the apparent impossibility of adding another component to an already full school day. If some knowledge facilitates other knowledge, then, in a beautifully paradoxical way, more can mean less!

The idea that learning more science and math necessarily means learning less of something else shows a wrong conception. If these domains are properly integrated into individuals' knowledge and into learning cultures, they will be supportive of, not competitive with, other learning. We believe in the possibility of integrating science, mathematical concepts, art, writing, and other subjects and making them mutually supportive. We also believe that in ISDP this principle of integration—which meant that young students learned fractions, Logo programming, instructional designing, planning, story-boarding, reflection, self-management, and so on, all at the same time and in a synergistic fashion—greatly contributed to the results.

Special Merits to Learning by Teaching and Explaining

As educators or teachers, producers, computer programmers, software developers, or professional people in general, we are rarely encouraged to draw on our own learning experiences to better understand the reasons, purposes, and processes of learning and teaching our subject matter. Too often we tend to forget what was really difficult for us to understand, or why one learning experience was more or less valuable for us than others in the course of our own intellectual and professional development.

It has been observed by students and educators in our group as well as by many experts that the best way to learn a subject is to teach it. Let us consider, for a moment, experiences that are common to professional people in all fields in the course of their everyday work or professional training. Teachers, for example, often remark that they "finally understood something today for the first time" when a student asked for an explanation of something he did not understand. Some of our friends (professional computer programmers) at MIT have told us that they "really" learned how to program when they had to teach it to someone else—or when they were involved in a real, complex, long, and meaningful programming job. Many university professors choose to teach a course on the theory of the topic of their research while they are actually working on it so that the process of teaching and discussing their work with students will enable them to clarify and refine their own ideas and theories. It certainly seems to be the case in the educational software field that the people who are having the most fun and are learning the most are the software designers and programmers. With most educational software today, especially the drill-and-practice kind, the users rarely gain deep understanding of the concepts taught, unless the software is supplemented by instruction and explanations from a good teacher. However, the designers, who spent a long and intensive period of time designing, learning, and thinking of ways to build explanations and graphical representations for given concepts (even for the simplest form of educational software), have probably mastered these concepts and gained a much deeper understanding of them than they were able to convey in the software product itself.

The intellectual benefit of generating one's own explanations has been stressed by a number of theorists. Piaget, for example, has argued that higher level reasoning occurs in a children's group in the form of arguments. These arguments, according to Piaget, help children construct and internalize ideas in the form of thought. Such observations prompted Piaget to conclude that the very act of communication produces the need for checking and confirming one's own thoughts (e.g., Piaget, 1955). Furthermore, in *The Child's Conception of Space* (Piaget and Inhelder, 1967), Piaget and his colleague emphasized how difficult it is for young children to *decenter*—that is, to move freely from their own point of view to that of another, in either literal or metaphorical senses. Increasing communication develops the child's ability to decenter and to come closer to an objective view of the whole. The process of decentering, says Piaget, is fundamental to knowledge in all its forms.

Among contemporary researchers, Brown, for example, has done many studies to elucidate the ways in which explanatory processes, as part of reciprocal teaching activities, motivate learners and encourage the search for deeper levels of understanding and subject mastery. Brown characterizes these explanatory-based interactive learning environments as ones that push the learners to explain and represent knowledge in multiple ways and therefore, in the process, to comprehend it more fully themselves. The interactions could be supported by computers, teachers, or other learners (e.g., Brown, 1988). Hatano and Inagaki (1987) also argued that comprehension and interest are enhanced where students have to explain their views and clarify their positions to others. In the process of trying to convince or teach other students, they explained, "one has to verbalize or make explicit that which is known only implicitly. One must examine one's own comprehension in detail and thus become aware of any inadequacies, thus far unnoticed, in the coordination among those pieces of knowledge" (1987:40). Their studies demonstrate how persuasion or teaching requires the orderly presentation of ideas, and better intraindividual organization of what one knows. It also invites students to commit themselves to some ideas, thereby placing the issue in question in their personal domains of interest.

Fourth-grade children seldom have such opportunities. Peer teaching or reciprocal teaching can be used to take a small step in that direction. We feel that ISDP took a much larger step.

Designing for Learning

In *Knowledge as Design,* Perkins (1986) discussed in detail the instructional philosophy that supports the creation of a design environment for learning, arguing that the act of designing promotes the active and creative use of knowledge by the learner—the designer. In the designing process, Perkins says, the problem's meaning is not given by the problem itself; rather, the designer imposes his own meanings and defines his own goals before and during the process. The goals and the subgoals may change over that period of time, and keeping track of these changes is a central interest when the design task is not for the purpose of "getting it right" but is instead aimed at producing something useful through the use of creative and critical thinking.

Schon's work (1987) is also relevant to this theme. He is interested in how different designers (e.g., architects) impose their own meaning on a given open-ended problem, and how they overcome constraints (created by themselves or given as part of the problem they solve) and take advantage of unexpected outcomes. This interactive process requires high levels of reflection and develops the ability to negotiate with situations in as-needed and creative ways.

What is the difference between programming as such and designing a piece of instructional software? How does it relate to the "knowledge as design" framework? A *computer program* is an independent entity consisting of a logically arranged set of programming statements, commands, or instructions, that defines the operations to be performed by a computer so that it will achieve specific and desired results. We use the term *instructional software design* to refer to the building of a computer program that has a specific instructional purpose and format— much more is involved than mere programming. In this context, the lessons constructed by children were composed of many computer procedures or routines (i.e., isolated units) that were connected to each other for the purpose of teaching or explaining fractions to younger children. A unit of instructional software is a collection of programs that evolve through consideration of the interface between product and user. The instructional software must facilitate the learning of something by someone.

Designing and creating instructional software on the computer requires more than merely programming it, more than merely presenting content in static pictures or written words, more than managing technical matters. When composing lessons on the computer, the designer combines knowledge of computers, programming, computer programs and routines, the content, communication, human interface, and instructional design. The communication between the software producers and their medium is dynamic. It requires constant goal-defining and redefining, planning and replanning, representing, building and rebuilding, blending, reorganizing, evaluating, modifying, and reflecting in similar senses to those described by Perkins and Schon in their work.

In terms of the programming end of it, software designers must constantly move back and forth between the whole lesson and each of its parts, between the overall piece and its subsections and individual screens (e.g., Adelson and Soloway, 1984; Atwood, Jefferies, and Polson, 1980; Jeffries, Turner, Polson, and Atwood, 1981). Because of the computer's branching capabilities, the designer has to consider the multiple routes a user might take, with the result that the nonlinear relationship between the lesson's parts can grow very complex. Moreover, the producer needs to design interactions between learner and computer: designing questions, anticipating users' responses, and providing explanations and feedback—which require sophisticated programming techniques. Finally, the child-producer who wants to design a lesson on the computer must learn about the content, become a tutor, a lesson designer, a pedagogical decision maker, an evaluator, a graphic artist, and so on. The environment we created in ISDP encouraged and facilitated these various processes and therefore, we believe, contributed to the results.

SUMMARY AND CONCLUSIONS

This chapter had a double intention: to describe ISDP and to situate this particular project in a general theoretical framework called constructionism. ISDP offered a realistic and comprehensive model for our constructionist vision of education in general and for the use of computers in education in particular. It also offered a model for the kinds of research that we find insightful and beneficial to our understanding of learning and development, thinking, teaching, education, and the use of computers to facilitate these processes. We described how the participant ISDP class, composed of 17 fourth-grade students, integratively learned mathematics, design, programming, and so on, in the course of using LogoWriter to develop pieces of instructional software for teaching third graders. We illustrated various aspects of our evaluation—quantitative and comparative results as well as qualitative ones. Our evaluation showed that the ISDP students achieved greater mastery of both Logo and fractions as well as improved metacognitive skills than did either control class. The ISDP approach of using Logo programming as a tool for reformulating fractions knowledge was compared with other approaches to using Logo, in particular, the traditional learning of programming per se in isolation from a content domain, and was also compared with other approaches to learning fractions. The ISDP experiment showed that simultaneously learning programming and fractions was more effective than learning them in isolation from each other.

The ISD Project recast fractions learning in essentially three ways:

(1) It emphasized more involvement with the deep structure (representations) over the surface structure of rational-number knowledge (algorithms);

(2) It made fractions learning instrumental to a larger intellectual and social goal, that is, having students think about and explain what they think and learn in an interactive lesson designed for younger children; and

(3) It encouraged both personal expression and social communication of rational-number knowledge and ideas.

We emphasized the fact that ISDP had little to do with the idea that learning Logo is in itself either easy or beneficial. We asserted that in different contexts the import of the phrase "learning Logo" can differ so greatly that the question borders on meaningless. Nevertheless, in the particular context of the ISDP, in which Logo was integrated into a total context and in which students programmed intensively and extensively, one can meaningfully begin to investigate the question of how various features of Logo contributed to the success of the children's work.

We found that Logo facilitated the ongoing personal engagement and gradual evolution of different kinds of knowledge; at the same time, it also facilitated the sharing of that knowledge with other members of the community, which in turn encouraged the learners to continue and build on their own and other people's ideas. In short, Logo facilitated communications about the processes and acts of cognition and learning. We do not maintain that only Logo could do this. However, looking carefully at what specific features of Logo enhanced individual cognition and social learning can help guide us in future technological developments. And indeed, ISDP provided us with many insights—cognitive/developmental as well as technological—into what kinds of thinking tools we want to develop for constructionist learning.

We mentioned that the ISDP should not be viewed as a "very controlled treatment" type of experiment. The pedagogical situation was quite complex, and one could formulate innumerable conjectures about the real source of the experimental children's learning. We concluded that ISDP allowed us to create a total learning environment in which some impressive integrated learning took place.

It was beyond the scope of this study to single out the contribution of the individual aspects of that environment. In our view, a more complete understanding of this learning process can come through an integrative and accumulative process of experimentation and theory-building (and there are several projects of this kind within our group at the MIT Media Laboratory, e.g., Harel, 1990b). This chapter is also intended as a contribution to that process, in which we shared our conjectures and the bases on which we formulated them. We hypothesized, for example, that improvements in performance among ISDP students could have been affected by factors related to (a) the affective side of cognition and learning; (b) the children's process of personal appropriation of knowledge; (c) the children's use of LogoWriter; (d) the children's constructivist involvement with the deep structure of fractions knowledge; (e) the integrated learning principle; (f) the learning-by-teaching principle; and (g) the power of design as a learning activity.

However, the main point we wanted to make here was that each one of those conjectures, when considered alone, would give only very partial information about the meaning of the results. By considering them together, and by speculating about their interrelations, we are endeavoring to make use of the very kind of holistic approach to knowledge and cognition, and to the development of learning technologies, that we believe informs and characterizes constructionism in general, and ISDP in particular.

ACKNOWLEDGMENTS

We are deeply grateful to Linda Moriarty, who made an essential contribution to the project and to the research ideas reported here. Over the years, many other teachers in Project Headlight at the Hennigan School contributed indirectly, but very importantly, to the work. We thank all the students and teachers of Headlight, without whom this project would not have been possible.

We thank Aaron Falbel and Beth Rashbaum for their editorial assistance, and other members of our Epistemology and Learning Group for their contribution in their inspiring discussions of the ideas presented in this chapter. We thank Yasmin Kafai for her help in the preparation of the statistical tables.

REFERENCES

Adelson, B., and E. Soloway, *A cognitive model of software design,* New Haven, CT: Yale University, 1984a. (Cognition and Programming Project, Res. Rep. No. 342)

Adelson, B., and E. Soloway, *The role of domain experience in software design,* New Haven, CT: Yale University, 1984b. (Cognition and Programming Project, Res. Rep. No. 25)

Atwood, M. E., R. Jefferies, and P. G. Polson, *Studies in plan construction I and II,* Englewood, CO: Science Applications Inc., March 1980. (Tech. Rep. No SA1-80-028-DEN)

Behr, M. J., R. Lesh, T. R. Post, and E. A. Silver, "Rational number concepts," in R. Lesh and M. Landau (eds.), *Acquisition of mathematics concepts and processes,* New York: Academic Press, 1983.

Behr, M. J., Wachsmuth, T. R. Post, and R. Lesh, "Order and equivalence: A clinical teaching experiment," *Journal of Research in Mathematics Education,* 15(5):323–341, 1984.

Brown, A. L., "Reciprocal teaching: Comprehension-fostering and comprehension-monitoring activities," *Cognition and Instruction,* 1(2):117–175, 1984.

Brown, A. L., "Motivation to learn and understand: On taking charge of one's own learning," *Cognition and Instruction,* 5(4):311–322, 1988.

Brown, A. L., J. D. Bransford, R. A. Ferrara, and J. C. Campione, "Learning, remembering, and understanding," *Handbook of child psychology: Cognitive development,* Vol. 3, New York: Wiley, 1983.

Brown, J. S., A. Collins, and P. Duguid, "Situated cognition and the culture of learning," *Educational Researcher,* 18(1):32–42, 1989.

Carver, S. M., *Transfer of LOGO debugging skill: Analysis, instruction, and assessment,* unpublished doctoral dissertation, Carnegie-Mellon University, Pittsburgh, PA, 1987.

Chipman, S. F., J. W. Segal, and R. Glaser, *Thinking and learning skills,* Vols. 1 and 2, Hillsdale, NJ: Erlbaum, 1985.

Collins, A., and J. S. Brown, *The new apprenticeship,* paper presented at the American Educational Research Association, Washington, DC, April 1987.

Goldman Segall, R., *Videodisc technology as a conceptual research tool for the study of human theory making,* unpublished manuscript, MIT Media Laboratory, Cambridge, MA, 1989a.

Goldman Segall, R., *Learning constellations: A multimedia ethnographic description of children's theories in a logo culture,* unpublished Ph.D. thesis proposal, MIT Media Laboratory, Cambridge, MA, 1989b.

Harel, I., *Children as software designers: An exploratory study in Project Headlight,* paper presented at the LOGO '86 International Conference, Massachusetts Institute of Technology, Cambridge, MA, July 1986.

Harel, I., *Software design for learning: Children's construction of meaning for fractions and logo programming,* unpublished doctoral dissertation, MIT Media Laboratory, Cambridge, MA, 1988.

Harel, I., "Software design for learning," in W. C. Ryan (ed.), *Proceedings Book of the National Educational Computer Conference (NECC),* Boston, MA: The International Council of Computers in Education, 1989a.

Harel, I., "Software design for learning mathematics," in C. Mather, G. Goldin, and R. Davis (eds.), *Proceedings Book of the Eleventh Annual Meeting of Psychology of Mathematics Education,* New Brunswick, NJ: Rutgers University, Center for Mathematics, Science, and Computer Education, 1989b.

Harel, I., "Software designing in a learning environment for young learners: Cognitive processes and cognitive tools," in *Proceedings of the FRIEND21 International Symposium on Next Generation Human Interface Technologies,* Tokyo, Japan, 1989c.

Harel, I., "Tools for young software designers," in *Proceedings of the Third Workshop of Empirical Studies of Programmers (ESP Society)*, Austin, TX: April 1989d.

Harel, I., "Children as software designers: A constructionist approach to learning mathematics," *Journal of Mathematical Behavior,* 9(1):3, 1990a.

Harel, I., (ed.), *Constructionist learning: A 5th anniversary collection of papers.* Cambridge, MA: MIT Media Laboratory, 1990b.

Harel, I. *Children Designers,* Norwood, NJ: ABLEX (1991).

Harel, I., and S. Papert (Eds.) *Constructionism,* Norwood, NJ: ABLEX (1991).

Hatano and Inagaki, "A theory of motivation for comprehension and its applications to mathematics instruction," in T. A. Romberg and D. M. Steward (eds.), *The monitoring of school mathematics: Background papers: Vol. 2, Implications from psychology, outcomes from instruction,* Madison, WI: Center for Educational Research, 1987.

Jackson, I. "Children's software design as a collaborative process: An experiment with fifth graders at Project Headlight," in I. Harel (ed.), *Constructionist learning: A 5th anniversary collection of papers,* Cambridge, MA: MIT Media Laboratory, 1990.

Janvier, C. (ed.), *Problems in representation in the teaching and learning of mathematics.* Hillsdale, NJ: Erlbaum, 1987.

Jefferies, R., A. A. Turner, P. G. Polson, and M. E. Atwood, "The processes involved in designing software," in J. R. Anderson (ed.), *Cognitive skills and their acquisition,* Hillsdale, NJ: Erlbaum, 1981.

Kafai, Y., and I. Harel, "The instructional software design project: Phase II," in I. Harel (ed.), *Constructionist learning: A 5th anniversary collection of papers,* Cambridge, MA: MIT Media Laboratory, 1990.

Lammers, S., *Programmers at work,* Redmond, WA: Microsoft Corp. Press, 1986.

Latour, B., *Science in action: How to follow scientists and engineers through society,* Cambridge, MA: Harvard University Press, 1987.

Lawler, R. W., *Computer experience and cognitive development: A child learning in a computer culture,* West Sussex, England: Ellis Horwood, Ltd., 1985.

Lesh, R., and M. Landau, *Acquisition of mathematics concepts and processes,* New York: Academic Press, 1983.

Minsky, M., *Society of mind,* New York: Simon and Schuster, 1986.

Motherwell, L., *Gender and style differences in a logo-based environment,* unpublished doctoral dissertation, MIT Media Laboratory, Cambridge, MA, 1988.

Papert, S. *Teaching children thinking* (AI Memo No. 247, and Logo Memo No. 2), Cambridge, MA: Massachusetts Institute of Technology, 1971a.

Papert, S., *Teaching children to be mathematicians vs. teaching about mathematics* (AI Memo No. 249 and Logo Memo No. 4), Cambridge, MA: Massachusetts Institute of Technology, 1971b.

Papert, S., *Mindstorms: Children, computers, and powerful ideas,* New York: Basic Books, 1980.

Papert, S., *Microworlds transforming education,* paper presented at the ITT Key Issues Conference, Annenberg School of Communications, University of Southern California, Los Angeles, 1984a.

Papert, S., *New theories for new learnings,* paper presented at the National Association for School Psychologists' Conference, 1984b.

Papert, S., "Computer criticism vs. technocentric thinking," *Educational Researcher,* 16(1):22–30, 1987.

Papert, S., "An introduction to the 5th anniversary collection," in I. Harel (ed.), *Constructionist learning: A 5th anniversary collection of papers,* Cambridge, MA: MIT Media Laboratory, 1990.

Papert, S., D. Watt, A. diSessa, and S. Weir, *Final report of the Brookline logo projects, Part I and II* (Logo Memo No. 53), Cambridge, MA: Massachusetts Institute of Technology, 1979.

Pea, R. D., and K. Sheingold (eds.), *Mirrors of mind: Patterns of experience in educational computing,* Norwood, NJ: Ablex, 1987.

Perkins, D. N., *Knowledge as design,* Hillsdale, NJ: Erlbaum, 1986.

Piaget, J., *The language and thought of the child,* New York: New American Library, 1955.

Piaget, J., and B. Inhelder, *The child's conception of space,* New York: W. W. Norton, 1967.

Resnick, M., *Lego Logo: Learning through and about design,* paper presented at the American Educational Research Association, San Francisco, CA, April 1989. (Appeared in I. Harel (ed.), *Constructionist learning: A 5th anniversary collection of papers,* Cambridge, MA: MIT Media Laboratory, 1990.)

Resnick, M., S. Ocko, and S. Papert, "Lego, LOGO, and design," *Children's Environments Quarterly,* 5(4), 1988.

Sachter, J. E., *Kids in space: Exploration into children's cognitive styles and understanding of space in 3-D computer graphics,* unpublished Ph.D. thesis proposal, MIT Media Laboratory, Cambridge, MA. (A short version of this proposal appeared in I. Harel (ed.), *Constructionist learning: A 5th anniversary collection of papers,* Cambridge, MA: MIT Media Laboratory, 1990.)

Schon, D. A., *Educating the reflective practitioner,* San Francisco: Jossey-Bass, 1987.

II

DEVELOPING TOOLS
FOR THE NOVICE DESIGNER

4

The Future of Computer-Assisted Design: Technological Support for Kids Building Artifacts

Mark Guzdial, Elliot Soloway, Phyllis Blumenfeld, Luke Hohmann,
Ken Ewing, Iris Tabak, Kathleen Brade
University of Michigan, Ann Arbor, MI

Yasmin Kafai
Harvard University, Cambridge, MA

Abstract *A project-based learning model emphasizes student design activities to engage the student with the domain material. Students, as novice designers, need support to be successful in building artifacts. The GPCeditor (Goal-Plan-Code editor) is a computer-based design support environment (DSE) that supports high school students as they learn and do software design. Case studies suggest that students using the GPCeditor do make use of its features in learning and doing software design. However, developing solutions to the problems students still face requires addressing both technological and educational issues as part of a complex interrelationship between instructional environment, curriculum, and technology.*

INTRODUCTION

The knowledge-transmission, didactic model of American education is no longer serving the needs of students and teachers. As has been described in many studies over the last five years, students are falling behind their counterparts in other countries, even compared with other American students of years past (Farnham-Diggory, 1990).

What seems to be needed now is a more project-based (or constructionist) approach to learning. Students who are actively engaged in designing and implementing projects in a domain are also actively engaged in the learning of the knowledge in that domain. Students building artifacts are creating critiquable, sharable externalizations of their knowledge, which provides both motivation and opportunity to exercise metacognitive skills.

However, students are notoriously bad designers. For example, studies of student software designers have indicated that students do not grasp design skills such as the ability to decompose problems into modules[1] (e.g., Jefferies, Turner, Polson, and Atwood, 1981; Pea and Kurland, 1986; Spohrer and Soloway, 1985).

This research was supported by NSF Grant #MDR-9010362. Equipment for this research was donated by Apple Computer. Mark Guzdial received support from the University of Michigan School of Education, and Luke Hohmann received support from Electronic Data Systems Corporation.

Without design skills, the designer is not able to cope with the complexity of the design process or the resultant artifact (Simon, 1969). It is important for students to be successful designers because producing bad designs can remove the incentive to engage in project-based learning. Thus, students require support to do design.

The Goal-Plan-Code editor (GPCeditor) developed by the HiCE research group[2] is a computer-based design support environment[3] (DSE) that supports high school students as they learn and do software design. The purpose of the GPCeditor is to provide an environment in which students can design software (the doing of design). Over the course of the semester, students are expected to produce higher quality artifacts of ever-increasing complexity by using good, systematic design process (the learning of design).

The GPCeditor implements a set of features called *scaffolding* that work together to support the student in the design process. These supports allow the student to concentrate on the salient parts of the overall task (Brown, Bransford, Ferrara, and Campione, 1983). The GPCeditor implements scaffolding for doing design through tools and representations that encourage students to think about software as an expert does and to use a design process based on empirical studies of expert programmers. Scaffolding for learning design comes through encouraging articulation (e.g., in names and descriptions of program components) and reflection (e.g., by providing multiple, linked representations).

The GPCeditor has been in continuous use in Community High School[4] in Ann Arbor for three years. We have observed that students do produce high-quality, complex artifacts with good, systematic design process. In our process of analyzing and measuring these outcomes, we undertook a case study of four typical students in the class. For these students we gathered programs, process traces, interview data, and think-aloud protocols. This chapter describes these four students and the situation in which they worked. The following four sections cover the following topics: (a) the components of instruction used in the class, that is, the features of the GPCeditor, the instructional environment that evolved, and the curriculum used in the classroom: (b) a description of the data collected and the criteria used in their review; (c) a presentation of case studies of four students selected as a representative sample to identify benefits and problems with our approach; and (d) an outline of future strategies.

COMPONENTS OF INSTRUCTION

GPCeditor

The GPCeditor must support the students as they do design but also support the students' learning. This dual goal is accomplished by providing a rich set of design tools whose use is structured to encourage learning. For example, a library containing program fragments (whose usefulness has been proven in prior programming experience) is provided, as one would expect to provide an expert designer in order to support doing programming (Guindon and Curtis, 1988). However, in the GPCeditor, students may not use something from the library until they have first articulated (a learning strategy) a goal for which the library entry will be used.

This enforced articulation is one way in which the GPCeditor provides a specific design process. By providing a design process, we encourage learning the components of the process while the order of the processes is structured. As students use the GPCeditor, the goal is that they internalize the process and begin using a more expert-like process resulting in the development of more expert-like products. Thus, learning occurs in a process of doing. The design process that is taught with the GPCeditor has three process stages.

Decomposition, or Analysis of the Problem

During decomposition, the student considers the problem requirements, formulates a goal, considers the potential alternative plans for achieving that goal, and finally chooses the plan for the given goal. For expert designers, the search for potential plans begins with plans already developed and used in previous plans, in the hope that the plan might be reused, thus reducing the complexity of the overall design.

The problems of student designers begin here. The skill of being able to modularly decompose problems is absolutely key in software design (Parnas, 1972) and yet is rarely developed by students even after a full semester (or more) of programming instruction (Pea and Kurland, 1986).

Composition, or Synthesis of the Solution

The student defines the particulars to make the generic plan fit the specific situation (instantiating the plan for the problem) and places the plans in the program in a particular order. Instantiating plans in software is the process of choosing appropriate data objects for the procedural plan and then ordering them in a predetermined manner to achieve a particular sequence of events.

This, too, is a key stage for student designers. A common source of error in programs, especially in student programs, is in the integration of plans (Spohrer and Soloway, 1985). Students find it difficult to take the decomposed elements and combine them into a final solution.

Debugging, or a Cycling of the Design Process

An expert programmer reviews the solution and develops predictions about the program's behavior. Testing the program, perhaps using debugging tools such as breakpoints, involves comparing expected results with actual results. If the comparison indicates that a bug exists, the programmer begins a new design cycle in which a goal may be to find the bug or perhaps to correct the bug if the cause is clear. Debugging must focus on the program as a whole to determine which plans are incorrect and then shift to concentrate on the localized interactions between component plans.

The GPCeditor provides two general sets of supports (scaffolding) in learning and doing design. The first set provides tools to aid in reflection, which is important for the learning of the goal-plan design methodology in the development of software. The second set helps students learn and do the process of design and is a critical component of the design stages described above.

Support for Reflection

The GPCeditor provides support for reflection at two levels. The first level is through the goal-plan approach, which encourages students to think about programs in a manner similar to experts. The second level supports the first by providing multiple representations for viewing the developing program.

Goal-plan approach. Students using the GPCeditor never type program statements. Instead, they construct programs by defining goals (statements of what they wish to achieve) and plans (how they wish to achieve these goals) and then assembling these plans. For each goal there are usually one or more alternative plans for achieving the goal. These plans can be thought of as components, or program modules, which are composed by the student to create the complete design or program.

Plans are either defined in terms of Pascal code (e.g., a `writeln` statement is a primitive plan available to the student which writes some data to a line of the text window) or in terms of a hierarchy of subgoals and their plans. A plan that is defined through subgoals is referred to as a plan grouping. The role of data in a GPCeditor program is to instantiate a plan for a particular program. For example, the `writeln` plan is always the same from use to use and program to program, but it is made specific for a particular purpose by the choice of data to write. In this way we encourage the important design skill of tailoring program components for specific use.

The goal-plan approach encourages modular programming by making clear the difference between the what and the how. The GPCeditor takes this approach a step further and allows the students to concentrate on the goals and plans of the program without the cost of learning specific, idiosyncratic rules associated with the Pascal programming language. Students using the GPCeditor can think about their programs as plan-oriented reusable pieces, without concern for arguments, scoping, or data type incompatibilities.

For example, consider the task of writing a program:

(1) to read two input numbers from the user,
(2) add them,
(3) write the result,
(4) ask the user if there were more numbers to be added, and
(5) repeat the process if the user answers in the affirmative.

A student using the GPCeditor would not be expected to address the problem in terms of `readln`, `writeln`, and `while-do` loops. Instead, he or she is expected to think about the following:

• a `GetInput` plan (a plan grouping consisting of a `writeln` to write a prompt for the user and a `readln` for reading a value), which asks users if they would like to begin adding numbers,
• some other `GetInput` plans for reading in numbers,
• a computation plan for adding the input numbers,
• an output plan for writing the result, and
• a `DoItAgain` plan (a plan grouping containing a `while-do`, a test for equality between a string variable and a string constant such as "Yes," and a `GetInput` plan at the bottom of the loop to ask users if they would like to do the computation again).

Research on expert software designers suggests that they use such a plan-based structure when thinking about programs. Soloway and Ehrlich (1984) showed that expert designers' activity could be described in terms of a goal-plan based knowledge structure. By thinking about the design in terms of what needs to be accomplished (goals) and plans that meet those needs, the expert designer changes the design task from thinking about code and syntax to thinking about higher level components.

A goal-plan approach reduces design complexity by fragmenting the task and providing a framework for component reuse. A plan defined in terms of subgoals defines a level of hierarchy in the program that can be dealt with almost as a program unto itself. Thus, a program in the GPCeditor is not a monolith, but a collection of small, manageable pieces. The notion of reuse is particularly important as experts reuse pieces such as these, attempting to solve new problems by using previously generated program fragments. This reuse of plans further reduces the complexity of design by allowing the designer to treat entire branches of the decomposed task as a solved problem.

The GPCeditor supports reuse with a plan library (lower left corner of Figure 1). The student's library initially contains plans based on language constructs included in traditional Macintosh Pascal implementations. Students can add their own plans to the library (such as `GetInput` and `DoItAgain`) for later reuse. Double-clicking on a plan in the library presents information on that plan, such as its description, what the code for the plan looks like, and what data objects are needed to instantiate the plan for a program.

Multiple, linked representations. The GPCeditor provides multiple, linked representations to support students using a goal-plan approach to programming. These representations support the student in manipulating and reflecting on the goal-plan structure. Multiple representations provide opportunity to consider the problem from more than one perspective (Larkin and Simon, 1987).

Figure 1 is a sample screen from the GPCeditor. The upper left window is the goal-plan list (or *bucket,* in the students' and researchers' common language), which contains lists of goals and plans. These identify, by name, each goal and its corresponding plan at a particular level of hierarchy (named above the lists). In the example, the named goals and plans implement the `initial_questions` plan. The upper right window presents the traditional code-oriented view of the program. The lower right window gives a graphical *overview* of the hierarchy of goals and plans. Each goal appears with its corresponding plan, and if the plan is defined in terms of lower level goals and plans, those appear below and connected to the goal-plan node.

These representations are linked such that corresponding elements in all the representations appear highlighted at the same time. Clicking on a goal name in the goal list highlights the corresponding plan in the plan list, the corresponding code in the *code view,* and the corresponding node in the overview representation. The purpose for the linking is to encourage students to ease the transition between working with one representation and working with several.

Support for Process

The GPCeditor enforces the model of design described earlier in this section: decomposition of the problem, composition of the solution elements into a whole, and debugging or testing of that whole solution. This model is similar to others developed for programmers (Adelson and Soloway, 1984; Spohrer, 1989) and has elements like those used to describe other design domains (e.g., Hayes and Flower, 1980, for composition). Though fixed, it is a reasonable model of expert-like design. Whereas design models of experts emphasize that the ordering of

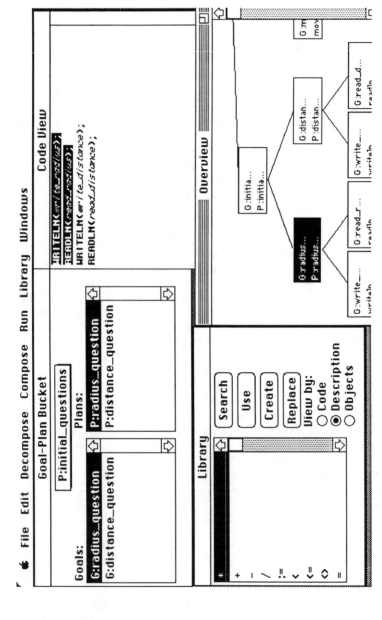

Figure 1 GPCeditor sample screen.

processes is not fixed (Hayes and Flower, 1980; Soloway and Ehrlich, 1984), students need a particular, initial ordering upon which to build their own design strategies (Corno and Snow, 1986).

The GPCeditor features scaffolding to support each of the three processes in its design model. The operations in this model are made explicit in the menus available to the student. Operations the student wishes to perform during decomposition are in the Decompose menu, and composition operations are in the Compose menu (Figure 2). Menus and their associated operations are enabled and disabled to reflect the current stage of the student's design.

Decomposition. During decomposition, the student uses New Goal . . . to formulate a goal, that is, to name and describe a goal. The library can be browsed at any time to identify potential alternative plans. The student may not select New Plan . . . to identify a plan for the program until a matching goal has been created. This means that students may not put components into their design without first identifying why the component is useful. The student can choose to create the new plan as a plan grouping or as a plan from the library by clicking on a plan in the library, then clicking on the Use button (Figure 1). As goals and plans are created, they appear in the goal-plan bucket and the overview window.

Some variation on this decomposition process does occur. For example, students sometimes use a *library-driven decomposition* strategy. They will browse through the library, check descriptions of various plans, and than create a goal and use one of the plans identified during the browse. Another variation that is not stressed within the curriculum is that a student can create any number of high-level, abstract goals that are not based on any particular order of composition. Only when plans are associated with these goals does the actual composition process occur. The important focus of the decomposition process of the GPCeditor is that goals are created before plans are chosen, with the implicit intent being the reasoned creation of these goals and articulations for the selections of a particular plan.

Composition. Once a plan is identified, the student enters the composition pro-

Figure 2 Decompose and compose menus.

cess. A plan just copied from the library is immediately instantiated for this program. A *match window* appears (Figure 3), listing the data objects needed to instantiate this plan for a program. From this window, the student can match each needed data object to an object already existing in the program or can create a new data object for the plan. Some required data objects might be left unmatched, to later be filled with plans consisting of expressions.

Students compose instantiated plans into the program using the Abutt and Nest operations in the Compose menu. The choice of operation depends on the kind of plan ordering desired. *Abutt* will place a plan either before or after another plan. *Nest* will place a plan within another plan, as when placing a plan between a `while-do` loop's `begin-end` block. The other compose operation, *Cut*, removes a plan from the program.

Debugging. Students change their programs during debugging by using the same metaphors used in constructing the program. Goals and plans can be removed or modified (i.e., changing names or descriptions). Plans can be matched to different data objects. However, the enforced ordering still prevails: A goal must be created before a plan can be identified, the plan must then be instantiated, and only then can the plan be composed into the program. In addition, program review tools are provided such as *Step* (see step through a program plan-by-plan to review execution) and an observe window to check variable values while the program executes.

Instructional Environment

The GPCeditor is used in Community High School, an alternative school in the Ann Arbor school district. The high school is loosely structured and emphasizes individual creativity and interdisciplinary efforts. Students do not have homerooms: They have forums that are as likely to meet in the evening at an area

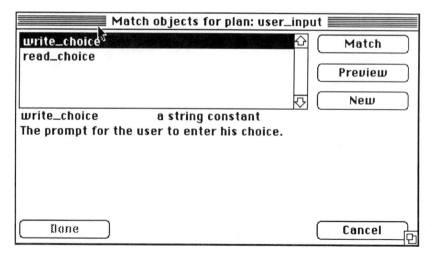

Figure 3 GPCeditor match window for instantiating plans for a program with data.

theater as in a formal classroom. Students are neither necessarily gifted nor learning disabled. They elect to come to this school because they are uncomfortable with more traditional schools.

Students apply to enter the course. Selection of students for the course is made by the administration, the course instructor, and members of the Highly Interactive Computing Environments (HiCE) research group. The goal is to fill the class with a wide range of students on dimensions such as gender, race, past computer experience, and academic performance. Ten to eleven students take the class each semester. The class using the GPCeditor has been run every semester since winter 1989. The students discussed in this chapter used the GPCeditor in fall 1989.

In the semester during which data were gathered for this chapter, the class met five days a week for two hours a day.[5] Because a two-hour class was unusual for Community High, the class was scheduled for the last hour of the normal day and one additional hour after school.

The instructor for the course, Robert Kinel, has been teaching mathematics (algebra, geometry, and calculus) for more than ten years, and computer science (specifically, Pascal) for seven years. He, with members of the HiCE group,[6] evolved the style of classroom interaction during the first semester of the course. Each student progresses through a set of worksheets at his or her own pace. The instructors wander through the classroom, providing individual instruction when asked and offering advice or asking students about their projects to encourage reflection. Thus, the instructor takes the role of the mentor, with the GPCeditor providing the needed technological support for the mentoring process. Occasionally, the class gathers to discuss a common issue.

For example, a common group discussion topic is on what makes a good design. The instructor presents students' programs in their overview representation on an overhead projector and has the students review and critique each design. The instructor might ask the students if the depth of decomposition and branching was appropriate, of if a different decomposition would have been better.

Although the course may sound teacher-intensive, in actual practice it is not. Students work alone or interact with their peers, for the most part. The teacher may provide coaching and instruction to an individual student for an entire class period without disturbing the activities of other students in the class. The GPCeditor provides enough support for many students in the class. However, even the amount of one-on-one interaction that is required might be too much for some classrooms. We address the point of needing to capture more of the teacher's expertise in the environment in the later section on future enhancements.

After approximately twelve weeks of the sixteen-week semester, some students will have progressed beyond the capabilities of the GPCeditor and begun using Lightspeed Pascal instead of the GPCeditor. Most of the students (50% to 75%) finish the portions of the curriculum that can be completed on the GPCeditor. They then use a traditional Pascal environment on the Macintosh to use features such as procedures and arrays that were not yet implemented in the GPCeditor at the time of this study.[7]

Curriculum

The goal of the curriculum is to teach students to develop Pascal software by using good design skills in the framework of the expert-based software design process described earlier. The curriculum is organized toward developing increasingly complex programs throughout the semester while simultaneously learning the design skills necessary to cope with this complexity. Design skills are introduced in stages as students learn more Pascal and are asked to synthesize ever more complex programs.

The curriculum used in the GPCeditor class was originally developed by Jeannine Pinto and Yasmin Kafai at Yale University for use in a course at a New Haven high school. Soloway and his group taught design using this curriculum with a traditional Pascal programming environment. Without support for the concepts in the environment, they found that students continued to focus on the code and not on the goal-plan structure of design. This curriculum was updated by Kafai for use with the GPCeditor.

The course is worksheet-based and self-paced. Students complete worksheets that discuss topics in Pascal and design. They file their completed worksheets and programs in individual notebooks, which the instructor collects, comments on, and grades every two to four weeks. Table 1 lists the GPCeditor worksheets. Each worksheet has a particular focus, as indicated by Table 1. The focuses were between Pascal constructs (e.g., the while-do loop and Macintosh graphics functions) and software design (e.g., identification of plans and the purpose of hierarchical decomposition). There are twenty-seven worksheets and forty-one assignments in the semester.

The assignments focus on Macintosh-style graphics and user interfaces. Students develop programs to move objects around on the screen, draw faces with blinking eyes, play games, and accept input through the keyboard or the mouse.

DATA AND CRITERIA

There were three foci that we used in considering the data gathered on the four case study students: student characteristics, learning and doing design, and use of the GPCeditor.

• The student characteristics of most concern were prior experience with computers, and motivation (both at the beginning and throughout the semester).
• The issue of learning and doing design breaks into four parts: quality of overall process and quality in each of the process stages.
  — In terms of the overall process, the use of reflection and explicit planning is key. Reflection is key to design (Jefferies et al., 1981) and to learning (Brown et al., 1983). Explicit planning is a measure of how systematic the student is about design.
  — The other three parts of learning and doing design are the three process stages: decomposition/reflection on the whole task, composition/reflection on the ordering of components, and debugging/reflection on the whole program with integrated components. Besides looking at performance on each of these processes, a subprocess for both decomposition and composition was identified for emphasis. For decomposition, how the student began the program was seen as significant, and for composition, the student's ability to handle data.
• To study use of the GPCeditor, two components were emphasized: the library and the alternative representations. Besides being the most significant physical

Table 1 GPCeditor worksheets and their foci

Worksheet	Focus
Planning, programming, and problem solving	Introduction to the GPCeditor. Students are asked to compose existing library plans and execute their programs.
Values and variables: Viva la differences	Students learn the difference between values and variables. They construct simple programs for performing math operations.
User friendliness: The key to popular programs	Introduction to the `GetInput` plan (prompt the user for data entry and input of data).
Getting coordinated: An introduction to the GPCeditor coordinate system	Students learn to specify locations in the graphics window in terms of horizontal and vertical offsets.
Graphics in the GPCeditor	Introduction to Macintosh graphics primitives, such as `paintoval` and `framerect`.
Looping in the GPCeditor	Introduction to the `while-do loop`.
Moving pictures in the GPCeditor	Combining iteration with graphics to achieve animation.
Writing good programs	Identification of named plans such as `GetInput` and `DoItAgain`.
Plans for moving pictures	Descriptions of plans used in animation.
Problem simplification	Discussion on program decomposition.
The word of the day: Hierarchy	Identifying program hierarchy.
Line drawings	Introduction to `moveto` and `lineto` graphics primitives.
Blinking eye face	Draw a face with animated, blinking eyes—a complex program requiring 20–50 lines of program code.
Decisions, decisions, decisions	Introduction to the `if-then`.
Apply your knowledge: Identifying plans	Identifying plans in other students' programs.
Finding out what you know about plans	Quiz on plans.
Working with plans	Introduction to debugging techniques.
Plan library	List of all programming plans met in the course.
Random numbers	Introduction to `random`.
Random numbers and game programs	Creation of computer games using `random` and `if-then`.
User-friendly interfaces	Using mouse-driven input.
Procedures	Introduction to procedures.
My life in disorganized crime	Methods for organizing code (procedures).
Or: Logical alternatives	Using logical conjunction.
Procedures revisited	More on procedures.
Handling user input errors	Handling data verification.
What you do when everyone wants to play: Arrays	Introduction to arrays.

features of the environment (Figure 1), they are the workspaces in which the students design.

Table 2 summarizes the data collected in the case study. The primary data source was the think-aloud protocol. These were used to observe the students' design processes and their use of the GPCeditor. The secondary data sources were questionnaires, interviews, review of the students' assigned programs, and trace files of GPCeditor usage (which are automatically generated by the GPCeditor).

Table 2 Summary of data sources and criteria

Topic/Issue	Data source	Frequency	No. of students	Criteria
Student characteristics				
Prior experience with programming and computers, and academic performance	Questionnaire	Twice (at beginning and end of semester)	All students	Asked students to describe previous computer experiences, programming instruction, and to write a program
Motivation	Interview	Twice (once at the beginning of the semester, and again mid-semester)	All students in initial interview, only students not in protocol in midsemester interview	Asked students why they were taking this class and what they thought of computers and the GPCeditor in particular
Learning and doing design				
Occurrence of reflection overall	Think-aloud protocols	Three times	Four students	Earlier and more frequent reflection as more expert-like
Occurrence of explicit planning	Think-aloud protocols	Three times	Four students	Explicit statement of plans or use of external aids (notebooks, pencil-and-paper)
Ability to begin program	Think-aloud protocols	Three times	Four students	Use of heuristic to determine first goal
Able to manage complexity in decomposition/reflection on whole task	Think-aloud protocols	Three times	Four students	Greater use of plan groupings to create levels of hierarchy; use of plan groupings to create functional decomposition; reuse of plans
	Assigned programs	Daily	All students	Reuse of plans

(Table continues on next page)

Ability	Data source	Frequency	Participants	Focus
Ability to manage complexity in composition/reflection on components	Think-aloud protocols	Three times	Four students	Tailoring of reused plans; use of composition features; correctness of program
Ability to instantiate plans with data	Assigned programs Think-aloud protocols	Daily Three times	All students Four students	Tailoring of reused plans; correctness of program Ability to recall data objects by function
Ability to manage complexity in debugging/reflection on whole program	Assigned programs Think-aloud protocols	Daily Three times	All students Four students	Naming of variables by function Use of review tools; skill in debugging—focus on goal and purposeful corrections
	Usage trace files	Daily	All students	Amount of program testing
			Use of GPCeditor features	
Use of the library	Think-aloud protocols Assigned programs Usage trace files	Three times Daily Daily	Four students All students All students	Reuse of plans; styles of library browsing Reuse of plans Reuse of plans; amount of plan saving
Use of alternative representations	Think-aloud protocols	Three times	Four students	Active reference to representations, i.e., use of the overview, goal-plan lists, and text view

Not all types of data were collected for all kinds of students, to reduce the complexity of review of the data and development of these criteria.

Each protocol had a similar structure. Students were asked to complete a series of small programs similar to ones they were doing in class. The programs were organized such that plans created in the early programs would be useful in the later ones, to encourage reuse. The worksheet from the first protocol appears in Appendix 1 as an example. In this protocol, the students were asked to write four programs: to draw a face, to draw two faces, to ask the user his name and greet him, and finally, both to draw two faces and to greet the user.

In addition to these formal data, less formal data were used to fill out the picture of the classroom. A researcher visited the class two to three times a week and kept a journal. Each student kept a daily journal on their problems, successes, comments on the GPCeditor, and comments on the entire class. Finally, the instructor's comments were often solicited.

Table 2 also summarizes the criteria used in evaluating student performance in each of these study foci using these data.

• For student characteristics, students were asked in questionnaires and in interviews what they felt about computers and the GPCeditor and what their prior programming experience had been.

• Criteria were developed for each of the subfoci to evaluate how the student did design. The data were compared over time by using these criteria to determine how well students learned design.

— Reflection in the overall process was evaluated on the frequency of reflection and where in the process it occurred. Reflecting late in the process was inefficient because decisions had already been made earlier in the process. Explicit planning was noted by verbal planning comments and use of notes.

— Decompositions were evaluated on the breadth and depth of the goal-plan trees, the use of plan groupings to create levels of hierarchy, and reuse of plans.

— Compositions were evaluated on the quality of the program, the student's ability to order the plans, ability to tailor reused plans, and ability to find and use data objects.

— Debugging was evaluated on kind and purposefulness of changes and use of debugging tools.

• Student use of the GPCeditor was evaluated on use of the library for saving and browsing and on use of the alternative representations for reflection or manipulation.

SUMMARY OF CASE STUDIES

Summary across Students

The four case study students are Sue, Allen, Lois, and Fred.[8] The data on these students is presented in detail in the Appendix 2 and are summarized in Table 3. These students were selected as a representative sample of the types of students using the GPCeditor. These students cover a wide range of prior knowledge and interests: from initial inexperience with programming to being self-taught in several languages, and from entering the class excited by computers to entering the

Table 3 Summary of data for case study students

Issues	Allen	Fred	Lois	Sue
		Student characteristics		
Prior experience	3.0 GPA, sophomore; less than a semester of Basic	Freshman; self-taught programming experience in Basic, Pascal, and Grasp	3.7 GPA, senior; self-taught programming experience in Basic	3.2 GPA, junior; less than a semester of Basic
Motivation	Interested in computer at initial interview	Interested in computers at initial interview; didn't like the GPCeditor at midsemester interview	Took class for transcript; experiences with computers, losing data at initial interview; didn't like the GPCeditor at midsemester interview	Took class for transcript; found computers frustrating at initial interview
		Learning and doing design		
Reflection overall	Early and often in first two protocols; only at beginning in last	Early and often in first protocol, only at beginning in last	Early and often in protocol	Late and little reflection in all three protocols
Explicit planning	Used notes in first protocol, and discussed where he was going; made some explicit plans in second protocol, few in third	Made explicit verbal and written plans in first protocol; none in last	Used notebook and made verbal plans in protocol	Little planning
Starting program	Had no problem starting in any of the three	Had no problem starting	Used a heuristic of doing something and then building on that	Frequently didn't know where to begin
Decomposition/reflection on whole task	Used composition to functionally decompose programs in the first protocol; only used groupings for difficult problems in second protocol; decomposition was not observable in third; no reuse of plans	No use of plan groupings; no reuse of plans	Reuse of plans observable in assigned programs; use of good functional decomposition	Little use of hierarchical decomposition in protocols, and only in rote manner; assigned programs had good functional decomposition and reuse, eventually

(Table continues on next page)

Table 3 Summary of data for case study students (*continued*)

Issues	Allen	Fred	Lois	Sue
Composition/reflection on components	No tailoring of reused plans; no problems composing plans; programs functioned correctly	No tailoring of reused plans; few problems composing plans in first program (choosing between *abutt* and *nest*); programs exceeded requirements	Tailored reused plans; programs functioned correctly	Tailoring of reused plans; programs exceeded requirements, eventually
Data handling	Poorly named data objects, but no problems finding data	Poorly named data objects; problems finding data in first protocol; no problems in later programs	Well-named data objects with no trouble finding data objects	Well-named data objects; many problems finding data in first protocol, fewer in later protocols
Debugging/reflection on whole program	Used hierarchy as a debugging technique; little debugging in later protocols	Used output and code view for simulation when debugging. Lost track of path in first protocol. Successful debugger later	Used simulation and tools	No identifiable debugging strategy; made random changes
Use of GPCeditor features				
Library use	Little use of saving, reuse, or browsing	Extensive browsing in first week; no saving or reuse	Little use until latter part of semester; saving and reuse	Frequent browsing throughout semester; saving and reuse
Alternative representations	Used code view, goal-plan buckets, and overview from first protocol	Used code view only in first protocol; occasional use of goal-plan buckets for plan selection in second protocol; never referenced the overview	Little active use of alternative representations	Used code view primarily, with occasional use of the goal-plan buckets

Table 4   Data collected for case study students

Student	Think-aloud protocols			Interviews	
	First	Second	Third[1]	Initial	Mid-Semester *r*
Sue	X	X	X	X	
Allen	X	X	X	X	
Lois			X	X	X
Fred	X		X	X	X

[1]Third protocol was with Lightspeed Pascal for all students except Sue.

class frustrated by computers. Their performance varied widely: On the first protocol, Allen completed all four programs, Fred completed the first two, and Sue finished only the first. The learning and doing of these students offers an representative sample of the kinds of activity seen when using the GPCeditor.

As mentioned in the previous section, not all data were collected for all students. The specific data collected for these four students are summarized in Table 4. The most data are available for Sue and Allen, the least for Lois.

In general, the students in the GPCeditor class seemed to succeed well using it. Table 5 describes the case study students' final projects by using a rough measure of program complexity, the number of lines of code in the program. For a first-semester high school programming course, these are large programs for students to make functional, especially considering how students in traditional courses rarely get beyond syntactic correctness in their programs (Pea and Kurland, 1986). Individually, the case study students point out the strengths and weaknesses of the GPCeditor approach.

Sue

Sue did seem to grasp the design concepts being taught with the GPCeditor. Sue used hierarchical decomposition, she reused plans, and she wrote working programs. The downside was that her progress was labor-intensive both for her and the instructor.

She needed more low-level support than the GPCeditor provided. For example, she might have found the GPCeditor more useful if it provided heuristics for beginning a program, more explicit process support (e.g., a prompt suggesting "Stop here and write down all the possible goals you might use"), and coaching (e.g., a phrase like "For this program, you will probably find move to to be very useful").

Table 5   Size of final projects in number of lines

Student	Size	Environment
Sue	41	GPCeditor
Allen[1]	33 and 88	Lightspeed
Lois	147	Lightspeed
Fred	144	Lightspeed

[1]Allen did two programs for his final project.

Allen

Allen began using the GPCeditor features and design skills it exemplifies, but then returned to novice-like skills. Though he continued to produce significant programs, they were ill-structured and he did not use the tools of the environment. He often complained that it was easier to work without the tools and that the GPCeditor slowed him down.

For Allen, the GPCeditor would have served him better if it provided more high-level support. The tools of the GPCeditor are well-designed for novice students, but as students became more expert the tools become more of a nuisance than an aid. Allen might have appreciated tools for structuring programs and for tracking data that are more like those appearing in expert-level CASE (computer-aided software engineering) tools.

Lois

For Lois, motivation was key. She was not successful in the course until she encountered problems that captured her interest. Once she had latched on to those, she used the functionality of the GPCeditor and learned the design skills being taught. By the end of the semester, she was one of the most proficient designers in the class.

Fred

Fred was an accomplished programmer entering the class. He did learn design skills in the course, but he did not explicitly use the ones being taught. From his comments, he may not have recognized the usefulness of the GPCeditor tools and design skills.

Fred might have found useful some instruction that explicitly modeled the design process. As design processes are dynamic, they are difficult to transmit through worksheets and thus require the instructor to model the design process (Collins, 1988). By performing the task, using the tools, and explicitly demonstrating good process, the instructor can provide a model for the students to follow (Paris and Winograd, 1989).

Instruction in the GPCeditor class did not include expert designers using the tools of the GPCeditor. Perhaps if Fred might have seen how the overview could be used effectively, where decomposition was useful, and what good debugging strategies were, he might have practiced them.

Summary across Study Foci

Though four students are too small a sample to make any statements of significance, the case studies themselves can be summarized across study foci. These provide some indication of how students are described under each of these foci.

Student Characteristics

Students' past experiences with programming did not seem to affect their performance with the GPCeditor as much as did other factors. Students with little experience were able to design complex programs with high quality. Students with a lot of experience generally did try the GPCeditor and used it in ways similar to other students. For example, Fred had significant programming experience before entering the class, but he had never done the kind of programming before (e.g., the size and complexity of the programs) that he did in the GPCeditor class. From his comments and performance, he seemed to be giving the GPCeditor a chance. The students' motivation seemed to be more significant than previous programming experience. Neither Lois nor Sue were particularly interested in the course or the GPCeditor at the beginning of the semester. Neither performed well during the first few weeks. Lois only began to improve when she grew interested in the programs she was writing. Sue did not show much improvement in the class nor interest in the programming assignments.

Learning and Doing Design

In this section we examine four distinct parts: the overall process and the process within the three stages of decomposition, composition, and debugging. The data indicate that even with the scaffolding of the software design process provided in the GPCeditor, our students still exhibited most of the problems associated with a novice-like approach to software design.

(1) *The overall process.* The students' overall process was not very good. Though several of the students began with good explicit planning and early and frequent reflection, these characteristics faded in the later protocols. Those students who did plan and reflect on the process performed well. Those who did not produced decompositions of a poorer quality relative to other students. In some cases the decompositions were unintelligible, although this was rare.

(2) *Decomposition.* The students' decomposition were, in general, quite good, and they did seem to improve over the course of the semester. Considering that students are notoriously bad at modular decomposition (Spohrer and Soloway, 1985), the quality and use of plan groupings to create hierarchy in their decompositions was impressive. Most students had good heuristics for handling problems such as determining where to begin a program. However, there was little reuse of grouped plans.

(3) *Composition.* The students' compositions were less impressive. Though their programs did run, data names were poor and the meaning of the data object associated with the variable name was often forgotten. The compositions were poorly structured and hard to read. For example, Allen's example program described in Appendix 2 has assignment statements (whose purpose is unclear because of variable names such as A and vari) interspersed among supposedly identical loops. Sue's composition, though much clearer and better structured, includes redundant plans not related to the problem at hand as well as data objects that are never used. The compositions did not seem to improve during the semester.

(4) *Debugging.* The students' debugging was interesting in its diversity. The students' use of debugging tools ranged from examination of the hierarchy as a debugging tool to use of mental simulation. Both Fred and Sue had significant difficulty keeping track of program bugs and following up on their correction. Students did develop debugging strategies across the semester.

The results are consistent with the previous claim that American students have more experience in the analysis skills of decomposition and less experience with the synthesis skills of composition and debugging.

Use of GPCeditor Features

In this section we summarize interactions of the students with various features in the GPCeditor. These observations motivate and direct changes to the existing environment and modifications to the course curriculum.

(1) *The Plan Library.* The plan library was mostly used for browsing, for finding information about plans. Though both Sue and Lois did use the library for saving, reusing, and tailoring plans (later in the semester), most students did not. Neither Fred nor Allen made any use of the library other than for retrieving plans and some browsing. The library use, however, did change during the course. Sue began saving and reusing plans early, but Lois did not until later. Fred began the semester doing a lot of browsing, but then he stopped browsing.

(2) *Goal-Plan Lists, Code View, and the Overview.* Most students used the goal-plan list (buckets) and the code view for reflection and manipulation. It is notable that they did not use just one, but it is surprising that they did not use the overview. Allen was unusual in his use of the overview, because most students were like Fred, who found it useless. Many students covered up the overview with other windows and never uncovered it.

(3) *Debugging and Other Advanced Features of the GPCeditor.* There was little use of any of the advanced debugging features of the GPCeditor. The Step and Walk program run options were rarely used, and students did not interact much with the observe window. The GPCeditor does provide the ability to set break-points (e.g., temporarily suspend the execution of a program so that the values of internal data objects can be easily examined or modified) but this feature was not used.

Other facilities provided by the GPCeditor as tools to support the design process were rarely used. For example, the plan library provides a search capability, allowing the student to search the plan library for all plans that contain a key-word phrase in their plan description.

FUTURE DIRECTIONS AND SUMMARY

Changes to the Instructional Environment, Curriculum, and GPCeditor

The problems described by the case study analyses are not answered by changing any one portion of the instructional package used in the GPCeditor class. The pieces of the package interact and require changes to all three components to be effective.

Changes to the Instructional Environment

The GPCeditor supports students as they learn and do software design, but our students had trouble learning which features of the GPCeditor should be used in various stages of the design process. Furthermore, it is unlikely that students will spontaneously discover certain key aspects of the design process (such as advanced debugging strategies or the use of alternative designs) without explicit instruction. The question is how to demonstrate the process of software design used by expert programmers that forms the foundation of the GPCeditor.

The question can be addressed most effectively by having the instructor model the use of the GPCeditor by solving problems similar to those given to the students. During this modeling the instructor would be expected to make explicit the rationale for using specific features of the GPCeditor. This would enable students to better realize how the instructor's actions in solving problems can be brought to bear on the problems they are attempting to solve.

Changes to the Curriculum.

The current focus of the GPCeditor curriculum is based on the analytical skills of decomposition and the synthesis skills of composition. Though the goal-plan approach is covered in a strong fashion, the curriculum does not talk about reflection, heuristics, and why the GPCeditor tools should be used. The curriculum needs to cover this material to enable learning of these design concepts.

The assigned programming tasks in the curriculum are not intrinsically motivating. They were designed to teach students to create the sorts of effects and interfaces that users encountered on the Macintosh. The assumption was that students would be interested in creating programs like those that they were using. Although this was effective for some students, it was not especially motivating for others. More motivating tasks might be those grounded in real-world problems (Collins, 1988; Harel and Papert, 1990).

Changes to the GPCeditor

The GPCeditor currently provides reasonable support to one type of student. It needs to change to provide a wider range of support for individual students (both low- and high-ability students) and to enhance the instruction and the curriculum.

A needed enhancement to the GPCeditor is adaptable scaffolding. The existing scaffolding of the GPCeditor, as exemplified by the strict process control of the student in the design process, is fixed. When first using the GPCeditor, the strict process control provides a structure that enables the student to handle the complexities of the design. As the student's skill grows and they become more expert-like in their problem-solving process, the strict process control can impede the student. The scaffolding of the GPCeditor needs to fade in such a way as to provide a less strict framework for the solution of problems.

Additional support the students might find helpful includes:

• Prompts that could be added to the GPCeditor to provide more explicit support for process learning. Example prompts might inform students when they should reflect or suggest what they might be thinking about for effective problem solving (Polya, 1945).
• Suggestions by the GPCeditor of plans, strategies, and heuristics, if it were aware of the kind of program being worked on. This kind of task-specific support might be useful as low-level scaffolding.
• New representations that could be added to insure complete coverage of the design process. In particular, tools could be created to ease the process of tracking data objects and of recalling past activity.

We do not anticipate that the implementation of adaptable scaffolding and advanced design support will be based solely on students' interactions with the GPCeditor. Rather, we expect to provide tools within the GPCeditor that allow the student with the advice of the instructor to customize the environment for a given student. Ultimately, we plan to provide a set of customization tools to the students themselves for more complete control over their own design process.

Summary

The GPCeditor has shown the validity of using computers as design support environments (DSEs) for students. The support provided in the GPCeditor has enabled the students to go beyond what they might achieve in a typical programming environment, to develop complex and interesting artifacts that motivate them and provide a focus for their learning.

We see DSEs as being the next stage in the evolution of computer-aided design (CAD) environments. Students are just one kind of novice engaged in design. The computer has made many design domains available to users, such as publishing and even architectural design. These domains are now available because the computer has taken over the mechanical skills previously necessary to work in that domain. However, design in these domains is more than simply mechanics—experts in these domains have knowledge structures and skills that make them capable of working on complex artifacts. For design novices to be at all successful in designing in these new domains, we must attempt to provide some of this expert knowledge in the form of design support in the environment.

The GPCeditor has provided useful information in our first pass at providing DSEs for students. Clearly, additional factors of instruction, curriculum, and the interaction with the environment must be considered and used to enhance the final result. Nevertheless, the direction is also clear that providing support for student design activities is key to making project-based learning a reality in the classroom.

ACKNOWLEDGMENTS

The GPCeditor was designed by Ken Ewing at Yale University. A team of programmers completed implementation at the University of Michigan: Luke Hohmann, Dave Koziol, Dan O'Leary, Charles Weaver, and Mark Guzdial. Luke Hohmann has maintained and updated the environment for the last three years.

REFERENCES

Adelson, B., and E. Soloway, "A cognitive model of software design," Technical Report #342, Cognition and Programming Project. Yale University, New Haven, CT, 1984.
Brown, A. L., J. D. Bransford, R. A. Ferrara, and J. C. Campione, "Learning, remembering, and understanding," in W. Kessen (ed.), *Handbook of child psychology: Cognitive development,* 77–166. New York: Wiley, 1983.
Collins, A., "Cognitive apprenticeship and instructional technology," Technical Report #6899. Cambridge, MA: Bolt, Beranek, Newman, 1988.
Corno, L., and R. Snow, "Adapting teaching to individual differences among learners," in M. Wittrock, *Handbook of research on teaching,* pp. 605–629. New York: Macmillan, 1986.
Farnham-Diggory, S., *Schooling.* Cambridge, MA: Harvard University Press, 1990.
Guindon, R., and B. Curtis, "Control of cognitive processes during software design: What tools are needed?" in *CHI'88: Conference Proceedings: Special Issue of the ACM/SIGCHI Bulletin,* 263–268, 1988.
Harel, I. *Software design for learning: Children's construction of meaning for fractions and LOGO programming,* Ph.D. dissertation, MIT Media Technology Laboratory, 1988.
Hayes, J. R., and L. S. Flower. "Identifying the organization of writing processes." In L. W. Gregg and E. R. Steinberg (eds.), *Cognitive processes in writing,* Hillsdale, NJ: Erlbaum, 1980.

Jefferies, R., A. A. Turner, P. G. Polson, and M. E. Atwood, "The processes involved in designing software," in J. R. Anderson (ed.), *Cognitive skills and their acquisition*, pp. 255–283. Hillsdale, NJ: Erlbaum, 1981.

Larkin, J. H., and H. A. Simon, "Why a diagram is (sometimes) worth ten thousand words," *Cognitive Science*, 11:65–99, 1987.

Paris, S. G., and P. Winograd, "How metacognition can promote academic learning and instruction," in B. F. Jones and L. Idol (eds.), in *Dimensions of thinking and cognitive instruction*. Hillsdale, NJ: Erlbaum, 1989.

Parnas, D., "On the criteria to be used in decomposing systems into modules," *Communications of the ACM*, 15(2):1053–1058, 1972.

Pea, R. D., and D. M. Kurland, "On the cognitive effects of learning computer programming," in R. D. Pea and K. Sheingold (eds.), *Mirrors of minds*, Norwood, NJ: Ablex, 1986.

Polya, G., *How to solve it: A new aspect of mathematical method*, Princeton, NJ: Princeton University Press, 1945.

Simon, H. A. *The sciences of the artificial*, Cambridge, MA: MIT Press, 1969.

Soloway, E., and K. Ehrlich, "Empirical studies of programming knowledge," *IEEE Transactions on Software Engineering*, 10(5):595–609, 1984.

Spohrer, J. C. *MARCEL: A generate-test-and-debug (GTD) impasse/repair model of student programmers*, Ph.D. dissertation, YALEU/CSD/RR #687, Yale University, New Haven, CT, 1989.

Spohrer, J. C., and E. Soloway, "Putting it all together is hard for novice programmers," in *Proceedings of the IEEE International Conference on Systems, Man, and Cybernetics*. Tucson, AZ, pp. 728–734.

NOTES

1. The skill of defining a task in terms of subtasks is *modular decomposition,* which reduces complexity of a large task by allowing the designer to concentrate on solving smaller, more manageable component tasks. Design researchers emphasize modular decomposition as key to coping with design complexity (e.g., Parnas, 1972).
2. Highly Interactive Computing Environments Research Group, directed by Professor Elliot Soloway at the University of Michigan Electrical Engineering and Computer Science Department.
3. The GPCeditor runs on Apple Macintosh computers with at least 2.5 Mb of memory, a hard disk, and a large monitor. The version used in this study required a 19-inch monitor, but a new version can be run on 13-inch monitors.
4. Through a donation from Apple Computer, eleven stations were placed in Community High School.
5. The class now meets three days a week for ninety minutes, with optional after-school sessions.
6. During the first month or two of the first semester using the GPCeditor, three instructors were present daily (the class instructor, Soloway, and Yasmin Kafai, one of his research assistants). Once a style of interaction was established, the number of instructors dropped to two (the class instructor and a research assistant).
7. Procedures have since been implemented in the GPCeditor.
8. Student names have been changed to protect subject anonymity.

APPENDIX 1: FIRST PROTOCOL WORKSHEET

Making Faces with the GPCeditor

This worksheet is a review of concepts already visited with the GPCeditor. Here you'll put them together.

There are several components to this worksheet. **Please read over the entire worksheet, then begin at Part 1.** Do as much as you can of the worksheet.

Part I: Drawing a Face (or Maybe a Bowling Ball)

You've drawn circles, lines, ovals, and rectangles in this class, sometimes as frames and sometimes painted. If you combine a big framed circle with three smaller, painted circles (two for the eyes and one for the mouth) you can draw a face as seen below.

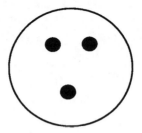

(It either looks like Mr. Bill, the clay figure from "Saturday Night Live," or a bowling ball with oddly spaced holes.)

Write A Program that draws this figure, then save the program as **PartOne.**

Part II: Draw Two Faces

The mouth can be made with a circle, above, or it could be made with other objects. For example, here's the mouth made with a circle and a new one made with moveto and lineto.

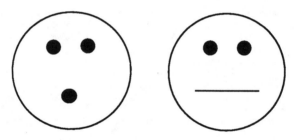

Or, if you're not comfortable with moveto and lineto, you could draw the second face using paintoval.

Write A Program that draws two faces on the screen, one next to the other. The leftmost face should be the face with a paintcircle mouth. The rightmost face has a mouth drawn either with moveto and lineto or with paintoval. When you're finished, save the program as **PartTwo.**

Part III. Get the User's Name

Now you'll write an entirely new program.
Earlier in class you wrote the Echo program. This program asked the user to type something, then displayed whatever the user typed. The program looked like this:

```
program echo;
var

    echo: string;

begin
    readln (echo);
    writeln (echo);

end.
```

Write a program like Echo, but reading and writing the user's name. Write the program to ask the user for their name and read their name as input. Then, display the word "Hello" and their name (on two separate lines.)

> **The program says:** What is your name?
> **You type:**   Mark

> **The program says:** Hello
>   Mark

Part IV: Making Friendly Faces

Now, write a program that contains parts of both programs.

First ask the user for their name (in the text window).
Then draw the faces (in the graphics window).
And finally display "Hello" and their name (in the text window).

Be sure that you get the order correct: ask for the name, then draw the faces, then say hello.
You may wish to use the library to copy plans between programs.

APPENDIX 2: EVALUATION OF CASE STUDIES

Each of the four case study students (Sue, Allen, Lois, and Fred) is discussed in some detail in the following subsections. The data for each are discussed under each of the study foci.

As representative of the programs that the students produced, each student's "Challenge" program is presented. This program involved extending a program written earlier by the students called "Triangles" which drew a moiré triangle by using multiple lines in an animation in which the triangle grew across the screen horizontally. The challenge was to draw four triangles so as to create a rectangle: the original horizontal triangle to form the top, then a vertical triangle to form the right side, another horizontal for the bottom, and a final vertical triangle for the left side. The instructions for "Triangles" and "Challenge" are in Figures 4 and

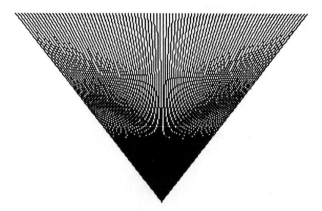

Figure 4 Instructions for Program 7: Triangles. Write a program
that produces a figure like the one shown above. To do
this, you will need to use both moveto and lineto
and the while loop. Hint: Each line is drawn between a
constant point and a variable point. The variable point
varies only horizontally. Vary the horizontal position on
this point according to a number that the user inputs
when the program runs. For example, this figure was
produced when a user input the number 3.

5. These programs appear in the worksheet "Moving Pictures in the GPCeditor,"
the seventh worksheet in the GPCeditor series of twenty-seven worksheets.

For each student, the complete Pascal program and a portion of the goal-plan
decomposition is presented. The decomposition is presented as it would appear in
the overview window. Plan names that begin with "P:" are plan groupings that
are created by the student, and all other plans are taken from the library. Goals and
plans appear left-to-right, top-to-bottom in the order in which the student created
them.

Sue

Student Characteristics

Sue entered the GPCeditor class as a junior with a 3.2 GPA. She had done some
programming in Basic. She admitted that she was taking the class only to have a
computer class on her high school transcript. In her initial interview, she expressed frustration in her experience with computers (verbal comment by the researcher appear in italics).

Do you like computers?

"If I know what I'm doing, I like them. If I don't understand, I get frustrated."

Is that (frustration) the hardest part of using computers?

"Yeah, just, in simple terms, I don't know, trying to express the ideas that you want, and trying
to get it onto the screen, trying to figure out what steps you have to do to get things onto the
computer or whatever."

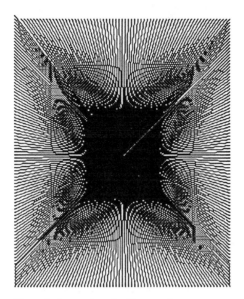

Figure 5   Instructions for Program 8:
Challenge. Enhance your Triangles
program to draw lines around all four
sides of the screen, clockwise. See
figure. Hint: You will need four
`while` loops, one for drawing each
side.

Use of Reflection and Explicit Planning

Sue did not reflect on the program until late in the task, when it was difficult to backtrack. For example, she would question her choice of goal or plan when instantiating the plan for the program in her protocols. This did not improve during the course of the semester.

She did not use explicit planning. She never wrote anything down, nor did she even make a verbal statement of what she was planning on doing. Not surprisingly, she often got lost in her protocols:

> "Oh! What did I do? Oh, I'll have to change that. The vertical. I forgot what I changed."

Decomposition

One of Sue's greatest difficulties was determining her first goal when faced with a new program. When given a new assignment, she would literally sit in front of her computer for an hour or more without creating any new goals or making any notes. She took longer than the other students and required extensive help. On a typical program, Sue took over three times as long as other students, ten days versus three days, and she mentioned in her journal receiving help on four of those ten days.

Part of the reason that she took so much longer in writing her programs was that she took great pains to have good hierarchical decomposition and plan reuse in her program, going so far as to redesign programs in order to achieve these goals.

The usage trace files show that she saved ten plans to the library during the course of the semester, more than twice as many as any other student in the class. The following quote from her journal exemplifies the effort that she went through for good decomposition and plan reuse.

"I retyped the Challenge so that I could have Hierarchy and reuse some of the same plans and goals. It really wasn't that hard because I knew what I was doing but now I have to change things so that it will make sense for the next loop in the programming."

During protocols, her use of hierarchy was rote. She announced during her second protocol that she was using "plenty of hierarchy." However, she only decomposed GetInput plans and bodies of while-do loops, two purposes explicitly suggested in the worksheets. She never used a new level of hierarchy, for example, to identify a logical partition in the program.

Sue's first protocol session was marked by a lack of planning. She did not reflect on the task and her process early, but late when it was difficult to backtrack, for example, while instantiating a plan for a particular program. In particular, she lost track of data objects and her rationale for the changes she was making. She created no hierarchical decomposition. In one of the programs in the second protocol, she was asked to write the result of a calculation. She created a new level of hierarchy, placed a writeln within it to write the result, then placed a readln immediately afterward—as if she was creating a GetInput plan. She did not realize that one could use a writeln outside of a GetInput plan and without a readln following.

Composition

Sue had little trouble composing her plans, but she had significant problems matching data objects. Though she chose good, descriptive names for her data objects, she still had difficulty matching the function of the data object to the name. In her second protocol, for example, she had variables named horizontal and vertical, but she forgot how this related to the output.

"I don't know—I'm just trying to figure out. Can I just match this? (*Pointing with her mouse to a data object.*) Left and right would be horizontal, up and down would be vertical? What should I do? I don't know."

Debugging

Her debugging strategies were typical for a novice programmer but did not improve through the semester. She made random changes that dealt only with surface characteristics of the program (e.g., changing the order of two plans) as opposed to reconstructing portions of the program (e.g., removing and creating a new goal). The following scene is from a debugging episode in her first protocol session.

(*Sue stares at the code view, clicking on various pieces.*)

"Hmm, I'm not sure . . ."

(*She clicks on a plan to draw a circle, moves it one statement further down in the program—a change that has no effect on execution. She runs the program and sees no difference. She clicks on the code view again.*)

"I had it right before."

(*Clicks on the output graphics window.*)

"Maybe it's here."

(*She changes the value of a data object, then re-runs the program.*)

"Okay, that did make a difference."

Gpceditor Use

Sue made more use of the library than any other student. She browsed the library and checked plan descriptions frequently. As mentioned, she saved and reused plans more than any other student.

She made little use of the alternative representations. Protocols and usage trace files showed no use of the overview and little use of the goal-plan buckets. Her primary program representation was the code view.

Sample Program

Sue's "Challenge" program and decomposition appear in Exhibit A. The program has a nice structure, is understandable, and is well composed. She uses descriptive data object names. Her program is not as efficient as it might be. In fact, she includes unnecessary components. For example, not only does she unnecessarily repeat center : = one_hundred; within every while-do loop (unnecessary because center is never changed), the variable center is never used at all. The repetitive nature of the program is highlighted in the identical structure used in drawing each triangle of the challenge.

Her decomposition is modular, easily understood, and easily modified. Each triangle in the challenge is made from the same three parts: a while-do loop, an expression to test for ending the loop (which she names prompt), and a body named while loop. This structure is repeated through all four components, and the while loop plan is reused in each case. Note that the while loop plan is not simply reused at each case—it is also tailored to fit the different requirements of each of the loops. Though she did not place all three components in one plan grouping, she does seem to understand the basic notion of modular decomposition and plan reuse.

Allen

Student Characteristics

Allen took the GPCeditor class because he was interested in computers. He had studied Basic for six weeks when he was in sixth grade. He took the class as a sophomore with a 3.0 GPA.

Use of Reflection and Explicit Planning

In his first protocol, Allen made frequent verbal statements of what he was going to do and what he was thinking about. In these examples from the first protocol, he makes explicit verbal plans, makes use of pencil and paper to plan what he is doing, and makes use of the overview window for reflection.

"How do we do this? Get their name, then draw the faces, and finally display hello and their name."

"The vertical would be . . . Let's draw a picture for a second."

(*While clicking in the overview window*) "I always like to see what's going on over here, just to see where I am, what it looks like."

Reflection and planning were not explicit in his second and third protocols. However, he completed all of his programs correctly in both of those protocols, and in less time than anyone else. It may be that the programs were too easy for him to demand reflection or explicit planning, or that these processes were internalized and were no longer being verbalized.

Decomposition

Allen used and seemed to understand the need for hierarchical decomposition from the start. In his first protocol, he created a plan grouping and explained its purpose to the researcher.

"Let's add a little hierarchy here . . ."

Why did you create that?

"So I can put all the circles, the face part in that. And then if I put the face part in that, then I can just . . . add the different parts of the program, add those in a different part."

Allen's other protocol programs and assigned programs used strange combinations of hierarchy and ungrouped plans. In his second protocol session, programs that he began with a comment like "this is easy" invariably had little or no hierarchy (i.e., he built his program entirely out of ungrouped Pascal primitives as opposed to defining levels of hierarchy.) However, when he encountered a program bug, for example, he would often define a new level of hierarchy and decompose the difficult plan there. For Allen, hierarchy seemed to be a method of coping with a complex problem.

It may be that Allen defined a new level of hierarchy in order to try an alternative design to meet the problem at hand. Because for Allen building a plan was more easily accomplished "from scratch," previously stored plans in his mental library were constructed in the problem-solving process. However, new plans, or alternative designs, required a new level of hierarchy to deal with the complexity.

Composition

Allen never exhibited any problems with ordering and composing plans or with instantiating plans with data. This is unusual because his names for variables were obtuse and seemed to lack any connection with their function.

Debugging

Allen's debugging strategies were difficult to observe because he made few mistakes. As mentioned, he used hierarchy as a debugging technique in his second protocol. By the end of the semester, Allen's process was expert-like. He made few mistakes in his third protocol session. His usage trace files showed few program modifications and few program executions.

During the first four weeks of the semester, Allen ran his programs an average of fourteen times a day. However, during the last four weeks (when he still used the GPCeditor before going on to Lightspeed), he ran his programs only three times a day. It may be that many repeated runs early in the semester helped solidify many of the design processes, thereby reducing the need for large numbers of runs at the end of the semester.

Gpceditor Use

Allen made little use of the plan library other than access to Pascal primitives. Over the course of the entire semester, Allen's usage trace files show that he saved only one plan to the library. When asked why he never reused plans, he replied that it was "easier to build it up [from scratch]."

Allen did make extensive use of all the representations. He seemed to use the goal-plan buckets to select goals and plans for operations and to navigate the hierarchy, to use the code view for reflection during debugging, and to use the overview for reflection during decomposition.

Sample Program

Allen's program and decomposition appear in Exhibit B. His program is not as understandable as Sue's. His poor naming and duplication of data objects is immediately obvious. His variables are named z, B, A, and x. He has three constants, vert_400, vert_400_b, and con_400, all of whose value is 400.0. His program does not make the repetitive nature of the program clear—the first loop of his program has a distinctly different construction from the latter three.

His decomposition is nearly indecipherable, with poor naming and mixed structure. Under a plan named inativate, he has the moveto and lineto (graphics primitives for drawing lines) of the first loop. He groups all but the first of the while-do loops in one plan named buncho loops. The meaning of goals named verblenumber and vernumB is unclear.

Lois

Student Characteristics

Lois took the GPCeditor class as a senior (3.7 GPA) interested in studying art. She applied for the class "to get an edge on college applications and stuff." She had typed in some programs from magazines in Basic a few times. One of her first comments on computers in the interview was how a computer once lost her data.

Do you like computers?

"I don't really know them. I never use them. I've never programmed before . . . They organize and store stuff. They can also mess things up. I lost a bunch of stuff once. We worked for two weeks to get it back."

At the midsemester interview, she admitted that she didn't like the GPCeditor: "It's interesting. But it's not one of my favorite things."

Use of Reflection and Explicit Planning

Lois was the only student who explicitly asked for her notebook containing her worksheets during her protocol. She used her notes to identify programs and plans that were similar to one she was facing.

"I'm looking through Moving Pictures [worksheet] and can't decide if I should take a whole program or part. COMET, SUPERNOVA [names of programs in that worksheet], it does increase the radius, doesn't it? I don't want to change the size of the square . . . Okay, I'll have to use a moveto."

Lois reflected early and often in the design process. She often paused to think about her program and how she was planning to complete it.

Decomposition

At the beginning of the semester, Lois had a hard time decomposing tasks and choosing the plans for the goals that she had chosen. Her comments in her diary, and the instructor's comments to the researcher, suggest that she received personal instruction almost daily. However, by midsemester, she appreciated and used hierarchical decomposition in her programs. In her midsemester interview, she explained why she liked it:

> "Actually, I think [hierarchy is] useful. I'll use it to sort of organize, so that if I have to change, like, values for something. Like for the face. I did the eyes in one thing and the nose in one thing. So if I needed to change something, I could go try to find it. It worked."

Lois had very good strategies for beginning programs. In her protocol, for example, she was asked to draw a square and move it (using animation techniques) across the screen. The first thing she did after reading the task assignment was to write a program to draw the square. Though she was unsure how to do the animation, she knew how to perform that part of the program, so her heuristic was to do the part that she knew how to do, and to develop the program from there.

> "Oh, now there's a square . . . now I just have to move it? This is what I don't know how to do. . . . It would help if I could have my notes, my old worksheets."

Composition

Lois had no problems ordering and composing plans. She used well-named data objects and seemed to have little trouble in finding data objects.

Debugging

Soon after the midsemester interview, Lois became very interested in one of a the assigned graphics programs, "Triangles." During the first eight weeks of class, Lois ran her programs an average of thirteen times per day. While working on "Triangles" and the "Challenge," she ran her programs an average of thirty-two times per day.

Her class programs began improving significantly, according to the instructor. She completed programs as fast or faster than Allen. For example, on one particularly difficult graphics-oriented program, Allen took two days, Fred took two days, and Lois took one day.

Lois used good debugging strategies during her protocol. Whenever bugs occurred, she stopped writing her program and mentally simulated it, stating predictions for what should happen.

> "It didn't work! No problem—I can deal with it . . . I have the framerect first, and it should be going down. So the right should be 500."

GPCeditor Use

Lois did not use the library much during the first part of the semester. In fact, during the midsemester interview, she claimed that she did not know how, though her usage trace files indicated that she had saved and reused a plan. However, she began saving, reusing, and tailoring plans by the end of the semester. Lois made little use of alternative representations. She relied mostly on the code view and the goal-plan buckets.

Sample Program

Lois's "Challenge" program and decomposition are in Exhibit C. Her program is well-composed with good data object naming. Her program has the same clear, repetitive structure of Sue's program but does not have the unnecessary redundancy that Sue had.

Her decomposition reflects the stage of her learning at the time of the "Challenge" program. She understood hierarchy and plan reuse but had not fully generalized it yet. Her first triangle (drawn horizontally) of the "Challenge" is created under the Create the Loop. This same plan is reused and tailored to draw the other horizontal triangle when achieving the goal Do 3rd Triangle. However, Lois did not seem to recognize that the Create the Loop plan could be tailored to draw vertical triangles as well. She used a flat hierarchy for drawing the second triangle under the plan Init. Values2, and then repeated the same flat order of plans to draw the fourth triangle (the other vertical one).

Fred

Student Characteristics

Fred entered the class as a freshman with extensive computer experience. He already had programmed in Basic, Pascal, and a graphics-oriented version of Pascal called Grasp. However, the longest program he had ever written previous to this class was only 20 lines long. He took the class because he wanted to learn more about Pascal.

Use of Reflection and Explicit Planning

Fred began the semester reflecting early and often. In his first protocol, Fred carefully considered what he should do in the program, stated constraints, and reflected on his program during debugging. When he found that he was forgetting what he wanted to do, he asked for pencil and paper to keep notes.

"I'm thinking of doing a paintcircle for the face with two invertcircles for the eyes and mouth. No, I don't think I will."

"The horizontal . . . the vertical should be the same as the second vertical because if they were different they'd be in the wrong place."

(*Clicks with mouse on right eye of face he's drawn so far.*) "If that's 600 . . ." (*clicks on left eye*) "And that's 100, no, 300 . . ." (*Moves mouse arrow up and down where the nose is going to be drawn.*) "Then that's the horizontal. The vertical will be . . . 500. About 500,500 ought to do it."

"Okay, I'll do a match to see what the numbers actually are . . . Aw, geez, I can't remember. Can I have a pencil so I can write some of this down?"

(Unfortunately, his strategy for using pencil-and-paper notes was incomplete. As he made changes, he forgot to update his notes. When he later modified his program based on his now inaccurate notes, he only implemented more bugs.)

Decomposition

Fred had little trouble starting programs, but he used none of the decomposition design techniques discussed in class. He rarely used plan groupings to create new levels of hierarchy and he never saved a plan to the library during the entire semester.

At one point in the first protocol, Fred created a new level of hierarchy. But when he found a bug, he deleted the entire level with several plans defined within it and then continued writing nonhierarchical code. He did not seem to understand or trust hierarchy.

Although he did not really take advantage of the structure within the GPCeditor, Fred seemed to appreciate it. During the midsemester interview, Fred said that he found goals and plans to be useful.

"I think (the GPCeditor) is okay. The first couple of weeks, I thought it was kind of lame, that goals and plans got in the way. But I can see that it's kind of helpful. I can see that in longer programs, it's kind of helpful."

Composition

Fred had several problems with composition. During his first protocol, he frequently confused the composition operations. Fred had significant problems with data handling in both his first and second protocols. He referred to his data objects in his protocols by their values instead of by their meanings, especially during the first protocol.

(*Pointing at the mouth of his face.*) "That's 500. It should be 450. 450 . . . 650. But which is which? That's 450 (*moving mouse up and down*) and that's 650 (*moving it side to side*). I'll put down 450 before I forget."

As the programs grew larger, Fred found it difficult to remember all the components and the meaning of terms like horizontal and vertical. While in the first program of the first protocol, he named his data objects meaningfully (e.g., `radius` and `horizontal`, but named his data objects in the second program of the first protocol based on their values (e.g., `sevenhundred` and `fourhundredfiftey`). This made it more difficult for him to remember the meaning of these data and to use them when instantiating plans for the program.

By the final protocol, he had learned to keep track of his variables, even with his poor naming schemes. Though he did not verbalize these strategies, he showed no difficulty in manipulating his data objects. In general, Fred's programs did work. In fact, he occasionally exceeded program requirements, adding interesting, new features.

Debugging

Fred had a great deal of difficulty with debugging. In part, his problem was due to forgetting data object meanings. In addition, however, he also forgot his goals in debugging. He would frequently begin work on a bug, switch his focus to a new bug, and forget about correcting the original bug.

GPCeditor Use

Fred never saved a plan to the library, rarely used any hierarchy, and found the overview useless. In general, he only used the code view and the program output when building or debugging his programs.

"No, [the overview] gets in the way."

Do you save things into the library?

"No, I don't remember how."

Sample Program

Fred's program and decomposition appear in Exhibit D. His program has a clear structure that shows the repetitive nature of the task. However, his data objects are so confused that one wonders how he was able to debug this program. The constant fiftey has the value of 200.0, the constant one has the value of 5.0, and his variable names are z, y, x, and vari.

His decomposition is almost perfectly flat. He uses a plan grouping once to link a while-do loop with its test expression. The rest of the program is not hierarchically decomposed and is difficult to understand.

EXHIBIT A: SUE'S CHALLENGE PROGRAM AND DECOMPOSITION

```
PROGRAM challenge;

  CONST

    one_hundred = 100.0;
    write = 'Enter the amount of spaces you would like between the
    lines.';
    two_hundred = 200.0;
    zero = 0.0;

  VAR

    center : REAL;
    read : REAL;
    vertical_start : REAL;
    Horizontal_start : REAL;
    vertical : REAL;
    horizontal : REAL;

BEGIN
    horizontal := zero;
    vertical := zero;
    Horizontal_start := two_hundred;
    vertical_start := two_hundred;
    WRITELN (write) ;
    READLN (read) ;
    WHILE (horizontal < = two_hundred) DO
        BEGIN
            center := one_hundred;
            MOVETO (horizontal, vertical);
            LINETO (one_hundred, one_hundred);
            horizontal := (horizontal + read);
        END;
    WHILE (vertical < = two_hundred) DO
        BEGIN
            center := one_hundred;
            MOVETO (horizontal, vertical);
            LINETO (one_hundred, one_hundred);
            vertical := (vertical + read);
        END
    WHILE (horizontal > = zero) DO
        BEGIN
            center := one_hundred;
            MOVETO (horizontal, vertical);
            LINETO (one_hundred, one_hundred);
            horizontal := (horizontal - read);
        END;
    WHILE (vertical > = zero) DO
        BEGIN
            center := one_hundred;
            MOVETO (horizontal, vertical);
            LINETO (one_hundred, one_hundred);
            vertical := (vertical - read);
        END.

END;
```

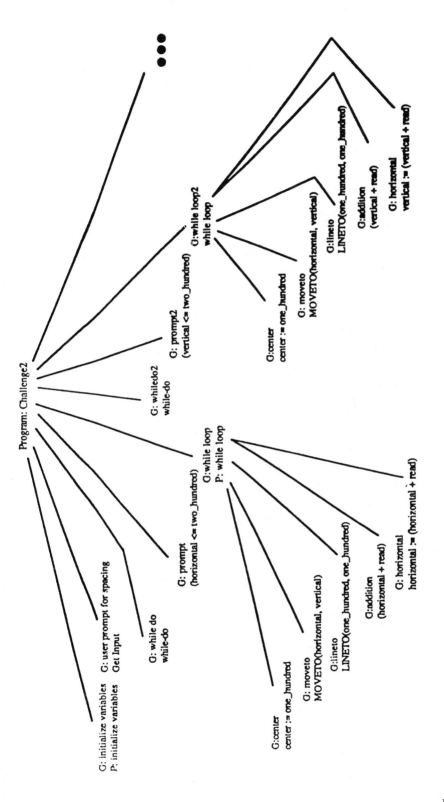

111

EXHIBIT B: ALLEN'S CHALLENGE PROGRAM AND DECOMPOSITION

```
PROGRAM chalgenge;

    CONST
        cont_0 = 0.0;
        vert_400 -= 400.0;
        vert_400_b = 400.0;
        five = 5.0;
        vert_linto = 0.0;
        vertcal = 200.0;
        hort = 200.0;
        con_400 = 400.0;

    VAR
        z : REAL;
        B : REAL;
        A : REAL;
        x : REAL;

BEGIN
    WHILE (x < con_400) DO
        BEGIN
            MOVETO (hort, vertcal);
            LINETO (x, vert_linto);
            x := (x + five);
        END
    A := con_400;
    B := con_400_b;
    WHILE (z < vert_400) DO
        BEGIN
            MOVETO (hort, vertcal);
            LINETO (con_400, z);
            z := (z + five);
        END;
    WHILE (A > cont_0) DO
        BEGIN
            MOVETO (hort, vertcal);
            LINETO (A, vert_linto);
            A := (A - five);
        END;
    WHILE (B > vert_linto) DO
        BEGIN
            MOVETO (hort, vertcal);
            LINETO (cont_0, B);
            B := (B - five);
        END;

END.
```

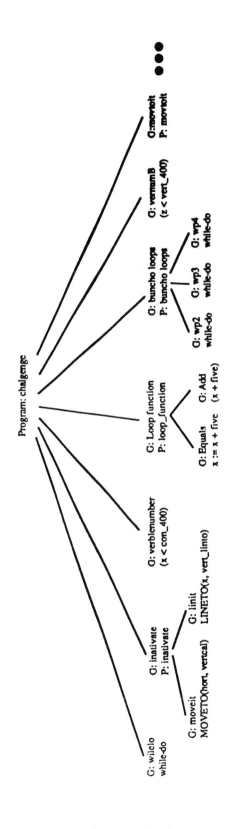

113

EXHIBIT C: LOIS'S CHALLENGE PROGRAM AND DECOMPOSITION

```pascal
PROGRAM Doing_the_Challenge;

    CONST
        five = 5.0;
        four_hundred = 400.0;
        two_hundred = 200.0;
        zero = 0.0;

    VAR
    final_vert : REAL;
    final_hori : REAL;
    vert : REAL;
    hori : REAL;

BEGIN
    hori := zero;
    vert := zero;
    final_hori := two_hundred;
    final_vert := two_hundred;
    WHILE (hori < = four_hundred) DO
        BEGIN
            MOVETO (hori, vert);
            LINETO (final_hori, final_vert);
            hori := (hori + five);
        END
    WHILE (vert < = four_hundred) DO
        BEGIN
            MOVETO (hori, vert);
            LINETO (final_hori, final_vert);
            vert := (vert + five);
        END
    WHILE (hori > = zero) DO
        BEGIN
            MOVETO (hori, vert);
            LINETO (final_hori, final_vert);
            hori := (hori + five);
        END
    WHILE (vert > = zero) DO
        BEGIN
            MOVETO (hori, vert);
            LINETO (final_hori, final_vert);
            vert := (vert - five);
        END;

END.
```

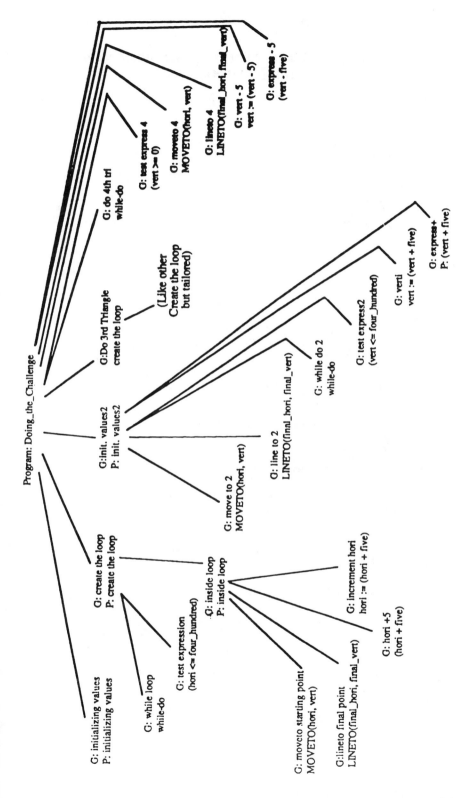

Program: Doing_the_Challenge

G: initializing values
P: initializing values

G: create the loop
P: create the loop

G: while loop
while-do

G: test expression
(hori <= four_hundred)

G: inside loop
P: inside loop

G: moveto starting point
MOVETO(hori, vert)

G:lineto final point
LINETO(final_hori, final_vert)

G: hori +5
(hori + five)

G: increment hori
hori := (hori + five)

G:Init. values2
P: Init. values2

(Like other
Create the loop
but tailored)

G: move to 2
MOVETO(hori, vert)

G: line to 2
LINETO(final_hori, final_vert)

G: while do 2
while-do

G: test express2
(vert <= four_hundred)

G: vert
vert := (vert + five)

G: express+
P: (vert + five)

G:Do 3rd Triangle
create the loop

G: do 4th trl
while-do

G: test express 4
(vert >= 0)

G: moveto 4
MOVETO(hori, vert)

G: lineto 4
LINETO(final_hori, final_vert)

G: vert - 5
vert := (vert - 5)

G: express - 5
(vert - five)

115

EXHIBIT D: FRED'S CHALLENGE PROGRAM AND DECOMPOSITION

```
PROGRAM Challange;

    CONST
        zero = 0.0;
        fiftey = 200.0;
        onehundred = 400.0;
        one = 5.0;

    VAR
        z : REAL;
        y : REAL;
        plusten : REAL;
        z : REAL;
        vari : REAL;

BEGIN
    vari := one;
    WHILE (vari < onehundred) DO
        BEGIN
            MOVETO (fiftey, fiftey);
            LINETO (x, onehundred);
            vari := (vari + one);
            x := (x + one);
        END
    plusten := onehundred;
    WHILE (plusten > = zero) DO
        BEGIN
            MOVETO (fiftey, fiftey);
            LINETO (onehundred, plusten);
            plusten := (plusten - one);
        END
    y := onehundred;
    WHILE (y > = zero) DO
        BEGIN
            MOVETO (fiftey, fiftey);
            LINETO (y, zero);
            y := (y - one);
        END
    z := zero;
    WHILE (z < = onehundred) DO
        BEGIN
            MOVETO (fiftey, fiftey);
            LINETO (zero, z);
            z := (z + one);
        END;

END.
```

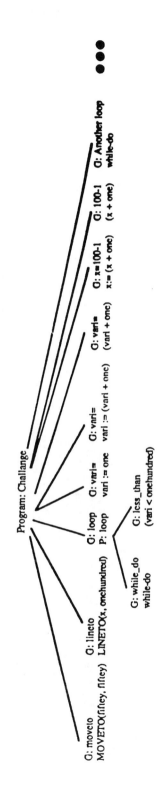

Program: Challange

G: moveto
MOVETO(fifty, fifty)

G: lineto
LINETO(x, onehundred)

G: while_do
while-do

G: loop
P: loop

G: vari=
vari := one

G: less_than
(vari < onehundred)

G: vari=
vari := (vari + one)

G: vari=
(vari + one)

G: x=100-1
x:= (x + one)

G: 100-1
(x + one)

G: Another loop
while-do

5

Writing: A Retrospective on Computer Support for Open-Ended Design Tasks

David S. Kaufer, Christine M. Neuwirth, Ravinder Chandhok, and James H. Morris
Carnegie-Mellon University, Pittsburgh, PA

Abstract *This chapter details our work on computer tools for writing since 1983. We discuss some of the concerns that originally involved us in software development for teaching writing as a design activity. We discuss our evolution from the WARRANT project to our current work on the PREP EDITOR. Our particular history lends support to the idea that teachers (and software developers) of open-ended design activities must remain flexible between what we call a* task focus *and a* tool focus. *Taken too far in one or another direction, software developers paint themselves into corners that they can avoid if they keep both foci in mind.*

Writing is an open-ended design task. A design task is a task that involves creating a product: an architect designs a building, a mechanical engineer designs a machine, a software engineer designs a computer program, a writer designs a article. An open-ended design task is a design task in which some of the specifications that the designer needs to create a finished product are not provided in the initial specification of the task, that is, some of the end-states are left open to interpretation by the designer. For example, the task description for an architectural problem may specify purpose and total cost, but omit specification of particular materials. To complete the design, the architect must construct additional constraints on materials. Open-ended design tasks contrast with tasks that cognitive psychologists call *well-defined* (cf. Simon, 1981). In a well-defined task, the end-states of the task (and sometimes the means for achieving them) are completely specified, or defined, in the initial task specification. The end-state for a simple algebra word problem, for example, is completely specified in the statement of the problem.

A popular conception associates mathematics, the natural sciences, and the more quantitative social sciences (e.g., economics and decision theory) with well-defined tasks and associates the humanities and the more qualitative social sciences (e.g., sociology and anthropology) with open-ended tasks. However pervasive this association, it is a misconception. All of these disciplines contain activities that can be characterized as open-ended design tasks: in mathematics, creating interesting

The first two authors are in the Department of English; the last two are in the Department of Computer Science.
We wish to thank David Ferguson and Diane Balestri for help with previous versions.

theorems; in the natural sciences, designing experiments, and so forth. The misconception may be due to the ways in which educators structure curricula. Educators often plan more basic courses in which students learn nuts-and-bolts technique on well-defined problems. The basic courses are intended to help students "get the mechanics out of the way" so that they can later focus on the larger interpretive issues they will need to address when working on real-world problems. In the 1940s, for example, Carnegie-Mellon planned its education curriculum for engineers. The curriculum then (and now) consists of basic courses, offering mathematical and engineering knowledge, and advanced design courses, teaching problem definition, analysis, and planning (Teare, 1948). The idea of the advanced courses then (and now) is to help engineering students see how they must interpret how to make the best use of their mechanical knowledge when addressing open-ended engineering problems. Likewise, many writing curricula reflect a similar duality of structure between basic courses focusing on "mechanics" (grammar, punctuation, sentence and paragraph forms, and limited classroom genres such as the five-paragraph theme) and more intensive "design" courses in which students are required to interpret what they know to address more open-ended writing situations (Balestri and Ehrmann, 1987a; Walton and Balestri, 1987). Thus, the popular misconception may be based on students' introductory experiences with the various disciplines.

Well-defined and open-ended design tasks are not dichotomous terms but lie on a continuum. For example, in writing education, grammar and punctuation exercises are relatively well-defined tasks because there is usually a "right" answer known in advance. Exercises in how to shape a good sentence or paragraph are more open-ended (less well-defined) tasks because there are many acceptable solutions, and whether a solution is acceptable or not depends on the writer's communicative intentions. Even more open-ended are the genres that have been developed specifically for the American composition classroom over the last one hundred years (e.g., the five-paragraph theme, the one-hundred-word book report, the five-page library research paper [requiring at least five citations and a smattering of footnotes]; Conners, 1985). Such classroom genres are open-ended, requiring the student to make choices, but typically not on a scale required of writers working outside the classroom.

A dilemma facing teachers of open-ended design in all disciplines is this: As the teacher puts an ever higher premium on making the student's experience more open-ended and realistic, the teacher is less likely to know the nature of that reality on which he or she is insisting. The simplicity—and most likely, at least part of the staying power—of reducing instruction in open-ended design to more well-defined tasks (e.g., reducing writing instruction to grammar and artificial classroom genres) is that well-defined problems have relatively complete task representations. Conversely, the difficulty of teaching open-ended design is that the task representation is, by definition, incomplete. The first two authors of this chapter became painfully aware of this difficulty when we set out to move our students beyond the classroom genre of the research report and to the more realistic genre of research writing as we, members of an academic discipline, understood it.

On the basis of their high school experience with the classroom genre, our students had matriculated to college with a well-learned—but incomplete—set of goals for writing a research paper. The student goals were to do the reading (which meant underline or mentally annotate for key words and main ideas) and then report on it (which meant turn these main ideas into sentences for one's own draft). The student goals represented a perfectly reasonable design strategy for using writing to display reading comprehension. Yet we assumed our students could read for basic comprehension; we wanted them to learn to associate academic writing with more. Academic literacy, we understood, includes but goes well beyond sentence facility and thematic unity. It also includes a detailed set of conventions established over hundreds of years for reporting new knowledge to intellectual peers. The academic writer must review an existing literature and then show how the rest of the article contributes new ideas to that literature. But how does a writer do this? We had no explicit or stable vocabulary for telling student writers how to move from their relatively well-defined task of research writing to the more open-ended task that we tacitly recognized in our practice as more valid. Similar to the experience of many teachers who insist on teaching their subjects as open-ended design, we found ourselves wanting our students to rise to a challenge we could not completely define for them. We wanted them to learn to represent and think through a research article in ways that broke with old ways of designing, yet we could not supply them with "correct" answers.

THE WARRANT PROJECT

The first two authors, along with Preston Covey and Cheryl Geisler, embarked in 1983 on a computer project called WARRANT in order to address these issues.[1] The idea behind WARRANT was simple. A long tradition of writing instruction has been based on the notion of using texts as models of instruction. According to this tradition, students can become skilled writers by studying the texts of renowned authors. Even today, the composition market is flooded with anthologies of the works of great writers, living and dead, in the spirit of this instructional tradition. In consonance with this tradition, we assumed that students could learn about more open-ended forms of research writing by being exposed to the example of experienced writers working on a research article. We thus intended to use experienced writers as models for students. Our one twist was to want to include process as well as product models in our instruction. We believed it was important for students not only to read the final research articles of experienced writers but to be able to track the thinking that led to it. Process models have the advantage over product models of making the expert writer's strategies more visible to the student. For example, our subsequent research on students' writing processes (Kaufer and Geisler, 1989, 1990; Geisler, in press) indicated that in the research paper, students seldom connect their ideas to prior authors during the composing process. The fact that experts make such linkages is evident in their texts. However, accessibility to the text alone, as a model, does not offer students a concrete mental picture of how these linkages are actually forged. Notice how concrete this picture can become with a process model, as in the following excerpt:

> [reads Dworkin, a source author, on the definition of paternalism] This definition is faulty in several respects, and is not made any better by Dworkin's admission that it is rough. First . . . Perhaps what Dworkin intends is something more like the following: [formulates new definition] But this will still not work. . . . There remains, however, the question of interference with liberty of action. . . . Buchanon [another source author], too, thinks this feature is important.

Readers of the author's final product—the text—may manage to figure out that the author had purposely made his definition of paternalism responsive to (though different from) definitions proposed by Dworkin and Buchanon. However, glimpses of an author's processes, such as the glimpse above, are, it seems, even more likely to drive home to students how experienced writers can make use of the definitions of previous authors to guide their design of new definitions. Arguably, process examples can help students more than can product examples, to dissolve unhelpful attitudes and rigid stereotypes about the writing process. Some of our students, for example, informed of the "expert strategy" of using the work of other authors as a scaffold to find something new to say, had previously discounted this strategy as a type of cheating ("You shouldn't let others influence your thinking or do your work for you") or a violation of natural law ("Experts can't be wrong").

Because in 1984 we had no process models for research writing at our disposal, a significant part of the WARRANT project was to gather our own. We conducted think-aloud protocols from expert writers working on a research article of the same kind we regularly assigned our students in the classroom. In a think-aloud protocol, a person thinks aloud while working on some task. We reasoned that if students could see examples of "experts in process" as experts worked on their (i.e., the students') assignment, we could give some direction to students who might feel a lack of direction. We expected that approach to work, in part, because writing instruction, more than many other areas of instruction, is lacking in expert process models. The general absence of extended process models in writing education is partly a result of the fact that writing consumes chunks of time much longer than normal classroom periods. A math or physics teacher can work out a problem in real time on the blackboard as illustration for students, that is, they can teach by demonstration. A writing teacher cannot, in real time, write an article from start to finish in eye- or earshot of students. Furthermore, many writing teachers in this country—hired as part-time instructors in exploited positions—are not themselves writers. Thus, it seemed to us, all the more need for bringing into the classroom some expert representations of writing a research article.

Over the course of two years, between 1984 and 1986, we collected hundreds of hours of protocol data from five expert writers as they worked on a standard freshman writing assignment. The goal of the research was to develop a series of expert representations for various phases of the research article that could be expressed in computer environments. Although many computer tools (text-editors, outliners, thesauri, and grammar aids) were then on the market (and many more since) to aid writers, none of these tools was "smart" about helping students organize the task of research writing. Our research was thus designed to build a theory of representation for the research article and translate this theory into new computer tools. Our software orientation in the mid 1980s was thus more task-driven than tool-driven. (We explain, in due course, how this orientation came to change.) Our work on expert representations of research writing has been reported in several places (Kaufer and Geisler, 1989) and is the subject of a book-length treatment in preparation (Geisler, in press). What is relevant to report here is that the initial assumption (Figure 1) with which we began our data collection proved false. Although we knew our students brought an incomplete understanding of research writing with them to college, we still assumed that it was essentially the same task as the one in which our experts had engaged (indicated by the thick line

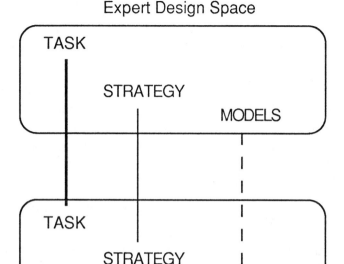

Expert Design Space

TASK

STRATEGY

MODELS

TASK

STRATEGY

MODELS

Student Design Space

Figure 1   A model underlying our basic assumptions of the WARRANT
project. We assumed the students and experts shared the
same task space and perhaps some of the same strategies. We
assumed that what students had most to learn from the
experts was the concrete examples (models) experts used to
achieve their strategies.

in Figure 1). We further assumed that, because they shared the same task understanding (just more or less complete versions of it) the students may have also
shared some (but not all) of the same strategies of experts (indicated by the solid
line in Figure 1). We further assumed that the major difference between experts
and students would be in the concrete examples (models) experts would use to
achieve their strategies (indicated by the broken line, Figure 1). For example, we
reasoned that a student might know at a particular point in the writing process that
he or she needed to work on the strategy, "find a counter-example," but the
student would have no model for going about doing this. This is where the expert
models should, we hypothesized, make a difference to student performance.

In its mature form, the WARRANT project was to include a sophisticated text
editor with note-taking and commenting facilities. It was also to have a data base
indexed by strategies and models. When the student came to a part of the design
process that used a particular strategy, he or she could access the various ways
different writers—both expert and student—worked on that strategy. The data base
would also contain any intermediate notes and jottings that our experts produced
while working on various strategies. Previous research in general design processes
(Reitman, 1965), the writing process (Flower and Hayes, 1981), and our own

protocol data (Kaufer and Geisler, 1989, 1990) suggests that writers accumulate a mass of intermediate drafts, doodles, and sketches and that retaining easy access to these objects can be important for the writer to work efficiently through a writing task. By allowing writers working with the WARRANT system to keep all these partial products in a data base, we reasoned, we could also increase their efficiency.

Limitations in the Assumptions Underlying WARRANT

After a preliminary analysis of our protocol data, it became apparent that many of our assumptions underlying WARRANT could not be sustained. The expert protocols, along with a couple of student protocols we took, suggested that students and experts were not engaged in parallel tasks drawing on parallel strategies and models. Rather, they were engaged in incommensurable tasks that made it impossible to draw parallels between strategies and models. Students were working to demonstrate their ability to read and order information with accuracy; experts were working for an angle on their sources that would allow them to say something new. We were forced to abandon the early WARRANT assumption that students could learn simply by following the process examples of experts.

Even if we had been able to confirm the comparability of what our experts and students did, we found further reason to doubt the instructional utility of process data. Process data can quickly get very dense and long-winded on the one hand, and elliptical and digressive on the other. Unlike a constructed example designed to illustrate one and only one point, it is difficult to listen to (or read) process data and efficiently extract points. Even for experts, process data are riddled with false starts and failed attempts, especially in a task as long and arduous as academic writing. Only a fraction of process information can be abstracted into information about progress, that is, information that can actually make a difference in moving the writer closer to an acceptable finished document. Moreover, for students, extracting this needle of useful information from a haystack of process data turns into a forbidding problem of induction.

From Process Models to a Theory of Progress

In light of the incommensurability of student and expert tasks and the limitations of using process data in direct instruction, our image of the WARRANT environment as a learning environment changed. Rather than use a computer system to house a data base of process information, we realized we would have to develop an overall model of the expert task that could structure for students an expert representation of "making progress" through a research article. We now worked on two fronts, abandoning the original hope of a full integration of our computer system and our empirical data. On one front, we worked on tailoring the computer facilities for note-taking and commenting, which we were developing as separate modules from the instructional data base so that they would eliminate some of the problems we had seen our experts experiencing while writing their articles. Work on the first front resulted in two computer programs, NOTES (Neuwirth and Kaufer, 1987) and COMMENTS (Neuwirth, Kaufer, Keim, and Gillespie, 1988).

NOTES had been designed to expedite note-taking from source texts. In our protocols, we had found that even experts lost information after taking notes on a reading. The note would maintain some, but not all, of the context of the original source. Thus, experts would regularly reread a source even after taking extensive notes on it, or, worse, experts would simply take verbatim notes, a kind of poor person's photocopy. The NOTES program maintained links between electronic source texts and notes so that a source would stay immediately linked (in a hypertext environment) with all the notes taken on it. In a field experiment (Ogura, 1989), we found that NOTES significantly increased the number of reflective notes and significantly decreased the number of verbatim notes taken by writers.

COMMENTS had been a network program designed to expedite feedback not only between teacher and student but also among students. A clear result of our protocol study was that experts relied heavily on feedback from peers between writing sessions. To provide student writers with this same kind of feedback, COMMENTS allows the passing of drafts back and forth across a campus network and even allows writers a very natural (hypertext) facility to engage in extended dialogues about a single passage or passages in a draft. An empirical study of COMMENTS confirmed its usefulness (Hartman et al., 1991). In a writing course emphasizing multiple drafts and collaboration, two sections used traditional modes of communication (face-to-face, paper, and phone); two other sections, in addition to using traditional modes, also used electronic modes (electronic mail, bulletin boards, COMMENTS, etc.). The study measured patterns of social interaction at two times: at six weeks and at the end of the semester. Results indicate that teachers in the networked sections interacted more with their students than teachers in the regular sections: Whereas teachers in the regular sections marginally increased their use of traditional communication over time, teachers in the networked sections substantially increased their use of electronic communication over time without significantly decreasing their use of traditional modes. In addition, teachers communicated more electronically with less able students than with more able students, and less able students communicated more electronically with other students. By the end of the semester, paper, face-to-face, and COMMENTS were the most frequently used modes of interaction.

On another front, we began turning information from our protocols into a curriculum presenting an expert representation of academic writing that (we hoped) was comprehensible to students. Work on this second front resulted in a textbook, *Arguing from Sources: Exploring Issues Through Reading and Writing* (Kaufer, Geisler, and Neuwirth, 1989). The textbook provided the opportunity to work out our "expert representation" of academic writing in a format designed to address students. The text was designed to illustrate our theory of "making progress" as an expert, step-by-step. We characterized these steps as summarizing, synthesizing, analyzing, and contributing. Each step culminated in the design of a written genre (i.e., a summary, a synthesis or review of literature, an analysis or critical review, and a final contribution or original essay). Yet, we also wanted students to see that each step provided an intermediate representation that made taking steps beyond it less difficult than they might otherwise be. For example, we tried to make a convincing demonstration argument to students that writing a synthesis is much easier when you have written good individual summaries than when you have to start from scratch. We also tried to help them see that, among the requirements of a good summary, there is the requirement that it reduce the difficulty of further steps—such as synthesizing. In the same way, synthesizing was designed to reduce the difficulty of analyzing, by contributing. Each step in our curriculum thus provided a battery of intermediate representations—notes, lines of argument, synthesis grids, synthesis trees, problem cases, and analysis trees (see Kaufer et al., 1989)—that both tried to reflect the work the writer had done and anticipated the work the writer had yet to do.

We should clarify at this point that the notion of a step in a theory of progress is quite different from and so should not be confused with a step in a theory of process. In the latter, a step means an action taken by the writer in real time and fixed in time relative to other steps. Within a process theory, in other words, a step is something the writer is expected to do at a specific time prior to some steps and subsequent to others. A cookbook relies on process steps (e.g., "add two teaspoons of salt and then stir"). In a theory of progressive representation, a step is quite different. Rather than a definite time period fixed in relation to others, a step within a progress theory is an *accountability* that is not fixed in time relative to others. An accountability is some constraint that is satisfied incrementally as a writing task proceeds. The important feature of an accountability is that it is done, not when it is done. At their discretion, writers can do an accounting at any time during the writing process. The purpose of this accounting—calling these accountabilities to mind—is to enable students to monitor the intersection between their current process and their current progress through the writing task. To help our students discriminate their process from their progress, we tell them that summarizing, synthesizing, analyzing, and contributing refer to a list of accountabilities to use to help monitor their progress through a research paper. We tell them that they need not start a research paper with summarizing, synthesizing, and so on, in lockstep order. They can start with contributing if they wish (drafting their original essay). But we remind them that they also have the responsibility of offering original ideas (a specific accountability of *contributing*), which rests on basing their new ideas on the strengths and weaknesses of existing positions (an accountability of *analyzing*), which requires in turn an accurate representation of existing positions (an accountability of *synthesizing*), which falls on an accurate representation of individual texts (an accountability of *summarizing*). Accountabilities in the research article thus form an interdependent system, and students must learn that making progress toward satisfying some systems of accountability typically requires making progress toward satisfying others. In light of the interdependence in systems of accountability, learning how to write the research paper (we tell students) requires learning how to coordinate these systems of accountability into their own writing process, which can only be done through extensive writing practice. We suggest to students that, wherever they start the research paper and however they order their activities in real time, they should not declare themselves "finished" until they have a draft that mutually satisfies the various accountabilities specified by summarizing, synthesizing, analyzing, and contributing.

Although the steps of our curriculum were derived mainly from our previous knowledge of writing and rhetoric, the fine points of many of the steps were extrapolated from our protocols. For example, we got a close look at synthesizing by noticing that many of our experts paid very close attention to disagreements across sources (students tended to ignore or suppress disagreements). Experts did not stop with the perception of disagreements, however. They used disagreements to hypothesize further agreements and disagreements that united and divided authors. In this fashion, they were able to assign a hodgepodge of texts into a few salient "camps" and "approaches" for a literature review (Kaufer and Geisler, 1989; Kaufer et al., 1989).

By 1989, NOTES and COMMENTS were in full use in selected sections of freshman writing at Carnegie-Mellon University, and we were designing further computer tools to fill out the synthesis, analysis, and contributing environments. However, our experience with NOTES and COMMENTS (approximately two hundred students in twelve sections over a three-year period) made us aware of serious limitations in our software design approach, and our thinking increasingly turned to ways of revamping rather than building further on the software design assumptions of the original WARRANT environment.

More Limitations in WARRANT

By the end of 1987, the various pieces of the WARRANT project (the computer software and the pedagogy) were in operation, but still without the unified theory that we had hoped from the start would envelop them. As we gained experience both with our pedagogy and with the software that delivered pieces[2] of it, we learned more about the limitations of both and, in particular, how each failed in some respects to hold up its end of the bargain for a more unified approach. As far as the software teaching us about the pedagogy, we found that the COMMENTS program was better received by students than the NOTES program. Student response to both programs was generally positive. However, we have found that when computer access is limited, students must see for themselves a very high added value in a particular piece of software to continue to prefer working with it. Students saw this higher added value in COMMENTS but not in NOTES. Unlike NOTES, COMMENTS allowed extended dialoguing between teachers and students and between students and students about a draft. NOTES, on the other hand, was a private design space that allowed students to build views of their reading that they could not easily share with others. What became increasingly clear to us was the importance of communication in the design process—the importance of allowing students to share their work at regular intervals with others and to receive feedback.

The COMMENTS program, in effect, taught us that our curriculum would have to be tweaked to allow for more collaboration. As for the pedagogy teaching us about the software, we had long realized that our pedagogy was based on students building multiple intermediate representations (notes, jottings, synthesis grids, trees, problem cases, sketches, and plans) of their progress to date, long before anything as official as a draft was ready to be written. Our success with the COMMENTS program indicated that we needed to make it easy for students not only to build these representations by computer but to share them with others. Yet neither NOTES nor COMMENTS was sufficiently general to allow students to build or share by computer all the immediate representations we had students construct as they passed through each phase of our curriculum. For example, our unit on summarizing required students to make trees of their notes. Although the NOTES program had a facility for making trees of notes, it was seldom used.[3] Our unit on synthesizing required students to make both grids and trees of notes culled from different source texts. Yet NOTES had no grid-making facility and the tree-making facility in NOTES did not work easily across source texts. Our units on analyzing and contributing were also affected by these limitations because they also required a device to design trees of information culled across source texts. Similar limitations hampered the COMMENTS program. COMMENTS allowed students to exchange drafts but not representations less formal or less linear, such as a tree, grid, outline, or network. As a result, many of our assignments beyond summarizing remained pencil-and-paper assignments, a situation we assumed would disappear as the WARRANT environment matured.

TAKING A NEW DIRECTION:
OVERTHROWING WARRANT

By the spring of 1988, WARRANT began to appear to us—like the Ptolemaic system of planetary motion—in need of overhaul. The problem had nothing to do with faith in our curriculum. We still believe in it and, to this day, teach it. The problem had to with the fact that we now saw our curriculum as an obstacle to the further development of our software. Keeping the curriculum at the center of the software effort defined various holes in what our software could and could not support. From the curriculum perspective, moreover, these holes seemed somewhat ad hoc and arbitrarily distributed, requiring us simply to add features when we found a particular functionality lacking in operations associated with summarizing, synthesizing, and so on. For example, we recognized the need for a good table editor to help students make grids as they synthesized across source texts. However, NOTES did not support tables and, given the architecture of NOTES, it was difficult to construct a table editor with the kind of flexibility we required. Our functionality requirements, in other words, began to outstrip our computer architecture. This turn made our continued software efforts seem unmotivated and lacking in a more powerful architecture for what we were trying to accomplish educationally. We eventually came to the conclusion that the holes in our software were far more unified and serious than we had first believed and that the deficiencies were in part related to a limitation in our educational theory. Insofar as our curriculum was succeeding in the classroom, it seemed to be succeeding because we had students working together in teams and exchanging early work and drafts both as co-authors and commenters. Yet our computer software and our educational theory, with a few exceptions already pointed out, did not bring collaboration into the core of a research project. Our educational focus had been *individual* design and nothing in the underlying architecture of our existing computer tools supported interpersonal or *social* design. We came to realize that as long as we tried to patch holes in software designed for individual use, we would never be able to support the curriculum we were coming to know better through field testing.

We resolved that a better strategy would be to uncouple our software and curriculum efforts and think more about a general computer architecture to support the social design of a document. A general architecture for social design would need to support the discussion and annotation of information along with its production. We reasoned that if our architecture were truly general, we should be able to deliver our existing curriculum through it. As a further test of the generality of the system, we reasoned that we should be able to deliver virtually any writing curriculum, rooted in a concept of social design, through it as well. A frequent criticism of our software was that it was too customized for too narrow a writing curriculum. Our response was that before we can design general writing software satisfying many curricula, we must first learn what it takes to satisfy even one in depth. We thus began the WARRANT project by supposing that writing software must reflect hard thinking about one extended writing task—and, indeed, this early supposition, we believe, bore much fruit. Nevertheless, by 1988 we had come to believe that the law of diminishing returns had set in in a way that made it easier to agree with some of our critics. That is, we felt we had learned about all we could from going deep into one task. It was now time to return to a higher level of generality, one that would support writing design, discussion, and annotation across a variety of writing tasks, including our own.

STUDYING PAPER AS A DELIVERY SYSTEM FOR COLLABORATIONS ABOUT WRITING

In pursuit of this redesign, we hooked up with a new team of collaborators (Chandhok and Morris) from computer science. Our work with WARRANT had given us a pretty good idea of the range of intermediate representations (e.g., jottings, outlines, trees, graphs, and pictures) that writers can design from reading to drafting. Although we had a reasonable idea of the kind of representations writers design, we had less understanding of how writers might most effectively talk about these designs collaboratively. We reasoned that because writers have had a millennium or more of practice—since at least medieval scriptoria—using paper (or parchment) as a medium for annotation, it would be useful to start by studying paper annotation and then moving to electronic annotation. Our initial work with Chandhok and Morris explored, as generally as we could, the art of how writers use paper to carry on a discussion of a text.

Whatever the limitations of paper, we found in interviews that many writing teachers would much rather "talk to a student" through marginal comments on paper than through a computer screen. Despite the hype of computers turning us into a "paperless society," we and other researchers have found that when people forsake a paper environment for a computer one, they often report important losses, three of the most important being the following:

Losing a Global Sense of the Text

In several studies, Haas has shown that writers working with paper do better at global planning and revision than they do when working with text on ordinary PC screens (Haas, 1989a, 1989b). Haas attributes these findings to the fact that computer screens eliminate a writer's "sense of the text," meaning visual and tactile cues about the text's length, its bulk, and the relationships between its parts. Anyone observing the browsing of library patrons knows that literate people have learned to examine books in the way that a careful shopper examines fruit—by getting an overall feel of the book through holding it, flipping pages, rummaging through a table of contents, an index, and so on. Computers have yet to provide readers with the ability to get an overall feel, which we now believe is a serious part of the reading or writing process. A great advantage of paper annotation is that it allows readers to scan many comments at once and so construct a global sense of what the comments are about and how they relate to one another. For us, one important feature of a design and discussion tool for writers was to make it easy for discussants to view one another's comments at a glance.

Losing Flexibility to Change and to Communicate Change in the Text

Paper is a flexible medium, easy to scribble over and copy (in the age of the photocopiers), and easy, within limits, for an editor to mark and rewrite in the margin and in the space between lines. Let us call the ability to annotate a paper while making permanent changes to the document *conventional* glossing. A number of computer systems have been designed or exploited to support the glossing of electronic documents (e.g., Mark-UP). However, these systems are almost always restricted to more static forms of conventional glossing than are possible on paper. Static glossing systems allow users to mark an electronic document as if they were marking a printed copy of the document: Users can add text, draw arrows, and so forth, to the electronic document but they cannot change the underlying document. This is a huge limitation because there are a number of important problems in texts (e.g., voice, persuasiveness, organization) that, though easy for a skilled writer to detect, cannot be easily described. For such problems, simply rewriting the text is often a more efficient strategy than trying to describe the problem, and skilled writers often choose this strategy when revising other's texts (Hayes, Flower, Schriver, Stratman, and Carey, 1987). Significantly, computer systems in use by some newspapers (e.g., the *New York Times*) have tried to maintain the feel of conventional paper glossing by allowing editors to change the author's document and to communicate these changes through special notations for adds and deletes or through change bars. But unlike paper, where much editorial communication takes place in margins, these systems intersperse author and editor text, potentially exacerbating the "sense of the text" problem and, in any case, creating clutter. For us, a second important feature of a design and discussion environment for writers was to give different persons (e.g., authors and editors) a visually distinct space in which to carry on their part of the discussion.

Losing the Margin as a Social Space

In traditional scholarship, the margin has played a historically dominant role in supporting communication between authors and commentators. Figure 2 shows a twelfth-century document with three levels of marginal commentary. The primary text is the writings of the Bible, and darkest in the largest handwriting. The first level of commentary is next to the primary text in smaller writing. The second level of commentary is offset as the column the farthest to the right.

Each level (column) of annotation was associated with a single commentator. It was understood that annotations reflected the theory of an individual reader and so annotations were best read as part of an integrated whole with other comments in the column. Margins thus allowed multiple commentators to represent their individual readings. It allowed a social space for author–commentator and author–author interaction.

The social space of the margin has been obliterated in modern hypertext systems, where any comment can be linked to any other, regardless of its owner. The COMMENTS program was hypertext in just this sense. There was no way for an author to see, at a glance, all the comments made by one commentator. Standard hypertext systems, including COMMENTS, use a "search and click" interface: The user must search for each comment and, to display it, must click on a link

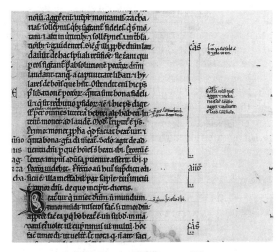

Figure 2 Columns of annotation in a twelfth-century
manuscript, Ms. AUCT. E. infra 6. This
manuscript was designed by Bosham. We thank
the Department of Western manuscripts at the
Bodleian Library, Oxford University, for
permission to reproduce this document. We thank
Todd Cavalier for pointing out this document to
us.

icon. (The comment is then often shown out of context). Although such localized link-following is adequate for browsing tasks (Halasz, 1987), it is problematic for writers who want to scan a set of comments quickly. An interesting line of research distinguishes (following Luria, 1976) between *simultaneous* information-processing tasks and *successive* information-processing tasks (Das, Kirby, and Jarman, 1975, 1979). Simultaneous processing tasks require all the information to be available at one time. For example, doing a jigsaw puzzle involves the scanning of all the pieces in the puzzle. In contrast, successive processing tasks require only the availability of the preceding and following elements in a series. This line of research allows us to predict an advantage for being able to see comments at a glance: An author typically needs to scan a set of comments rapidly to get an overall sense of the comments, both to come to some understanding of the relationship among them and to make some overall plans for how to proceed with responses and revisions. Then the author can proceed with successive processing, dealing with each comment in turn.

These considerations led us to increasingly appreciate the role of margins in historical scholarship (Cavalier, Chandhok, Morris, Kaufer, and Neuwirth, 1991) and question the appropriateness of general hypertext systems as an adequate environment for managing the wealth of objects created during the writing process. We began to consider computer architectures that would allow us to retain the advantages of computers without losing what seemed to be some of the traditional advantages of paper. We considered designs, that is, that addressed the text-sense problem, the problem of change and communicating change, and that restored the margin as a social space.

One can argue that new technologies have the largest impact when they build on the familiarity and strengths of the older technology while minimizing many of the older technologies' weaknesses. One can argue, for example, that word processing software has had such impact because it builds on the typewriter while minimizing the frustrations of typing. Spreadsheets have a similar relationship to the paper art of bookkeeping and the ledger. We now saw ourselves needing to make a similar argument for writing—to create a new technology mimicking the advantages of paper conventions for annotation but extending these conventions to intermediate objects and to the general flexibility of a computer environment.

PREP EDITOR: AN ARCHITECTURE FOR WRITING DESIGN, DISCUSSION, AND ANNOTATION

We are currently working on a new program called PREP (which stands for work in preparation) and are building a tool called the PREP EDITOR (Neuwirth, Kaufer, Chandhok, and Morris, 1990).[4] PREP is a construction kit that supports both writing design and discussion. As a construction kit, PREP is not a tool locked into any one writing curriculum, writing task, or type of discussion. Rather, it is a tool out of which writers can create and fill in their own writing designs and then discuss these designs with other writers. In its generality as a writing tool, PREP EDITOR approaches some of the versatility of STORYSPACE (Bolter, 1991).[5] As a comment on this versatility, we have found that other teachers of design process, going beyond writing, have used PREP for purposes we had never envisioned—commenting on computer code, writing screenplays, keeping gradebooks, taking field notes, and as a classroom lecture tool, allowing a teacher to annotate texts and slides during a lecture.

What makes PREP EDITOR work as a tool that enables both general design and discussion? We are still trying to answer this question for ourselves, but the best answer we have is that it allows the writer free access to plan with unlimited horizontal as well as vertical space. One reason why writers often like real desks more than small computer screens and (sometimes) large walls of whiteboard rather than desks is the amount of open horizontal space available. To design any object, including an article, requires one to see relationships; it is much easier to detect relationships, it seems, when one can place the objects being related side-by-side. When the objects being positioned are actual elements of the design (e.g., texts, plans, or outlines), one has a design space. When the objects being positioned are elements of communication about the design, we have an annotation space (when the communication is abbreviated and one-way) or a discussion space (when the communication is extended and two-way). Side-by-side alignment, we believe, is a fundamental structure underlying the design, annotation, and discussion of textual information in our everyday world; it only stands to reason that we should try to preserve these structures when adapting textual design, annotation, and discussion within computer environments. Built on the architecture of a column view, PREP EDITOR facilitates side-by-side alignment with the ease that normal editors facilitate single-column vertical alignment.

When side-by-side alignment in PREP EDITOR is used to support annotation,

PREP EDITOR has the look and feel of a paper margin. An implicit convention of paper is that commenters are individuated by their interaction in separate columns. The author's column is more conventionally called the draft or text. The commenter's column is more conventionally called the margin or annotation column. PREP EDITOR has the resources to create an indefinite number of margins in a single file, allowing multiple users to see one another's annotations at a glance and allowing an annotation environment to scale up to a discussion environment, where the discourse between the authors and the annotators becomes (at least temporarily) more important than the author's text itself. To support the dynamic nature of electronic documents, we are pursuing a line of research that we call *dynamic glossing*. Implementing glosses in a dynamic medium in which users can create new columns, add and delete comments, and so forth, requires a layout algorithm that can handle changes in arbitrary shapes and links (Smolensky, Bell, Fox, King, and Lewis, 1987). Figure 3 provides an actual screen dump of the collaborative work of three professional writers—Rob, John, and Phil. In Figure 3, John and Phil have annotated Rob's text (the content column). The column marked "Plan" was written by Rob to explain to John and Phil what he was trying to accomplish with various passages and so provide some focus for John and Phil's commenting.

The column architecture provides an alternative to unconstrained hypertext annotation, including an alternative to our original COMMENTS program. It also provides an alternative to NOTES, insofar as columns are composed of "chunks," with roughly the same properties of notecards in the original NOTES program.

Used as a design tool, this same side-by-side layout has similar advantages. PREP EDITOR transforms from a discussion/annotation to a design environment when the information in the chunks is associated with the raw materials of a paper. For the past two years, we have been teaching our research writing curriculum— summarizing, synthesizing, analyzing, and contributing—within PREP and finding that we can support many more aspects of our original curriculum than we could

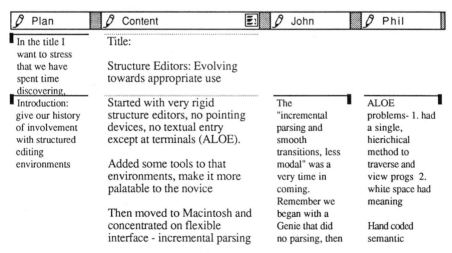

Figure 3   Use of columns to individuate authors and reviewers in the PREP EDITOR.

with NOTES and COMMENTS combined. For example, the column architecture provides a natural environment for the flexible table-making facility that we had hankered after in the NOTES environment but that had not been supported. Figure 4 illustrates how students use PREP EDITOR to create flexible tables of information as they synthesize. The left column is the *issue* column, which contains key questions that unite or divide a community of authors. Working alone or in groups, students generate questions in the issue column and then create separate columns for each author, indicating where that author stands on the question. For example, in Figure 4, two students have worked together to synthesize four authors (Hashimoto, the authors of the National Assessment of Educational Progress [NAEP] statement, Lapointe, and Connor) by generating questions in the issues column to which each can respond.

In our original WARRANT data, we have found experts creating such grids on paper when synthesizing, but it was beyond the architecture of WARRANT to supply these grids within the program itself. PREP EDITOR, with its more general architecture, has allowed us to reproduce virtually all the functionality of NOTES and COMMENTS along with additional features. Although they are not specifically implemented, trees and networks are supported by PREP's general architecture. PREP EDITOR also handles picture chunks as well as text chunks and supports automatic edits. Automatic editing is the ability to compare two columns of text and construct a third column which records all the changes between one column and the next. This is an especially useful feature for writers to have when

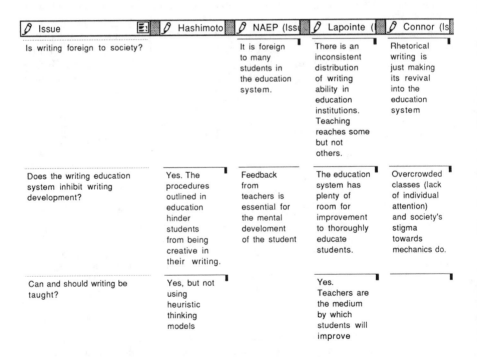

Figure 4   The use of columns to structure synthesis across authors.

they want to discuss changes from one version of a text to another and they don't want to spend hours logging each change. We have been currently testing PREP EDITOR in experimental writing classrooms (a base of about 100 students so far) and with a couple of research teams (in English and computer science) who rely on co-authoring and commenting as part of their routine practice.

LESSONS LEARNED ABOUT DESIGN: THE NEED FOR BALANCING A TASK FOCUS AND A TOOL FOCUS

The most important lesson we have learned from trying to support design as teachers is the need to be both task focused and tool focused and (especially) to know when a given focus is more appropriate. As we mentioned at the outset of this chapter, as the design task increases in reality, teachers of design are likely to have hazier impressions of the reality they want to teach. They are likely to know little, at first, about how to coach students through the task and how to fairly evaluate student work after the fact. Students, for their part, are likely to question how a teacher can expect to grade an assignment that the teacher is still struggling to understand. To resolve classroom tensions such as these, the teacher must become highly task focused to extract a representational theory of progress through the new task. In the early phase of our project, we had to take this advice—more reluctantly than we are dispensing it now—because we had no idea what made a "good move" through the assignment we wanted to teach. Although the computer can define limitless possibilities (i.e., features) for quickening a student's pace from A to B, unless we have a theory that defines A to B as a positive, critical path and recurring move, the power of the tool will seem a quite useless power. When a teacher of design is still trying to understand the assignment, a task focus seems more warranted than a tool focus. The task focus seems the more enlightened alternative; the tool focus, the more narrow.

However, as we also learned the hard way, a task focus can lose its welcome when it paints the teacher into too small a corner of specialization. If the task focus is justified on the reasoning that a support tool will need to support at least one task in depth to be able to support any, the tool focus redeems itself on the equally compelling reasoning that if a support tool is designed with only one task in mind, it will probably not have enough generality to support even that. It was the cold water of this second insight that moved us from WARRANT to PREP EDITOR and that impelled us to think about how to take the ideas about making progress in a single writing task, to generalize aspects of these representations to other tasks, and to embed these ideas as tools available as part of a more general computer architecture. In this context, the tool focus seemed to be the enlightened alternative to what had come to seem to us the narrowness of the task focus. Although PREP EDITOR is far from complete, we are satisfied that our more recent tool focus is appropriate at our current phase of development. However, even at this stage, opportunities to shift to a more concentrated task focus are becoming increasingly clear to us. Some of these opportunities will arise as we study PREP EDITOR in the following contexts:

(1) Co-authors who must search a subject domain (electronically and conventionally) prior to selecting information and incorporating it for writing.

(2) Co-authors who must decide who will compose what parts of a text prior to or in the midst of composition and discussion.
(3) Co-authors who must work at sites remote from one another.
(4) Co-authors who must write together in specific institutional settings.

Our research on academic writing taught us little about how authors (a) learn prior to their engagement in writing; (b) make decisions to organize themselves as a writing group; (c) work at a distance from one another; and (d) work under the demands of specific institutional settings. We lack strong representational theories of progress for writing design and discussion in these contexts, and so as we enter these arenas, a strong task focus will again be needed before committing ourselves too fully to a tool focus. Some of these lessons, learned the hard way, were adumbrated in previous observation. Balestri and Ehrmann (1987a, 1987b) wrote that the computer helps make implicit tasks more explicit and that the computer "provides leverage" (1987b:10) for assessing the roles of designing in the curriculum. Looking back on these statements five years later, we can appreciate how prophetic they have become. Ostensibly, the computer helps us teach what we want to teach better. However, as our experience suggests, computers do much more. They teach us about the tasks we want to teach; then they can be molded into the types of general tools that can teach these (and, potentially, other) tasks better.

REFERENCES

Balestri, Diane, and Stephen C. Ehrmann, "Introduction," *Machine-Mediated Learning*, 2(1-2):3-9, 1987a.
Balestri, Diane, and Stephen C. Ehrmann, "Learning to design, designing to learn: A more creative role for technology," *Machine-Mediated Learning*, 2(1-2):9-34, 1987b.
Bolter, Jay. STORYSPACE. Eastgate Systems, 1991.
Cavalier, T., R. Chandhok, J. Morris, D. Kaufer, and C. Neuwirth, "A visual design for collaborative work: Columns for commenting and annotation," in *Proceedings of the Twenty-Fourth Annual Hawaii International Conference on System Sciences*, Kauai, Hawaii, January 8-11, 1991, Volume III, 729-738, IEEE Press, 1991.
Conners, Robert J., "Mechanical correctness as a focus in composition instruction," *College Composition and Communication*, 36(1):61-72, 1985.
Das, J. P., J. R. Kirby, and R. F. Jarman, "Simultaneous and successive synthesis: An alternative model for cognitive abilities," *Psychological Bulletin*, 82:87-103, 1975.
Das, J. P., J. R. Kirby, and R. F. Jarman, *Simultaneous and successive cognitive processes*, New York: Academic Press, 1979.
Flower, L., and J. R. Hayes, "A cognitive process theory of writing," *College Composition and Communication*, 32:365-387, 1981.
Geisler, C., *The nature and development of expertise in essayist literacy*, Hillsdale, NJ: Erlbaum, in press.
Haas, Christina, "How the writing medium shapes the writing process: Effects of word processing on planning," *Research in the Teaching of English*, 32(2):181-207, 1989a.
Haas, Christina, "A sense of the text: Problems writers encounter in building text representations," Center for Educational Computing in English, English Department, Carnegie-Mellon University, Pittsburgh, PA, 1989b.
Halasz, F. G., "Reflections on notecards: Seven issues for the next generation of hypermedia systems," in *Hypertext '87 Proceedings*, 345-365, Chapel Hill, NC, Nov. 13-15, 1987, ACM, 1987.
Hartman, K., C. Neuwirth, "Patterns of social interaction in learning to write: Some effects of network technologies," *Written Communication*, 8 (Jan.):79-113, 1991.
Hayes, J. R., L. Flower, K. A. Schriver, J. Stratman, and L. Carey. "Cognitive processes in revision," in S. Rosenberg (ed.), *Advances in applied psycholinguistics, Volume II: Reading, writing, and language processing*, 176-240. Cambridge, England: Cambridge University Press, 1987.

WRITING 137

Kaufer, D. S., and C. Geisler, "Novelty in academic writing," *Written Communication*, 6(3):286–311, 1989.

Kaufer, D. S., and C. Geisler, "Structuring argumentation in a social constructivist framework: A pedagogy with computer support," *Argumentation*, 4:379–396, 1990.

Kaufer, D. S., C. Geisler, and C. Neuwirth, *Arguing from sources: Exploring issues through reading and writing*, New York: Harcourt, Brace, 1989.

Luria, A. R. Cognitive development, its cultural and social foundations. (trans. M. Lopez-Moriallas and L. Solotaroff) ed. M. Cole. Cambridge, MA: Harvard UP, 1976.

Mainstay Software. *Mark-UP* Agoura Hill, CA: Mainstay Software, 1989.

Neuwirth, C., and D. Kaufer, "The NOTES program: A decision-support tool for writing from sources," in *Hypertext '87 Proceedings*, 121–141, Chapel Hill, NC, Nov. 13, 1987, ACM.

Neuwirth, C., and D. Kaufer, "The role of external representation in the writing process: Implications for the design of hypertext writing tools," in *Hypertext '89 Proceedings*, 319–341, Pittsburgh, PA, Oct 16, 1989, ACM, 1989.

Neuwirth, C., D. Kaufer, R. Chandhok, and J. Morris, "Issues in the design of computer support for co-authoring and commenting," in *Proceedings of the Conference for Computer-Supported Cooperative Work*, 183–195, Oct. 7–10, 1990, Los Angeles, CA, Baltimore, MD: ACM SIGCHI and SIGOIS, 1990.

Neuwirth, C., D. Kaufer, G. Keim, and T. Gillespie, "The COMMENTS program: A computer tool for response to writing," Technical Report, Center for Educational Computing in English, Carnegie-Mellon University, Pittsburgh, PA, 1988.

Ogura, A., "Reflective vs. verbatim notes: A study of the NOTES program," paper presented at the Conference on College Composition and Communication, March 1989.

Reitman, Walter Ralph, *Cognition and thought: An information processing approach*, New York: Wiley, 1965.

Simon, Herbert A., *The sciences of the artificial*, Cambridge: MA: Massachusetts Institute of Technology, 1981.

Smolensky, P., B. Bell, B. Fox, R. King, and C. Lewis, "Constraint-based hypertext for argumentation," in *Hypertext '87 Proceedings*, Chapel Hill, NC, Nov. 13–15, 1987, Chapel Hill. ACM, 1987.

Teare, B. Richard, "The use of problems and instances to make education professional (in engineering)," *Education for Professional Responsibility*. Pittsburgh, PA: Carnegie Institute of Technology Press, 1948, 215–243.

Walton, Richard, and Diane Balestri, "Writing as a design discipline," *Machine-Mediated Learning*, 2(1–2):47–66, 1987.

NOTES

1. The WARRANT project was funded by FIPSE (Fund for the Improvement of Postsecondary Education) in 1984, Preston Covey, David Kaufer, Chris Neuwirth, and Cheryl Geisler, principal investigators.
2. By no stretch of the imagination did our implementation efforts keep pace with our pedagogical aspirations. NOTES, for example, allowed students to take notes on electronic sources but, because of its lack of portability, was not convenient for taking notes on printed texts in the library. Furthermore, NOTES proved to be much better at helping students to take and search notes than to organize them into rhetorical patterns. Although NOTES had these organizational capabilities, students did not widely use them. See the main text for more disjunctures between our software and the requirements of our curriculum. Generally speaking, we have found, no matter how tightly coupled the educational planning and the software development efforts, there are bound to be fissures that push these enterprises toward a life of their own. Our project was no exception.
3. See Note 2.
4. PREP EDITOR has been supported by the National Science Foundation under Grant No. IRI-8902891 and by a grant from Apple External Research and the Bellcore Corporation. We thank Dale Miller and Paul Erion for work on programming PREP EDITOR prototype and Todd Cavalier for work on graphic design for PREP EDITOR interface.
5. Because our experience with STORYSPACE is limited, any comparisons between it and PREP EDITOR are tentative at best. One point of contrast, perhaps, is that PREP is being designed to handle writing design, discussion, and annotation in a seamless way. STORYSPACE is a more dedicated writing design tool with asymmetrical focus on the discussion and annotation process.

III

LEARNING TO THINK
LIKE A DESIGNER:
TWO MICROWORLDS
AND A TUTOR

6

Science Through Design Practica, Where Students Actively Investigate and Persuade

John R. Jungck
Beloit College, Beloit, WI

Nils S. Peterson
From The Heart Software, Monmouth, OR

John N. Calley
University of Arizona, Fayetteville

Abstract *Design learning in science is greatly facilitated by computer simulations and tools that enable students to solve open-ended problems that require them to pose problems, iteratively probe the problems that they frame, and persuade their peers that their hypotheses are warranted and significant. Collaborative group work in such problem-solving activities facilitates the collection and analysis of large amounts of complex data, the development and examination of multiple working hypotheses, peer learning, and the construction of persuasive propositions. As with design in the arts, students learn that scientists construct meaning in the world rather than passively discovering facts. Thus, we assert that there are fundamental similarities between science and the creative arts and that these similarities can be readily experienced by students in a practice that engages them in generating useful fictions (hypotheses or theories). Our example of design learning in science uses computer simulations that involve design at many levels of application.*

INTRODUCTION

Science educators have much in common with creative writing teachers. Teachers of creative writing routinely ask students to write original compositions in a variety of genres (poems, plays, short stories, novels, etc.) on subjects about which students frequently care deeply. Students assume that their teachers have an excellent grasp of craft and that their goal is to help students become better writers. In addition, teachers of creative writing ask students to read some of the best examples of each genre of literature, examples that have captured the academic vernacular for creativity. Similarly, teachers of what may be called "creative sciencing" develop courses in which the students are expected to generate their

Expanded and updated from an article entitled "A Design Approach to Science," by N. S. Peterson, J. R. Jungck, D. M. Sharpe, and W. F. Finzer, *Machine-Mediated Learning*, 2(1–2):111–127, 1987.

own hypotheses and experimental protocols and are judged by the scientific papers that they produce.

In the 1960s, without inciting the academic community's acrimony by calling such courses "creative sciencing," a group of science educators experimented intensely with a series of courses or sections of courses entitled "Investigative Laboratories" (Thorton, 1972). Students were asked to come up with their own problem, define a critical test, develop or adopt a methodology, order their own materials and/or collect their own organisms, possibly travel to an appropriate ecosystem, perform their experiments, analyze their results, produce a scientific article, and make a scientific presentation to their peers. The open-endedness of facilitating so many different kinds of projects, the financial difficulties in supporting diverse projects, and the lack of correlation to what was occurring in the lecture courses of their curricula ultimately led to the disappearance of all but a few of these ventures. Nonetheless, this historical tradition of teaching in a "creative sciencing" way did not disappear but instead has been the source of a great deal of curricular innovation over the past twenty-five years. In particular, the advent of powerful, graphically rich microcomputers has allowed the instructors to facilitate open-ended problem solving in a research-like environment and to simulate economically prohibitive laboratory and field projects in diverse coursework domains. These computer exploratoria offer the potential to address all three problems associated with investigative labs and to enable several new opportunities.

Our central theme is that fundamentals of scientific practice can only be learned in a design practicum. Rather than learning about or for the sake of problem solving, we argue for learning through problem solving. This chapter explores how scientific problems are design problems, why design problems are difficult, why scientific design must be learned through practice, and what benefits students derive from doing scientific design. We believe that science education should be more concerned with the history, construction, and communication of problems than with the conclusions drawn from problems that have been well defined in advance for students. Computer exploratoria (Jungck, 1991) are practica encapsulating a simulated investigatory world that enable teachers and students to frame a particular area of open-ended scientific research. These exploratoria have been designed so that there are authentic parallels between using them and learning science through practice in research laboratories. In addition, they parallel learning in the practica of other design disciplines.

To make clear the parallels between science and other design disciplines, we use the general terms *design learning* to describe a type of learning process and *practicum* to describe a learning setting. Design learning stresses three things: (a) The learner is always self-directed and active; (b) problems are open-ended, with multiple working hypotheses and solution pathways; and (c) the viability of solutions is established by the judgment of problem solvers and their peers. The last point is important to stress. We believe that it is important for science students to understand that the viability of a solution depends both on its pragmatic utility and on its being convincingly communicated to peers, in a way that coheres with their knowledge and appeals to their aesthetic sense. Thus, we promote scientific realism, which House (1991:2) claims:

Must be distinguished from naive realism, which is clearly wrong. For example, a naive realist would hold that a lemon is really yellow. A scientific realist would hold that a lemon appears yellow because of the refraction of light off its surface, the particular nature of light waves, and the structure of the human eye, thus invoking the causal entities and structures that produce the phenomenon, that is, the yellow lemon. The analysis does not stop with surface events but examines the underlying patterns and tendencies.

Students need to understand that the art of scientific design lies in choosing appropriate lenses and in understanding their limitations as tools for examining "underlying patterns and tendencies." Demonstrations will not suffice because: (a) the student is a passive observer; (b) the "event" is a rehearsed exercise rather than a problem; (c) they "deal with well-established phenomena, not new and contentious phenomena" (Collins, 1989); and (d) there is an element of science as "magic" that frequently closes the student off from the contingencies involved in the preparation of a well-honed demonstration.

We illustrate this chapter with one of a number of pieces of computer software that have been designed to create scientific practica, namely, the Genetics Construction Kit (Jungck and Calley, 1986/1990).[1] Other software for biology practica can be found in two major software development projects from the late 1980s: BioQUEST[2] and the Cardiovascular Function Laboratories.[3] These examples are illustrative, but not exhaustive. The techniques and philosophies described here can be applied not only across biology education but also across science instruction in general (e.g., for a discussion of workshop physics and discovery chemistry, see Laws, 1991).

SCIENCE AS A DESIGN ACTIVITY

When we propose that the student's work in a science practicum is a design-like activity, we are drawing a parallel to other design activities such as architecture or music composition. We are informed in our notion of design primarily by William Morris's nineteenth-century vision of design as both a creative and a utilitarian art. Particularly, Morris inveighed against the mechanical and exploitative aspects of what many had previously distinguished as design (Stansky, 1985). In each design setting there are some initial constraints, such as slope of the land in architecture and tonal range of an instrument in music composition, and some assumed hypotheses. There is also some goal: the building of a single-family house, the composition of a concerto, or the explanation of a set of observations. The design methodology for reaching a goal is the heart of professional education in each of these disciplines.

Let us return to the initial example of creative writing to examine the teaching methods being used there. If creative writing teachers were only to have students reproduce the narrative structure, syntax, mood, and plot technique of canonized literature, we might accuse the students of plagiarism or simplistic mimicry rather than laud them for creative writing. Mentoring creativity in writing, instead, must engage the instructor as a writing collaborator and critic. In a similar manner, this kind of mentoring collaboration is what a science educator must do if students are investigating the causal mechanisms for unknown phenomena.

Herbert Simon (1982) has described the science (as opposed to the art) of design as a "science of the artificial"—a science, that is, which contains knowledge about artificial (i.e., human-made) objects and their creation. Simon contrasts sciences of the artificial with sciences of the natural (i.e., nature-made), but for us this distinction is not meaningful. Knowledge about natural systems does not represent absolute truth; rather, it represents human-made explanations for observations of the natural world. For example, the alleles[4] hypothesized by early Mendelian geneticists are now being found to have a chemical basis in differences among DNA molecules, but the human-made explanation of alleles predated and did not depend on knowledge of whether genes existed as regions on the DNA molecule. Collins (1986) has described scientific activity as the development, articulation, testing, and defense of hypotheses, which we argue are design activities, whether the phenomena are artificial or natural.

Problems

Science is often taught through analytical problems that take the form of some initial data and an evaluation algorithm. For example, the question "Does this car get at least twenty-five miles per gallon?" can be solved by analysis, as diagrammed in Figure 1.

A analytical problem in genetics looks similar:

> In Drosophila *the allele for long wings [W] is dominant to the allele for short wings [w] and the allele for tan body [B] is dominant to the allele for ebony body [b]. What phenotype and genotype ratios are expected when a heterozygous long-winged and ebony-bodied fly [Ww, bb] and one that is short-winged and ebony-bodied [ww, bb] are crossed? (Stewart, 1988)*

It is analytical problems like these, typical of secondary and undergraduate science curricula, that leave students with the perception of science as an activity in which data are to be properly combined to give a single correct or "provable" answer. Teaching science solely by analytical problems creates the myth that scientists work by progressing logically from known givens (causes) to universally recognized "truths." We would characterize these activities as exercises, not problems. In sharp contrast with this normative image of the rational, logical scientist, Imre Lakatos, a philosopher of science, has stated that there is "no magical

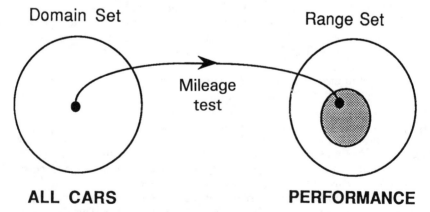

Figure 1   An analysis problem uses an algorithm to map a car to its performance. The gray region represents performance that meets a criterion, for example, 25 miles per gallon. Viewed more generally, this figure shows an analysis function that maps an element in the domain to one in the range.

Domain Set   Range Set

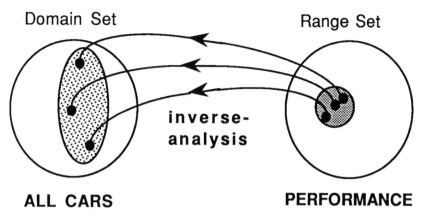

inverse-
analysis

ALL CARS   PERFORMANCE

Figure 2 The inverse-analysis (synthesis) function goes from desired performance to car designs. Designs that meet the performance criteria are in the oval region. This inverse-analysis function is multivalued and does not exist.

method for instant rationality" (1976). By way of confirmation, Kern, Mirels, and Hinshaw (1983) tested scientists from physics, psychology, and biology and found that none of them fared better than 25 percent on a simple test of propositional logic!

A synthetic problem, "Design a passenger car that gets at least 25 miles per gallon (mpg)," is diagrammed in Figure 2. This is a much harder problem than the first one we looked at, because there are many possible car designs that will get least 25 mpg: The relationship between desired performance and cars is multivalued. The problem is further complicated because the inverse-analysis function (the relationship between performance and cars) does not exist. If it did, General Motors would probably apply it. A common method for solving a design problem is to create a prototype and analyze it. If the design fails, the designer modifies the design to improve the performance. Often this process can be conducted with one or more types of models. This is a difficult process for the designer because the design variables that can be manipulated (number of cylinders, wheelbase, body materials, etc.) have a complex relationship to one another and to the performance measures. Thus, it may not be clear to the designer if increasing the wheelbase will increase or decrease the mileage of the car.

To summarize, we have argued that there are two kinds of scientific problems: analytic and synthetic. They are interwoven in the process of designing. Stewart (Stewart, 1988; Stewart and Hafner, 1991) has described a typology of genetics problems that categorizes analysis problems as *cause-to-effects* and synthesis problems as *effects-to-cause*. He has explored the role of each kind of problem in genetics education. Analysis problems require students to implement conceptual knowledge they have been given; these problems often lead students to a deeper understanding of the analytic model. Synthesis problems help students develop (a) a deeper understanding of genetics-specific content; (b) content-independent problem-solving heuristics; and (c) an understanding of science as an intellectual activity. Thus, for robust science instruction, we believe the pedagogic challenge is to engage students in both analytic and synthetic designing activities.

With these concerns in mind, we have identified three important elements in any scientific practicum. These "3 Ps" of science are problem posing, problem solving, and persuasion (Peterson and Jungck, 1988).

Problem Posing

The science practica that we have developed eschew pre-posed, finite analysis problems like those presented in textbooks. Real problems do not come pre-posed to scientists—a problem is much less difficult if it has been well posed. Problems have a historical thread woven into them and the perceptions used to pose problems may, in themselves, be theory-laden. Problem posing is important to learning about science as an intellectual activity because it is where so many of the biases of culture and ideology enter. Prejudices based on race, gender, and ethnicity, as well as reductionism, teleology, and anthropomorphism creep into many formulations of problems. If hidden assumptions are ignored during problem posing, it is difficult to address them at the later stages.

Problem posing is also an important opportunity for students to address the "What should I do?" question themselves. In actual scientific practice, no problems will come to them out of thin air. Students can only begin to appreciate the tremendous agenda-setting issues in problem posing if they are presented practica that facilitate their posing of problems for themselves. When students begin asking questions, they will rapidly see that their problem-posing and problem-solving activities are inseparable and that drawing warranted inferences depends on knowing the assumptions that were made at the posing stage.

The program, Genetics Construction Kit (GCK; Jungck and Calley, 1986)[5] provides an example of a practicum created with a computer simulation. The program is a simulation of a classical genetics laboratory. It starts by creating a set of organisms with unknown patterns of inheritance, called the *field population* (see Figure 3), and provides the tools needed to design and perform an experimental strategy to infer the inheritance patterns. The practicum is realistic because it permits students to cross the unknown organisms and analyze the crosses with the same types of tools that are used by practicing scientists.

GCK is not meant to replace work with live organisms, but the constraints of time, space, money, and laboratory technique (important parts of scientific research) make it practically impossible for most students to experience the excitement and challenge of an actual research problem. Consequently, we often use live fruit flies concurrently with the simulation. The wet lab allows students to learn from living organisms; the simulated lab allows them to practice intellectual skills and perform many more crosses than time permits in the wet laboratory. The phenotypes (but not necessarily the genetic phenomena) that appear in the GCK program are those associated with *Drosophila,* commonly known as the fruit fly.

What is the problem in Figure 3? Answering this question is an important experience in a scientific practicum. For example, students might observe that there are two forms of the arista (a bristle-like part) and pose the problem, "Develop a true-breeding strain." Other problems are equally possible: "Develop a strain that doesn't breed true"; "Determine if the Minute trait is dominant or recessive." All of these problems can be addressed, and in any order that they occur to the student. For each of these problems, student groups will produce a hypothesis, for example, "From the following crosses, we hypothesize that the

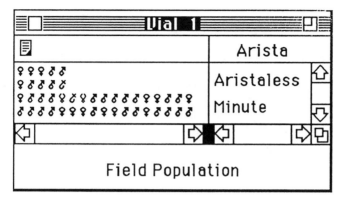

Figure 3 The field population collected (created) when the Genetics
Construction Kit (GCK) is started. There is one trait (the
Arista) recorded in this example and it appears in two variants
(Aristaless and Minute). The rows of sex symbols on the left
represent individual fruit flies. To perform a cross, two flies of
opposite sex are selected with the Macintosh mouse and then
the Cross operation is chosen.

Minute trait is recessive." Two hypotheses are diagrammed in Figure 4 as functions from a mating pair domain to a offspring phenotype range.

Student groups find that problem probing frequently generates their greatest
frustrations because they have had little experience in determining whether a problem that they have framed is significant, soluble, "what the teacher wants," and so
on. However, like Piet Hein's *Grooks* (1966), students quickly learn that "problems worthy of attack prove their worth by hitting back."[5] No matter how long
they stand in the lab or in the field, problems do not come pre-posed to them and
students need to engage actively in constructing problems for themselves.

Problem Solving

Theories are fictions that are useful for successful problem solving and the
communication of science. We describe them as *fictions* to remind ourselves that
although theories are explanatory, even predictive, they do not represent an absolute truth, only an artificial construct that is a parsimonious and functional description of current observations. To help students see this viewpoint, we propose that
they learn through problem solving in realistic, open-ended domains. Here they
must proceed by forming one or more working hypotheses from data they collect,
testing the hypotheses with new experiments, and concluding which hypotheses
are most parsimonious and defensible to themselves and their peers.

Our approach is driven by the view that acquisition of knowledge is not a static
activity; it is not a matter of training students to respond in a set fashion. Knowledge goes beyond factual understanding; it is a literacy in the *process* of construction. This literacy makes a body of knowledge dynamic and keeps the learner open
to continual learning. To achieve this dynamic state, we require practica that pose
realistic problems for which there is no unique solution path or endpoint. For these

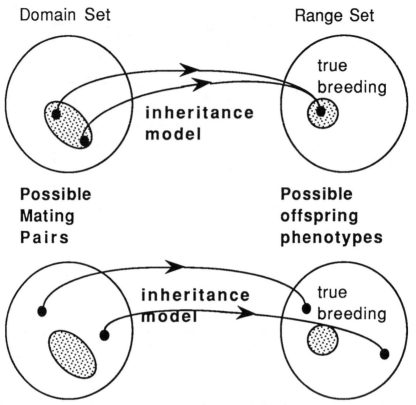

Figure 4   A diagram of two genetics hypotheses. In the upper panel, all possible mating pairs in the oval are hypothesized to produce offspring of only one phenotype (e.g., true-breeding). In the lower panel, all possible mating pairs outside the oval are hypothesized to produce offspring of more than one phenotype. The former is somewhat like the cross represented in Vial 2 in Figure 5 and the latter is somewhat like the cross represented in Vial 4 in Figure 6.

problems, the solution is a hypothesis. Students should understand that scientific theories have traveled the same road as their own hypotheses and that these theories are open to challenge and change. However, unlike student hypotheses in student experiments, theories have withstood a longer test of time and may be generalizable to a wider class of observations.

Teacher's Role as Collaborative Researcher/Coach

Realistic problem solving is messy; students need to experience going down blind alleys. The wise instructor resists the urge to correct these errors by solving the problem in his or her own heuristic approach. In our simulations, students have posed their problem, performed their own experiments, and collected their own results. In this situation, experienced teachers will recognize that it is more important for their students to be learning and negotiating with one another than for teachers to be reinforcing them with heavy guidance into a few heuristic strategies.

Donald Schön (1987) has studied the role of the practicum in professional education. His study focused on architectural design, master classes in music, and clinical psychology. In each case, the core of the education involved realistic practice with the tools and problems of the profession: designing buildings, playing music, or psychoanalyzing patients. Schön describes the teacher as a *coach* who alternates between demonstrating for the student as they work jointly on a problem and critiquing the student's solo performance.

In science, the metaphor of teacher as coach is less apt; therefore, we usually stress the role of a research colleague, particularly one from a nonhierarchical social setting. However, Schön's approach is suggestive. Consider the problem of learning to swim. It cannot be learned well by expert swimmers lecturing about swimming or swimmers. Rather, learner and coach get in the water and practice. The learner must swim in order to understand what swimming is. Swimming research might involve swimmers' invention of new strokes out of an understanding of the relationship between human biomechanics and the fluid dynamics associated with propulsion. This model is very different from the practices in a typical undergraduate biology course in which the instructor expounds and the student memorizes.

Jungck and Calley (1986) have described their style of teaching in a genetics practicum as a "post-Socratic pedagogy," because the software they use creates an environment in which the teacher has no more idea than the students about what an answer or optimal strategy might be. They designed the GCK software to enable students to pose their own problems and create their own problem environments of varying complexity, rather than having problems posed for them in the Socratic method. The student and teacher swim side-by-side, navigating their study through uncertain waters. Nonetheless, the teacher demonstrates techniques and earns credibility, like Schön's *coach,* but also is allowed to participate in the research (something that we teachers do too infrequently!).

Multiple Hypotheses

Realistic problem solving should include the possibility of multiple hypotheses and avenues of research. As an example, we work with the theory of simple dominance and design experiments to create two true-breeding strains. If we denote the dominant allele for the Arista as A and the recessive allele as a, then true-breeding strains will have parents with either AA or aa genotypes (homozygotes). Non-true-breeding strains will have Aa or aA genotypes (heterozygotes). The heterozygotes will have the same appearance (phenotype) as the dominant homozygotes.

Figure 5 shows vials containing the results of two crosses. In Vial 2, we performed a Minute–Minute cross of two field population flies and got only Minute Arista progeny. We can now create four initial working hypotheses: (1) Minute is a phenotype generated by a homozygous recessive (aa) genotype; or (2) we were very lucky and crossed two homozygous dominant (AA) Minute individuals and Aristaless is the homozygous recessive (aa) condition; (3) we crossed a homozygous dominant (AA) Minute individuals with a heterozygous dominant (Aa) Minute individuals and Aristaless is the homozygous recessive (aa) condition; or (4) we crossed two heterozygous dominant (Aa) Minute individual and Aristaless is the homozygous recessive (aa) condition, but in our small progeny sample, by chance, none of the recessive phenotype appeared. The results of the cross in Vial 3

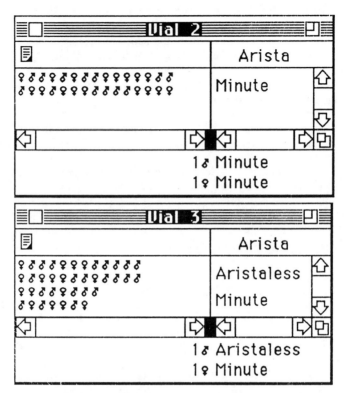

Figure 5 The upper panel shows a GCK vial containing the results of a
Minute–Minute cross. The lower panel shows the results of an
Aristaless–Minute cross.

(Figure 4) are most consistent with the first hypothesis; however, none of the
others can yet be ruled out. A Minute–Aristaless cross produced mixed progeny. A
chi-square calculator exists in GCK for statistically testing the likelihood that the
observed progeny distribution of 24 : 15 is in concordance with an expected 1 : 1
ratio (19.5 : 19.5) if we had crossed an heterozygous dominant (*Aa*) individual
with a homozygous recessive (*aa*) individual. After computing the chi-square
value, students would learn such a large deviation from their expected values could
be expected, on chance alone, to occur between 10 percent and 20 percent of the
time. Because this value is greater than the scientifically accepted 5 percent value,
we could not reject the hypothesis that the result is a cross between a heterozygote
and a homozygote; however, we still do not know which phenotype is produced by
a heterozygous condition.

All of our four models presumed only the simplest of genetic models (one locus
and two alleles) and did not consider the range of genetic and environmental
influences that are well known. Nonetheless, such assumptions have great heuristic value in getting students started in the investigative process. They need only
give up their assumptions when confronted by data that they can no longer explain.

Solving the Meta-Problem

Our assumption of the theory of simple dominance has shaped the description of our problem solving so far. However, when we begin to seek a true-breeding Aristaless strain by crossing two Aristaless flies, a problem appears in Vial 4 (see Figure 6). With the assumption of simple dominance in our problem posing, we hypothesized that only Minute and Aristaless traits could appear, to illustrate the pitfalls of assumptions made during problem posing. The last cross produced a new trait that is unexplainable using the simple dominance theory, that is, the analytic model we are using cannot account for the progeny from the cross. Our problem solving now unexpectedly shifts to a meta-level: We suddenly need to design a new theory of inheritance, a theory (expressed as an analytic model) that explains all of the data collected to date, including Vial 4. This type of meta-problem can arise in GCK problems because the program contains a number of important inheritance models, including simple dominance, codominance, sex-linkage, autosomal linkage, and multiple alleles.

Design learning requires students to construct meaning actively while they work, by which we mean that beyond discovering a "fact," students are continuously being challenged to evaluate three structures of their knowledge: methodology (strategies), justification (how do you know that you know), and the perception of which components are under investigation (what is the real problem). Dyke (1988) describes the process of interaction between methodology, epistemology, and ontology as "structuring structured structures." The failure of the third cross to meet our expectations demonstrates the need to restructure the problem dynamically during its investigation. In contrast, the positivistic, normative tradition of science education has been grounded on a given methodology (the scientific method), a notion of warrant (*scientific proof*), and an assumption of realism (*observable facts*). We believe that design learning is much more emancipatory than teaching students within the positivistic, normative tradition because it more

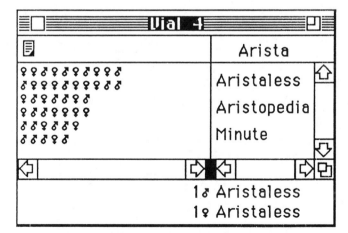

Figure 6 This vial shows that an Aristaless–Aristaless cross produced fourteen offspring with the unanticipated Aristopedia phenotype.

honestly reflects the dynamic nature of both science and knowing. We usually find that students become very engaged in GCK problem solving and that they ask us new and interesting questions about their research.

Persuasion

As was illustrated above, the development and defense of a hypothesis might progress unevenly through multiple pathways with side trips for tentative confirmation or rejection of alternatives. During this process, scientists may entertain several hypotheses simultaneously, weighing and evaluating each. Ideally, all but one can be ruled out with a degree of confidence, but none can ever be stated with absolute certainty.

Presenting the hypothesis as a solution requires that problem solvers satisfy a community of other problem solvers. A persuasive argument must be presented that defends the utility of the solution; it cannot be judged *right* according to an external truth or outside authority. A hypothesis is credible because it is consistent with all data collected so far, probable alternative hypotheses have been refuted, and it can be persuasively argued to colleagues in a fashion that coheres with their knowledge.

Because scientific literature is frequently seen by students as reporting or communicating, it is important to share examples of persuasion that transformed the very nature of scientific and cultural discourse. For example, Margot Norris (1985:30) describes the impact of the *Origin of Species* thus:

> But Darwin further abolished the individualization of the Author at the levels of metaphor and analogy by substituting the many for the one, the dispersed for the unitary, the gradual for the instantaneous, the trivial for the portentous, and the oxymoron of unconscious choice for the anthropomorphism of deliberate decision.

The germ theory of disease, the theory of genes, and the nutritional view of vitamins all posited initially invisible entities as responsible for an enormous range of human conditions; Semmelweis was hospitalized as insane for one such view. Although few scientists establish such new forms of persuasion, students need to recognize the breadth of opportunity available to them.

For instance, the degree to which a student's solution to the dilemma of the third cross fits accepted scientific theory will vary. In further explorations the student will measure the utility (or dis-utility) of each tentative hypothesis as it facilitates the solution of new problems. We believe that students will learn about science *qua* science when answers are recognized as hypotheses that can always be qualified or questioned further. We find that students are most receptive to changing their worldview when they are regularly confronted with situations that are surprising, challenging, and perturbing to them. Our simulations have provided them with many such opportunities; a number of master's and doctoral dissertations in science have recorded conversations that have been full of controversy, even though the students are usually only considering classical textbook phenomena.

Returning again to our example, we still need to resolve whether the Minute phenotype was recessive. The problem solver decides how many crosses are required before the chosen hypothesis is warranted. To persuade peers of the results, the problem solver must also decide how many crosses, and which types of crosses, will succinctly, elegantly, and convincingly communicate the results. In this process, many blind alleys and superfluous experiments may be dropped from the report and new experiments may be added to refute alternate hypotheses most clearly. The design audience is continually being persuaded either by appeal to aesthetic tastes (elegance, parsimony, and reproducibility) or by development of new aesthetic principles. Defensibility and coherence with other knowledge complement the utility of the result as criteria for judging the aesthetic quality of the design.

The Role of Persuasion and Student Evaluation

Using the design pedagogy in science education transforms the focus and purpose of evaluation in science education. In design practica we encourage students to test how well their ideas work in explaining and analyzing data, making predictions, duplicating experiments, and convincing their peer community. Problems on traditional exams do not adequately evaluate these skills. Furthermore, final exams do not fit with a constructivist philosophy of learning. We advocate a more formative approach, similar to that taken by other design professions. Students' design learning should be evaluated in the same way that professionals are evaluated, just as student musicians give recitals and student architects present drawings for critique, so should student scientists should present talks and papers. In talks and papers, several aspects of the student's learning are made audible and visible for students as well as others. Self-reflection on the process and outcomes provides a meta-cognitive window into one's own reasoning (the individual student's self-assessment). Peer review serves to establish credibility within the discipline (or class). Thus, actions taken in the course of problem solving can be explicitly analyzed for efficiency, robustness, generality, and aesthetics in a community of self and others.

Computer software can make available sets of tools for helping students to reflect on their work, construct their science, and prepare their papers. GCK, for example, includes note pads, visual displays of histograms, chi-square tables, charts of crosses performed, and tools for reorganizing the display of information in a vial or organisms. These scripts and displays can all be exported to a word processor and developed into a persuasive article. The data can be exported to a spreadsheet, graphics package, or statistical package for further manipulation, and conclusions can be incorporated into the word-processed text. The construction of such an article not only informs instructors and peers about the strategies that were used in the investigation but also says much about the aesthetics that inform the students' science. For example, did they develop pedigrees for examining their data? If so, were these pedigrees wide and shallow or narrow and deep? Reflection and conscious articulation by students of reasons for actions taken while constructing meaning leads to problem solving with understanding. Therefore, we focus evaluation on students' self-reflection and narratives of complex systems rather than on the mastery of individual components of systems. Our purpose in evaluation is to stimulate self-assessment through such reflective and communal interactions. Just as scientists may be judged by the quality of their published work, our goal is that students will experience this approach to assessment as more authentic and empowering.

CURRICULAR CONSEQUENCES

When science is taught through design practica, there are enormous curricular consequences. Instead of teachers being authoritative disseminators of information, they must earn credibility as coresearchers on problems that students have posed and probed. Doll (1986:10) says:

> Any curriculum which emphasizes the active and reflective—the only way to achieve internality—must by nature run the risk of disequilibrium. . . . Disruption, or disequilibrium, is the motor which drives reorganizational behavior. . . . The teacher must intentionally cause enough chaos to motivate the student to reorganize. Because no preset formula can tell the teacher what [the right amount of chaos] will be for individual students, teaching becomes an art. Behavioral objectives with their set predeterminations have no place in this art. Immense responsibility is placed on the teacher, and curricula need to be teacher manipulated, not teacher proofed.

Val Woodward (1972:23), a geneticist, situated investigative labs in the larger context of creative design:

> Highly creative people honor the attitude of discovery and they trust, in some measure, their senses. Yet it is important to consider that creativity is not merely present or absent, but, rather, that different people possess different degrees of creativity and different motives for and modes of expression; meaning, of course, that environmental circumstances act as determinants or repressants of expression. If, for example, there exists an environmental threshold below which curiosity is curbed and above which it is unleashed, the appearance would be that some people are creative and that some are not. Environmental circumstances, i.e., the educational apparati, act to raise or lower the threshold, depending on the values of society. Leaders may wish to raise the threshold simply because noncurious people are easier to lead. On the other hand, a society may conclude that species survival is directly proportional to species creativity, and choose to lower the threshold. In either case, education is the handle by which the threshold is manipulated.
>   Science is an example of concerted activity within which the relationship between the investigative attitude and increased awareness is apparent, but appreciation of the fullness of this relationship demands historical perspective. Recall the social pressures exerted upon scientists a few centuries back, when their discoveries were negated simply by reference to dogma. Some were executed, some exiled, and many of their discoveries annulled. . . . A large part of this resistance can be traced to the way we teach young people. Certainly we have never applied the methods we use in discovery to the processes of teaching . . . Our mode and manner of teaching signals whether, as a society, we are ready to live with sustained and open-ended uncertainty, or whether we will persist to encircle ourselves with limited dimensions which, in time, demand the kinds of upheavals that negate the advances we have made toward an understanding of our higher qualities.

CONCLUSION

We have argued that scientific investigation is a practice much closer to the traditional design fields of composition, graphic design, and architecture than is commonly recognized. The process begins from a set of tentatively accepted theories (resources and constraints) and seeks to understand a phenomenon. Understanding (expressed as a hypothesis) is the product to be created. The goals are fuzzy, very fuzzy, when compared to the concise statements that will ultimately be published in the scientific literature, and the nature of the goals is refined (even "discovered") during the process of pursuing them. The decision that the goals have been reached is subjective, decided by the scientist. This decision may be based on external constraints, such as available time, but preferably is based on personal judgment that the hypothesis is convincing, defensible, reproducible, parsimonious, and, in some sense, elegant.

A scientific practicum helps students develop a deeper understanding of domain-specific concepts, while it develops content-independent heuristic skills and an understanding of the nature of science. We have found it an engaging and powerful way to teach. Papert (1980:31) contrasts the impact of a design learning environment with that found in typical school experiences:

> *[A design environment] offers children an opportunity to become more like adults, indeed like advanced professionals, in their relationship to their intellectual products and to themselves. In doing so, it comes into head-on collision with many aspects of school whose effect, if not whose intention, is to "infantilize" the child.*

A practicum also helps students mature because it lets them appreciate the role of failure in learning. Henry Petroski's (1985) book *To Engineer Is Human* is subtitled *The Role of Failure in Successful Design.* For Petroski, design is iterative revision and "success is foreseeing failure." Furthermore, he weighs the risks and rewards of innovation with the futility of trying to produce the perfect product. Schwartz (1983:33), a director of first-year college English, describes the design metaphor in a similar manner:

> *To learn to debug is to overcome the fear of being wrong, replacing it with the drive to untangle the problem. This is the real goal of making writing personally meaningful and relevant. It encourages the student to become an active participant and creates a truly collaborative relationship with the writing teacher.*

Scientific practica give students the opportunity to engage in the activities of design: choosing materials and objectives, posing problems, fabricating, editing, and retouching solutions. Students do not merely mimic professionals in a practicum; no requirement is made that students develop hypotheses in an historic sequence, or in any other fixed way.

The GCK software has been used with a wide variety of students, from primary school to postdoctoral fellows. We find that learning is most effective in small groups of three students at one computer. Contrary to the projections of some, we find this type of computer-assisted learning both stimulating to, and demanding of, the teacher. Computer software enhances successful practica when the student–teacher–computer interactions are strong, when the computer is a microcosm of the world, and when together they solve a realistic problem and using realistic tools.

Dwyer (1974) states that "deep technology is of little value without a deep view of education." The deep view of education that is used in computer software for scientific practica is one of design learning. Practica that facilitate design learning and literacy in science are the hallmarks of our approach. We value this approach to science education because it provides novices with an opportunity to participate in the scientific tradition while it moves them toward a literacy that cannot be easily learned in textbooks. Furthermore, we value the new role of the teacher as strategist, motivator, and co-explorer. Finally, the practicum gives students an appreciation for the hypothetical and debatable nature of scientific theories, an appreciation that prepares them to be educated citizens in our society.

REFERENCES

Collins, Angelo, "Content knowledge and thought processes for solving transmission genetics problems," Ph.D. dissertation, University of Wisconsin—Madison, 1986.

Collins, Harry M., "The meaning of experiment: Replication and reasonableness," in Hilary Lawson and Lisa Appignanesi, *Dismantling truth: Reality in the post-modern world,* 82–92, 169–170, New York: St. Martin's Press, 1989.

Doll, William E., Jr., "Prigogine: A new sense of order, a new curriculum," *Theory into Practice,* 25(1):10–16, 1986.

Dwyer, Thomas, "Heuristic strategies for using computers to enrich education," *International Journal of Man-Machine Studies,* 6:137–154, 1974.

Dyke, Charles, *The evolutionary dynamics of complex systems: A study in biosocial complexity,* New York: Oxford University Press, 1988.

Hein, Piet, *Grooks,* Garden City, NY: Doubleday & Company, Inc., 1966.

House, Ernest R., "Realism in research," *Educational Researcher,* 20:2–9, 25, 1991.

Jungck, John R., "Constructivism, computer exploratoriums, and collaborative learning: Constructing scientific knowledge," *Teaching Education,* 3(2):151–170, 1991.

Jungck, John R., and John N. Calley, "Strategic simulations and post-Socratic pedagogy: Constructing computer software to develop long-term inference through experimental inquiry," *American Biology Teacher,* 47(1):11–15, 1985.

Jungck, John R., and John N. Calley, *Genetics: Strategic simulations in Mendelian genetics,* Wentworth, NH: COMPress, 1986.

Jungck, John R., Nils S. Peterson, Jim Stewart, and John N. Calley, (eds.), *The BioQUEST Collection,* College Park, MD: University of Maryland Multimedia Press, 1992.

Kern, Leslie H., Herbert L. Mirels, and Virgil G. Hinshaw, "Scientists' understanding of propositional logic: An experimental investigation." *Social Studies of Science* 13:131–146, 1983.

Lakatos, Imre, *Proofs and refutations: The logic of mathematical discovery.* London: Cambridge University Press, 1976.

Laws, Priscilla, "Workshop physics: Learning introductory physics by doing it." *Change: The Magazine of Higher Learning* 23(4):20–27, 1991.

Norris, Margot, *Beasts of the modern imagination: Darwin, Nietzsche, Kafka, Ernst, and Lawrence,* Baltimore: The Johns Hopkins University Press, 1985.

Papert, Seymour, *Mindstorms: Children, computers, and powerful ideas,* New York: Basic Books, 1980.

Peterson, Nils Sören, Managing Editor, *The Cardiovascular Function Laboratories,* Monmouth, OR: From the Heart Software, 1991.

Peterson, N. S., and J. R. Jungck, "Problem-posing, problem-solving, and persuasion in biology education," *Academic Computing,* 2(6):14–17 and 48–50, 1988.

Peterson, N. S., J. R. Jungck, D. M. Sharpe, and W. F. Finzer, "A design approach to science," *Machine Mediated Learning* 2(1&2): 111–127, 1987.

Petroski, Henry, *To engineer is human: The role of failure in successful design,* St. Martin's Press: New York, 1985.

Schön, D. A., *Educating the reflective practitioner,* New York, NY: Jossey-Bass, 1987.

Schwartz, Lawrence, "Teaching writing in the age of the word processor and personal computers," *Educational Technology* (June):33–35, 1983.

Simon, Herbert A., *The sciences of the artificial,* 2nd ed., Cambridge, MA: MIT Press, 1982.

Stansky, Peter, *Redesigning the world: William Morris, the 1880s, and the arts and crafts movement,* Princeton, NJ: Princeton University Press, 1985.

Stewart, Jim, "Potential learning outcomes from solving genetics problems: A typology of problems," *Science Education,* 72(2):237–254, 1988.

Stewart, Jim, and Robert Hafner, "Extending the conception of 'problem' in problem-solving research," *Science Education,* 75(1):105–120, 1991.

Thorton, John W., *The laboratory: A place to investigate,* CUEBS Publication Number 33, Washington, DC: American Institute of Biological Sciences, 1972.

Woodward, Val, "Teaching and learning through investigation: A case for participatory evolution," in John W. Thorton, *The laboratory: A place to investigate,* 15–25, Washington, DC: American Institute of Biological Sciences, 1972.

NOTES

1. John R. Jungck and John N. Calley originally published the Genetics Construction Kit for the Apple II computer in *Genetics: Strategic Simulations in Mendelian Genetics,* Wentworth, NH: COMPress, 1986. It has been revised and translated for the Macintosh computer and is included in the BioQUEST collection (1990).
2. Funded by the Annenberg/CPB Project, Apple Computer, and the Foundation for Microbiology. BioQUEST has developed materials for a general undergraduate biology curriculum. BioQUEST may be contacted at the Biology Department, Beloit College, 700 College Street, Beloit, WI 53511. In June 1990, fourteen modules began a nationwide field test.
3. Funded by the National Institutes of Health, R44 HL37790. The Cardiovascular Function Laboratory project developed a monograph and accompanying software for use in first- and second-year medical physiology courses. Published by From The Heart Software, P.O. Box 25, Monmouth, OR 97361.
4. An allele is any of a possible group of mutational forms of a gene.
5. See note 1.

7

Using Structure as a Design Tool in Algorithmic Problem Solving

Peter B. Henderson and David L. Ferguson
State University of New York at Stony Brook

Abstract *Computer scientists seek to express the solutions to many problems as sequences of unambiguous steps. The ultimate goal is to express such solutions, called* algorithms, *in formal programming languages. However, there is a wide gap between a problem statement and its solution as given in a formal programming language. Even when one puts aside the syntax and semantics of specific programming languages, algorithmic problem solving is a complex mental activity. It requires that students develop several cognitive skills: the abilities to discover relationships, discern structure, develop plans for solutions, and express solutions precisely and concisely. In this chapter we clarify the meaning of* structure *in the context of algorithmic problem solving and show how students can come to use the structure of the problem to guide the design process. The relationships between the concepts of* abstraction *and* structure *in the design process are explored. We show how technology can be used to help students better understand the structure of problems and discover algorithms. Furthermore, we show how the technology can aid students in expressing their algorithmic solutions.*

There is a distinction between teaching students how to program and teaching them how to design software systems. The former is primarily conveying details of syntax and semantics and some notion of how to organize and present an algorithm in the programming language they are learning. The latter is concerned with the process of taking a potentially complex problem and creating a usable software application. This requires software engineering design principles and a good understanding of the problem domain. Most computer science students somehow succeed in learning this process after several years. They learn, by trial and error, to see the relationships between problems and their algorithmic solutions, something we do not explicitly teach them.

Computer scientists seek to express the solutions to many problems as sequences of unambiguous steps. The ultimate goal is to express such solutions, called *algorithms,* in formal programming languages such as Pascal, FORTRAN, BASIC, and so on. However, there is a wide gap between a problem statement and its potential solutions, as presented in a specific programming language. Even when the details of the language such as syntax and semantics are hidden, algorithmic problem solving is a complex mental activity. It requires that students develop many diverse cognitive skills including the ability to discover relationships in problems, abstract and decompose problems, look for structure in problems, outline processes and develop plans, and understand ways of expressing solutions precisely and concisely. Computer science students must develop these problem-solving skills.

The focus of this chapter is using the structure of a problem to guide the design process and the role technology might play in teaching design-oriented activities for software development. One must first understand what is meant by structure in algorithmic problem solving, and how structure is used in the context of the other aspects of this form of problem solving mentioned above.

In this chapter we examine this relationship between the structure of a problem and the structure of its algorithmic solution as a guiding principle in the design of algorithms. This is primarily achieved through the use of examples illustrating this process. The second section introduces issues relating to student design activities in software development. The third section examines the meaning of the term *structure* and studies its use in problem solving and the development of software. The fourth section looks at issues regarding algorithmic problem solving. The fifth section gives a detailed example: the "Connect-Four" game. The sixth section gives a description of the role of our computer-aided instructional environment in helping students to design algorithms. Specifically, we look at the role structure and abstraction play, and the difficulties students experience with algorithmic problem solving. The section addresses design-related activities in more detail by working through the design of a simple game. The seventh section gives an overview of the role of technology in software design. It discusses some of the ways technology is evolving to assist with design-oriented activities in software development. The Conclusions section summarizes the key points made in the chapter.

STUDENT SOFTWARE DESIGN ISSUES: AN INTRODUCTION

Software design differs from design in most other disciplines, for example, engineering and architecture. In many other disciplines, designers work with tangible materials or representations of tangible materials; however, software designers must deal with concepts that often have no physical referents. Although software design is primarily an abstract activity, designs can be directly implemented and tested by using the appropriate computer technology (programming languages, editors, compilers, etc.). Hence, despite the abstractness of the design activity, students can get immediate feedback regarding the correctness of their design. The quality of the design is best judged subjectively, however.

Like design in other disciplines, software design is open-ended. Such open-endedness is difficult for students who are used to a more rigorously structured learning environment. Indeed, software development instruction is far too open-ended. Students are given too many design and implementation choices. This freedom of choice makes it very difficult for novice programming students to design and implement good computer programs. They experience difficulty using abstraction techniques at the design level and translating those designs to implementations. Students easily get confused with all the syntactic and semantic details of the programming language they are learning. In addition, details of the operating system, editor, compiler, printers, and so on, interfere with the focus on design. They suffer from the traditional problem of being unable to see the forest for the trees.

This "forest-for-the-trees" problem was the primary factor motivating the development of a computer-aided instructional environment for guiding students toward the discovery of algorithms (Henderson, 1987; Henderson and Ferguson, 1986, 1987). The goal is to permit students to design algorithms at a much higher level of abstraction. This is achieved in several ways.

First, students are given a visual model of the problem. They use this to learn about the problem domain. For instance, if students are to develop algorithms for controlling elevators in a building, then they are provided with a visual simulation of the building and elevators. In addition, they must perform set tasks, such as manually moving elevators in response to requests for service. Indeed, students are not permitted to progress to the design and implementation phases until the instructional environment establishes that the student clearly understands all aspects of the problem.

In the design and implementation phase, the environment provides students with the algorithmic primitives specific to the problem they are solving. For instance, for the elevator control problem, primitives for moving an elevator to a specific floor, for getting requests for service, and so on, are provided. The environment includes an easy-to-use structured editor and interpreter for developing and testing algorithms. The interpreter permits students to visually see an animation of the execution of their algorithm. For example, students may watch images of elevators move on the display in response to requests for elevator service.

The environment guides students in the design of their algorithms, eliminating details that typically confuse students. An example environment is discussed in the section on the role of technology in teaching. By watching students trying to design algorithms by using this environment we learned some things about how students use structure in the design process. By identifying and using the proper structures for each problem, students developed much better designs.

WHAT IS STRUCTURE?

The term *structure* arises frequently in computer science instruction (e.g., structured programming, data structures, and structured design; Yourdon and Constantine, 1979). At the basic programming level, students may be expected to match problems to traditional structures, presented as templates, that exemplify the use of specific constructs of the programming language (Linn and Clancey, 1991; Bonar, Soloway, and Ehrlich, 1989). At a more fundamental level, students may be expected to discern structure through exploration in their attempt to discover and express algorithms. Computer scientists love structure but rarely understand it. One objective of a good computer science curriculum should be to teach students to identify structure in the problems they are trying to solve and to use this structure in the design of software systems. As noted earlier, teaching this process is currently very ad hoc. This chapter explores approaches to explicitly identifying structure in problems and using this structure in the design of algorithms.

So, what is structure? It is looking for patterns, and exploiting these patterns to understand and solve problems. A very simple example of structure in mathematics is algebraic expressions, such as the following:

$$(5 + 4) \times (37 \div (6 - 3))(x \times y) \div 6 \qquad (1)$$

Such equations represent a familiar structure. People understand this structure because they understand both the syntactic structure (nested parentheses and infix operators $+$, $-$, $\times$, $\div$) and the semantic structure (meaning of numbers and the operators).

Quick Sort, which sorts a list of elements, is a good example. Here, the structure of lists is exploited, first by partitioning the list into two lists with the property that all elements in the first list are less than all elements in the second list. This process is continued recursively (a pattern) for each of these lists until each list contains one element. Now a sorted list is obtained by simply appending the resulting lists together. This process is illustrated in Figure 1.

The most fitting brief dictionary definition of the word *structure* is "the arrangement of all the parts of a whole." There is structure, or a sense of well-being, in almost everything we encounter in our daily lives. Many structures occur naturally in nature—trees, clouds, snowflakes, and so on. Others, like buildings, phone systems, maps, and so on, are man made. The structure we identify in these objects and tools is meant to simplify our lives. For example, consider the map of New York City shown in Figure 2. This map is an abstract representation of the city streets. Observe the structure inherent in this map. Streets and avenues are laid out by using an easily recognizable pattern. This structure makes it easy for us to solve navigational problems in New York City. The arrangement of all the parts (streets and avenues) forms the whole (map). Could you recognize similar structure in a map of the city of Boston?

We use structure every day to solve problems, whether it be navigating on highways or in buildings, making a phone call, or brushing our teeth. In design-oriented problem-solving tasks our goal is to identify and express the most natural parts of the whole problem, and to use these parts to derive a solution. This is true no matter whether we are designing buildings, automobiles, highways, bridges, electronic circuits, or software systems. In every case, we need a convenient language for expressing our solutions, one that can capture the natural structure we have identified in the problem. Blueprints represent one language for expressing the design of many physical structures. Schematic circuit and block diagrams are used for expressing electronic circuits. For software systems, bubble, structure, and flow charts are common representations for expressing structure (Yourdon and

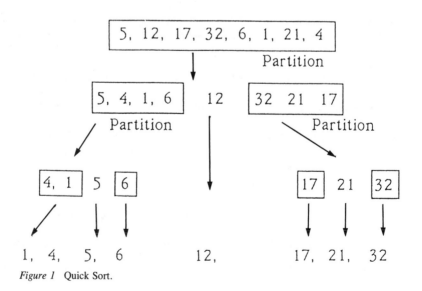

Figure 1 Quick Sort.

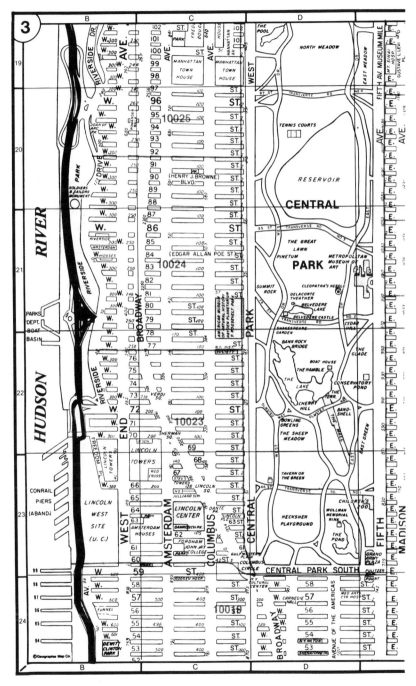

Figure 2 Map of New York City (mid-Manhattan section). Reprinted from *Pocket Road Atlas* © 1988 by Geographia Map Company, 1992 Rand McNally. R. L. 92-S-115.

163

Constantine, 1979). An example of a structure chart for a text-editing software system is illustrated in Figure 3.

Frequently the sheer number of parts may be overwhelming, or the complexity of some component parts may be intellectually unmanageable. This is when the concepts of abstraction and structure are integrally linked. Stated simply, abstraction is hiding details. It addresses the traditional forest-for-the-trees problem. Abstraction permits us to view the problem or solution at a more comfortable level by hiding those extra parts that might overwhelm us, or by looking only at specific, limited features of a complex component. For instance, consider the module, *Delete a string,* in Figure 3. We can understand the purpose of this module in the context of this design solution without understanding the actual steps that module *Delete a string* uses to achieve its task.

Abstraction is one of the more powerful tools we use in problem solving. It can be used for all phases of the design-oriented problem-solving process. For example, abstraction can be used for understanding a problem, problem decomposition, integrating component parts to form a solution, testing the design/solution, debugging, and understanding a solution for the purpose of maintaining or modifying it. In design, abstraction is the process whereby the structure of a problem is used to decompose the problem into smaller problems. That is, this structure is usually understood and expressed abstractly. Some simple examples may help to clarify this concept of structure.

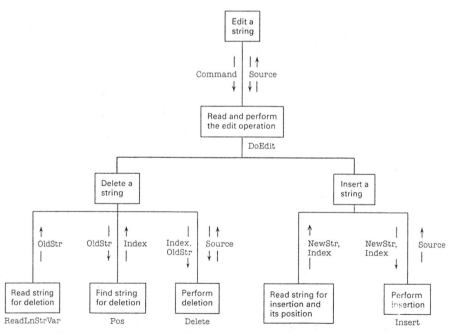

Figure 3 Structure chart for a text-editing system. Elliot B. Koffman, *Pascal: Problem Solving and Program Design,* copyrighted 1989, by Addison-Wesley Publishing Company Inc. Reprinted with permission of the publisher.

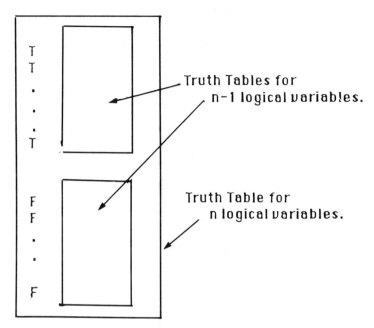

T
T
.
.
.
T

F
F
.
.
F

Truth Tables for
n-1 logical variables.

Truth Table for
n logical variables.

Figure 4   Truth table for *n* logical variables.

Example 1. In propositional logic we know that a truth table with 2 logical variables has 4 rows, one with 3 variables has 8 rows, and so on. That is, it is easy to see structure, or patterns here. Knowing that a truth table with $n - 1$ logical variables has K rows, then one with n logical variables must have $2 \times K$ rows. Generalizing this further by using mathematical induction, there are 2^n rows in a truth table with n logical variables.

Knowledge of the structure of truth tables can be exploited further. For instance, assume you have constructed a truth table for $n - 1$ logical variables. How can this table be used to construct a truth table for n logical variables? A solution is illustrated in Figure 4.

Example 2. N coins are arranged in a row on a table, some with heads facing up, the others with tails facing up. The following two actions are permitted to manipulate these coins: Action 1: If two adjacent coins are opposites (one heads and the other tails), then you may turn over these two coins. Action 2: If the coin at the left end (of the row) and the coin at the right end (of the row) are the same (both heads or both tails), then turn over these two coins. Find a general strategy, if one exists, for getting tails facing up on all N coins.

The best way to understand this problem is by taking out some coins and arranging them on a table or other convenient flat surface and experimenting with different initial configurations of coins. Problem solving requires active engagement (Levine, 1988). In looking for a general strategy, one must first ask whether or not the goal of getting tails facing up on all N coins can always be achieved. Here, we are looking for structure in the problem.

After playing with some coins one quickly discovers that there do exist initial configurations for which the goal cannot always be achieved. An example is the following initial configuration of five coins. Can you find the general property that ensures the goal can be achieved for a given initial configuration?

T H T H H

Although it was not explicitly specified in the statement of this problem, what is sought is a general algorithmic strategy for obtaining the goal, when possible, given an initial configuration of coins. This raises many questions. How do we derive an algorithm? How is it expressed? Can others understand it? Is the algorithm correct? Is our algorithm efficient? Is it the *best* algorithm? What do we mean by *best*? These issues are addressed in the following section.

ALGORITHMIC PROBLEM SOLVING

Algorithmic problem solving is designing and expressing an algorithmic solution to a problem. Consider Example 2 above—the N coins problem. We are looking for structure in this problem. First, we found the condition under which the goal can always be attained: The number of heads in the configuration must be even. In deriving an algorithmic solution we seek general patterns. Again, one of the best ways to identify these patterns is to experiment with sample configurations. Initially, we avoid patterns that deal with low-level details because we do not wish to get trapped in the forest-for the-trees dilemma.

After experimenting with this problem we observe that the only way to eliminate heads is using Action 2. Accordingly, we have identified one subgoal; that is, moving coins with heads facing up to each end of the row whereupon Action 2 can be applied. Observe that this is a high-level subgoal. We have not yet addressed certain low-level details such as how to achieve this subgoal. These have been "abstracted away." The problem-solving process described is similar to stepwise refinement (Dijkstra, 1972).

How can our algorithm be expressed? In English it might be stated as follows:

> Ensure there are an even number of heads. If not, the goal cannot be achieved. If there are an even number of heads, repeat the following process until there are no heads facing up. Get coins with heads facing up on both ends of the row. Now use Action 2 to flip these coins.

This algorithm may be expressed more formally by using pseudo-code, a form of expression that uses both English and certain programming language statements.

```
Ensure there are a finite even number of heads.

WHILE there are more heads facing up DO
    |
    |
    | Get coins with heads facing up on both ends.
    | Use Action 2
    |
```

Does this algorithm make sense to you? Do you think it is correct? If you had to convince a friend that this algorithm will always work correctly (achieve the stated goal given any initial configuration with a finite even number of heads), how would you formulate your argument? Now we must reason about the algorithm we have developed. Our argument might go as follows:

There are an even number of heads on entering the WHILE iteration for the first time. Assume repeated applications of Action 1 can be used to get heads facing up on the two coins at each end of the row of the coins. Now, applying Action 2 will flip these two coins, changing the two heads to two tails. We exit from the WHILE iteration when there are no more heads facing up; that is, the goal has been attained.

To complete the argument, we must also demonstrate that eventually we will exit from the WHILE iteration. This is easy. We start with a finite even number of heads. Repeated applications of Action 1 do not change the number of heads. Applying Action 2 reduces the number of heads by two. Eventually, the number of heads will be reduced to zero, terminating the WHILE iteration.

Although this problem may now seem relatively trivial, few students develop an initial design as simple as the one above. They cannot identify the property necessary for a solution to exist, and they typically seem to get lost in the details of the problem (e.g., the process for getting heads facing up on both ends). That is, they are unable to use abstraction as an effective design tool. Students do have difficulty seeing the structure in such problems, using this structure to design algorithmic solutions, and reasoning about their solutions. All three are crucial to the development of good computer software. Here is another familiar example, which is a bit more complex than the coin-flipping problem.

Example 3. Consider the problem of developing a spelling checker that accepts input text in machine readable form (ASCII, perhaps) and outputs a list, in alphabetical order, of all the misspelled words in the input text. Assume there is a dictionary available on the system that includes the proper spelling of all desired words.

At first glance this problem may appear to be simple; however, there are numerous hidden traps. For example, dealing with upper- and lower-case letters in words (i.e., MacDonald) or punctuation symbols, such as hyphens or apostrophes in words. Most of these details can be abstracted away if the initial design is done properly. For example, one assumes the existence of a routine that extracts words from the text while ensuring that these words conform to our specification of valid words. The details of such components are delayed until later on in the design process. An outline for one solution is presented as follows:

```
WHILE there are more words in the input text DO
|
| Extract the next word from the input text
|
| IF this word is not in the dictionary
|    THEN add this word to the list of misspelled words
|
| Advance to the next word in the input text
|


Sort the list of misspelled words
Output the list of misspelled words
```

Again, this high-level representation of an algorithmic solution is very easy to understand. Can you see how it reflects the fundamental structure of the stated problem while hiding unnecessary details? For example, the term *word* is not clearly defined yet. It should be very easy for you to convince someone that this basic algorithm performs correctly.

There are several lessons we have learned by observing students attempting to design algorithms for this problem. First, they fail to understand the problem before deriving a solution. This was expected because there are numerous details that are easily overlooked (hidden traps, as noted above). Students cannot identify structure in the problem and use it to design a good solution. That is, they cannot abstract; rather, a bottom-up approach is used. This is like trying to put the pieces of a puzzle together when the pieces are not clearly defined.

A better approach is top-down, in which abstraction is used to identify the most natural pieces, or components, of the problem—those that match the structure of the problem. This is the algorithmic problem-solving technique we try to convey in our computer science courses. However, this mode of thinking appears to take a long time to develop. We have observed that even experienced upper-division computer science students seem to think "bottom-up."

A DESIGN EXAMPLE: "CONNECT-FOUR" GAME

Here is a sample software development problem assigned in the Computer Science I course at Stony Brook. The objective is to develop a computer program by using Pascal for this problem.

> You are to write a program that allows two people to play the game "Connect-Four." The playing board has six rows and seven columns (and in real life stands vertically with openings in the top of each column). The object of the game is to get four of your pieces in contiguous locations before your opponent does. The four pieces may appear in any four adjacent spaces of a row, a column, or a diagonal. Pieces can only be added from the "openings" in the top and the pieces will "fall" (due to "gravity") to the lowest available position. Only one piece may fall to a given location. Once in place, pieces cannot be removed.
>
> Your program should provide instructions, then prompt for the names of the players, then begin play. When a player wins, your program should report this and offer to run another game. If they decide to play another game, the prior game's Player #1 becomes the new game's Player #2, and vice versa. When the players decline to play another game, your program should print out the number of games won by each player.

Many students start by trying to develop Pascal code, even before understanding the problem. They use instinct rather than reason in the design of the software. Before doing anything, a model for better understanding this problem should be developed. A good approach for students to understand this problem is to purchase the "Connect-Four" game (at a local game store) and devote some time to actually playing the game, that is, actively engage the problem (Levine, 1988). Lacking the actual game, the student can create a suitable visual model, such as the one shown in Figure 5. To build an accurate mental model, students should use visual imagery and play example games.

Once they understand the problem, students can begin developing a solution. Again, novice programming students tend to work bottom-up. They are overly concerned with the low-level details such as the representation of the playing board. Accordingly, they lose sight of the overall problem and its inherent structure. Let us pursue an alternative top-down problem-solving approach, which

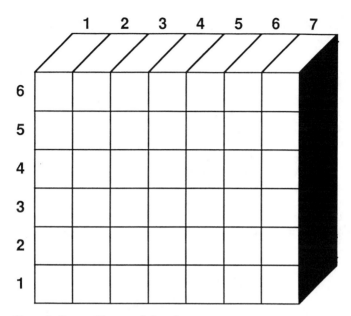

Figure 5   Connect-Four sample board.

makes use of the structure of the problem and more accurately reflects the evolutionary process of software development.

On close examination, there is a significant amount of structure in this problem. Let us start by identifying the relevant objects of the problem. These objects include the playing board, the pieces, and the players. The playing board may be further decomposed into objects such as rows, columns, diagonals, and locations. Identifying objects is a very natural way of finding structure in problems. When developing an algorithmic solution, and ultimately the computer program, we ensure that these objects are accurately reflected in the solution.

Associated with each object is a state. For example, the state of the playing board consists of the positions of all the pieces. Operations on objects permit the state of the objects to be changed. For example, dropping a piece into a specified column changes the state of the board. We may also inquire about the state of an object to make decisions in our algorithm. For instance, is there a winner after a piece has been dropped? Or is a certain column filled?

Before developing a solution, students should ask several pertinent questions. For example, is there always a winner? What happens if a player specifies an invalid column to drop a piece into? What action does the system take when a player attempts to drop a piece into a column that is full? In a user-oriented system such as the "Connect-Four game," over 60 percent of the software code can be devoted to dealing with special or exceptional cases. Typically, these extra details overwhelm students.

Our approach is evolutionary. That is, first focus on getting a basic system working, one which does not deal with all the exceptional cases or has a fancy user interface. We have observed students devoting exorbitant effort to creating visual interfaces and code for every possible exception but whose system fails to solve the basic problem. Initially, let us assume there will always be a winner, a valid column is always selected, players do not drop pieces into full columns, and so on. Once we get the basic system operational, it can be evolved into a complete, robust system by adding the appropriate code. This forces students to be more disciplined in their approach to design and development.

One potential design for the basic Connect-Four system is illustrated in Figure 6. Here we assume the first player's piece is marked with an X and second player's piece with an O. In this structure chart the fundamental procedural components (e.g., `Get Player #1 Move`) and objects (PlayingBoard) are shown, along with the interactions between these components. For example, procedure `PlayGame` must use procedures `Get Player #1 Move` and `Get Player #2 Move`, and the operations and decisions associated with the PlayingBoard.

Now a preliminary design for the `PlayGame` component can be developed. This is illustrated in the example below, and is expressed by using high-level pseudo-code. Again, the objective is to represent the details as simply as possible.

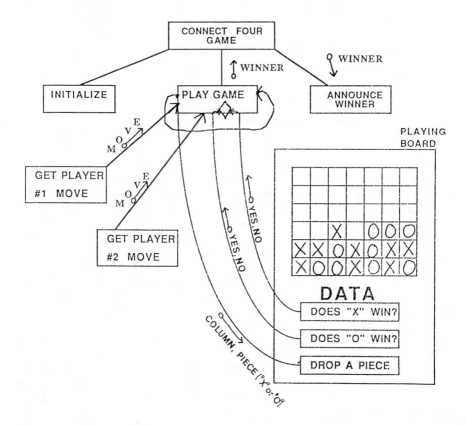

Figure 6 Structure chart for Connect-Four system design.

This makes it easier for us to reason about our solution and for others to understand our solution. Once we have a high degree of confidence that our design is correct, it can be transformed to a computer program. Please note that this approach to the design of software systems is independent of any particular programming language.

Observe that some aspects of the problem, as noted earlier, have been intentionally overlooked here. We assume that there is a winner, that invalid player moves are ignored (either invalid ColumnNumber or full columns), and that there are only two players.

```
REPEAT
   | Get Player #1 Move (ColumnNumber)
   | Drop a Piece (ColumnNumber, X)
   |
   | IF Player #1 wins
   | THEN Return Winner is Player #1
   | ELSE
   |       | Get Player #2 Move (ColumnNumber)
   |       | Drop a Piece (ColumnNumber, O)
   |       |
   |       | IF Player #2 wins
   |       | THEN Return Winner is Player #2
   |
UNTIL there is a winner
```

For now, we consider only the design and implementation of the simplest system. Later we can elaborate further by using an evolutionary development approach building from this basic system. Here we are following the advice, "It is best to develop something simple that works than something complex that does not work."

In earlier comments we have noted some of the problems that novice students encounter with the design of algorithms. Another problem is a failure to identify common functionality in design. Common functionality is patterns that are identical or very similar. An example appears in the above example. Note that the sequences of operations for Player #1 and Player #2 are very similar: They differ only in the player number (1 or 2) and the piece X or O. Is there a way to capture this common functionality?

This question can be viewed from a different perspective. One potential extension of this game is the inclusion of more than two players. Software developers should try to develop systems in which design decisions are not locked in. The term *software* implies that things should be easy to change, as opposed to hardware where design is more rigid. Unfortunately, common functionality and potential changes are often overlooked in software design, making software maintenance extremely difficult and expensive.

Taking this lesson to heart, let us examine an alternative design for the Play-Game component—one that uses a general procedure for performing a player's move. This procedure, called Perform Player Move accepts as arguments a Player, that is, information about the player including player number and the symbol for that player's piece, and returns (Wins), which is true if the player won with that move and false otherwise. This alternative design is shown below.

```
Player <-- FirstPlayer

REPEAT
  |
  | Perform Player Move (Player, Wins)
  |
  | IF Player did not win                    {NOT Wins}
  |    THEN
  |       | Player <--  NextPlayer
  |
UNTIL there is a winner                      {Wins = true}

Return Winner is Player
```

We hope the elegance of this simple design is evident. Most of the details are relegated to lower-level procedures and functions, making this design very flexible. For example, the first player to move and the sequencing of players to move are relegated to the lower-level functions, FirstPlayer and NextPlayer, and are not the concern of PlayGame. Moreover, the details of procedure Perform Player Move are hidden; however, the brief description in the previous paragraph suffices to define its purpose.

We will not elaborate further on this example. We hope the reader has gained some insights into the activities associated with software design, and the difficulties in conveying these ideas to computer science students. Some of the key points are (1) look for structure in the problem and reflect that structure in the design solution, (2) build a basic system first, (3) evolve a complete system incrementally from the basic system, (4) seek common functionality in the design, and (5) always plan for change (evolving or expanding the system).

ROLE OF TECHNOLOGY IN TEACHING
SOFTWARE DESIGN: AN EXAMPLE

The Algorithm Discovery Project was initiated six years ago at Stony Brook in response to the observation that algorithmic problem solving is a conceptual hurdle for many students (Henderson, 1987; Henderson and Ferguson, 1986, 1987). Given a simple problem statement, students can usually grasp the meaning of the problem and even mentally simulate the behavior of an algorithmic solution for specific problem instances. However, they frequently encounter difficulty in trying to formulate a general algorithmic solution that conforms to these thought processes. Students have difficulty generalizing and expressing abstractions. They get so involved with the details that they lose sight of the most important aspect, the problem-solving process itself. Current instructional programming languages (Pascal, Modula, Ada, etc.), which lack adequate support for abstraction, only serve to further exacerbate this problem.

Algorithm discovery courseware provides a computer-aided instructional environment that assists students with the discovery, creation, testing, and debugging of algorithms for well-defined problems. As an example, consider the card-stacking problem described below.

The Card-Stacking Game

This is a simple game consisting of three stacks of cards (labeled Stacks A, B, and C). Initially, cards numbered 1, 2, 3, 4, through N (where N is between 0 and 10) are placed bottom-to-top on Stack A, and Stacks B and C are empty. Cards may be moved from one stack to another using only the following three *moves*:

(1) Move the top card from Stack A to the top of Stack B.
(2) Move the top card from Stack A to the top of Stack C.
(3) Move the top card from Stack B to the top of Stack C.

The objective is to determine a sequence of *moves* that achieves a specified ordering of these N cards on Stack C, the desired goal being Stack C.

Sample initial configuration with four cards:

4444			3333
3333			1111
2222			2222
1111			4444

Stack A	Stack B	Stack C	Desired Goal, Stack C

During the first phase, students are introduced to this problem through an intelligent tutoring system (Henderson, 1987). Students are first introduced to the constraints of the problem and are then provided with example problems to be solved. The tutoring system progressively introduces new features, which students discover by graphically manipulating representative configurations of the problem (e.g., cards can only be moved to stacks to the right). The tutoring system incorporates feedback to ensure that students understand all aspects of the problem. It also guides students toward an algorithmic solution by displaying progressively more abstract representations of the problem. Figure 7 illustrates the display for one stage of this problem-understanding phase. (Note that the cursor is shark shaped, a true "card shark.")

Once a student has demonstrated a complete understanding of the card-stacking

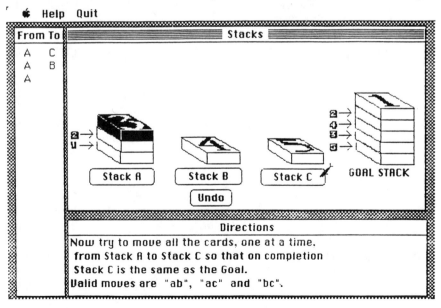

Figure 7 Problem-understanding phase of card-stacking problem.

problem and the representations required to derive a good algorithmic solution, he or she begins the second phase—algorithm development. As noted earlier, the major hurdle that students must overcome is generalizing their knowledge of how to solve specific instances of a problem to create a valid algorithmic solution and then expressing it in a suitably expressive language. To facilitate this process, a simple card-stacking algorithmic language and associated environment have been developed. This language provides only primitive features required to solve the card-stacking problem (e.g., "Move top card from Stack A to top of Stack B"; "Is Stack A empty?"). Students can focus on the problem-solving process without extraneous language details (such as those in general-purpose programming languages) distracting them.

The new screen-oriented language-knowledgeable editor allows students to create programs in our target algorithmic language. This language will support standard structured flow of control constructs such as **WHILE-DO, IF-THEN, IF-THEN-ELSE, CASE, REPEAT-UNTIL** and **FOR-DO**. Primitive operations and conditionals, tailored for each specific problem, are provided. The language-knowledgeable editor makes it easy for students to create programs without extensive typing. Templates for all of the flow-of-control constructs and primitives are available from a menu or by entering the appropriate key word. For example, by selecting the template corresponding to the primitive, **Move** (or by simply typing the word *move* to create the template), the appropriate template is expanded as follows:

Move top card of ⟨from stack⟩ to top of ⟨to stack⟩

The student completes this template by specifying the ⟨**from stack**⟩ and the ⟨**to stack**⟩. This is done by moving the cursor to the appropriate unfilled field ⟨**from stack**⟩ or ⟨**to stack**⟩. and typing the appropriate stack designator (A, B, or C). Note that the editor catches possible semantic errors here also. Only the specified stack designators may be entered, and useless (moving from Stack A to Stack A) or invalid moves (moving from Stack C) are caught and the student is appropriately warned. Because knowledge of the language syntax, semantics, and display format can be specified externally to the editor—in table form—it is easy to adapt this editor for different problems and target languages

For any problem, the complexity of the algorithmic solution can be adjusted according to the representation and granularity of the primitive operations and conditionals provided. For example, students could either be provided with the English-like move primitive, **Move top card of Stack A to top of Stack C** or the prefix operand version, **Move(Stack_A, Stack_B)**. The former might be more appropriate for children, and the latter for high school and college students. The granularity of the conditional primitives can affect the solution. For example, testing for termination of the card-stacking algorithm can be done easily with the primitive, **While there are more cards to be moved**. However, if only lower-level primitives like **Empty (⟨stack⟩)** and the Boolean operations **NOT, AND,** and **OR** are furnished, students would have to derive the equivalent of the primitive, **While there are more cards to be moved**, by creating the expression **NOT Empty (Stack_A) OR (NOT Empty (Stack_B)**.

The interpreter is linked to the graphical images that students manipulate during the problem-understanding phase. In this way, execution of the algorithm provides direct visual feedback to the student. Feedback is provided in a number of other ways. The system shows the text of the algorithm and highlights the statement that is currently being executed. In addition, students have complete control over the speed (single-step or slow to fast) and direction (forward vs. backward) of execution. This is a fantastic assistance for debugging and understanding algorithm behavior. Ultimately, most students are able to develop a complete algorithm solution. A sample solution is given below. Note that statements enclosed within brackets are comments—not executable statements.

```
WHILE (there are more cards to be moved) and (a valid move sequence
exists)

DO

        IF (the desired goal card is on top of Stack B)

            THEN

                (move top card of Stack B to top of Stack C)

                (advance to next desired goal card on Stack C)

            ELSE
                [try to locate desired goal card in Stack A]

                WHILE (Stack A is not empty) and (desired goal card is
                not top card on Stack A) DO

                    (move top card of Stack A to top of Stack B)

                [Either the desired goal card is on top of Stack A or Stack A is empty, which
                implies that no valid move sequence exists.]

                IF (Stack A is not empty)

                    THEN
                    (move top card of Stack A to top of Stack B)
                    (advance to next desired goal card on Stack C)
                    ELSE
                    (no valid move sequence exists)
```

I.M. MARSH LIBRARY LIVERPOOL L17 6BD
TEL. 0151 231 5216/5299

FUTURE ROLE OF TECHNOLOGY
IN TEACHING SOFTWARE DESIGN

Technology plays a critical role in the teaching of software design and development. It is clear that computer technology (hardware and software) is necessary for creating executable software. However, in software design one must realize that the technology is much broader than simply running software on computers. For example, the languages and notations used for expressing and implementing designs, and understanding the cognitive issues relating to design are part of the technology. This technology appears to be even more important in software design than other types of design, primarily because of the multiplicity of existing design and programming languages and the ease with which new languages and forms of communication with the computer (e.g., visual, voice, etc.) evolve. This is evident from the large number of programming languages in use today, and the evolution of new languages.

To date, most of the effort associated with teaching introductory software design has been devoted to building better tools for computer programming. These include, among others, text editors, compilers, and debuggers. More advanced projects focus on integrated programming environments for computer science instruction (Archer and Conway, 1981; Teitelbaum and Reps, 1981). There is a belief that, for novice students, programming and design are synonymous. Unfortunately, students are poorly prepared for either (Henderson, 1990).

Teaching programming does help to improve software design skills. Unfortunately, much computer science instruction suffers from the "toy programming" syndrome, that is, writing simple programs without much practical value. This is somewhat analogous to having architectural students building tree houses for several semesters. Much of what is learned is not easily transferred to architectural design principles for actual structures.

How can technology help? Here are some general areas in which technological innovation and related studies can help improve software design instruction. First and foremost is the development of more expensive or powerful design languages (for both learners and experts). This must be coupled with tools and environments to support these new languages, preferably tailored individually to novices and experts. A better understanding of how novices learn design is also important. Educators should use new approaches and technology for teaching design. This presentation is not meant to be comprehensive; rather, it provides a glimpse into future possibilities and directions.

To illustrate these ideas, we examine several emerging languages and environments for expressing design. Perhaps the most dramatic advances will be made in the area of visual programming and design (Shu, 1988), that is, creating designs and programs that use visual images rather than words. In the software engineering community, there already exist visually oriented computer-aided design tools. For instance, graphic tools for creating structure charts exist. Unfortunately, most of these tools are simply graphical editors, providing little assistance with the design activity itself or the ability to test designs.

Standard ML is a state-of-the-art functional programming language (Harper, MacQueen, and Milner, 1986; Milner, 1984; Wikström, 1987) that has been used effectively for computer science instruction (Henderson and Romero, 1989). Its expressive power is derived from a simple and uniform syntax, a system that automatically infers the type of data items, powerful data and function declaration facilities, and recursive programming features. A sample ML function that performs a pre-order traversal of a labeled binary tree is illustrated as follows:

```
fun preorder (tree) =
    if tree = empty {Is tree an empty binary tree?}
        then [] {if tree is empty, return the empty list []}
        else prepend (label(tree), appendlist(preorder(left_ sub-
        tree(tree)), preorder(right_subtree(tree))));
```

This function definition uses several other simple functions such as **prepend** and **appendlist**, which prepends an item to a list and appends two lists, respectively. After several weeks, novice students can develop such powerful functions. Students learning an imperative programming language, such as Pascal, require at least one semester of experience in programming to develop an equivalent program, and it would consist of over fifty lines of code.

With very little experience, it becomes easy for novice students to identify the structure in problems necessary to develop ML programs. The language has a rich expressive power. Some of the lessons learned and student experiences with ML are described in an article by Henderson and Romero (1989).

In computer science education, there has been interest recently in using graphics to motivate and understand concepts and ideas. This includes visualizing program execution and data structures, animation (Pattis, 1981), developing graphically oriented computer programs (Niguidula and van Dam, 1987), and visual programming (Shu, 1988). Standard ML is not a graphically oriented language, although we are currently adding features that permit students to create and display data structures such as trees, lists, graphs, and so on, graphically.

One example of visual programming language is Prograph (Cox and Pietrzykowski, 1988). Prograph is visually oriented in several different ways that attempt to make effective use of the structure of a problem. First, it is an object-oriented language. That is, icons representing the objects of the problem can be created from existing or other user-defined objects. For example, students are people and thus inherit all of the attributes of a person such as name, age, sex, and so on. The relationships between these objects are graphically displayed, and icons representing the various attributes can be viewed. An example is shown in Figure 8.

Prograph also uses graphics to define the operations that manipulate and test the states of the objects. All programs are created visually by using a powerful visual data flow language. There is no coding in the traditional sense. An example is illustrated in Figure 9.

Prograph has been used for computer science instruction as an introduction to programming for high school students, with great success. This language and its graphical programming environment are representative of the new directions in visual programming. That is, evolving visual languages should be created on the basis of new paradigms and problem-solving approaches, not simply emulations of existing verbally oriented languages. Visually oriented versions of Pascal, BASIC, or C would still suffer from the weaknesses and constraints of underlying language.

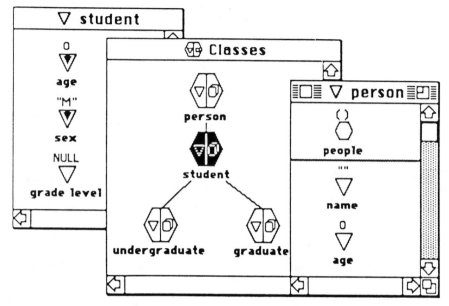

Figure 8 Prograph object display. Reprinted from The Best of MacTutor, Volume 5, by permission of TGS Systems, publisher of MacTutor Magazine.

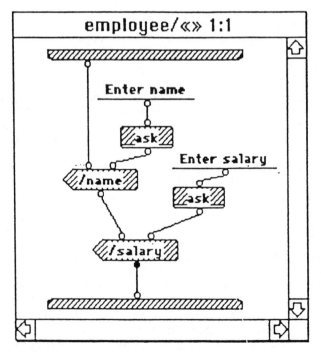

Figure 9 Prograph visual program. Reprinted from *Prograph Technical Specifications* by permission of TGS Systems.

The distinction between a programming language and a design language is unclear. Programming languages can be used for design but are confined to using the syntactic and semantic details of the specific language, which are not always suitable for expressing the desired design. To overcome this deficiency, emerging visual software system design languages attempt to express design details at a higher level of abstraction. One example is state charts (Harel, 1988).

State charts were developed by David Harel as a visual design tool for software development. A graphically oriented environment for developing and executing state charts has been developed. State charts provide a graphical representation of the objects of a problem and changes to the states of those objects as execution proceeds. A sample state chart describing the operation of a digital watch is shown in Figure 10.

There has not been much experience in using state charts and their associated design environment for educational purposes. State charts were presented to illustrate the potential of emerging design notations and computer-aided tools supporting these notations. In time, we anticipate that similar visually oriented design techniques will become more commonplace in introductory computer science education.

CONCLUSIONS

Learning design, in any discipline, requires time, patience, and practice. Design in software development is particularly difficult because there are numerous notations for expressing designs, including both visual or graphical design representations and traditional character-oriented programming languages. Ideally, the notation used should match the structure of the problem to be solved. Unfortunately, notations tend to be general and problems tend to be domain specific. This often makes it difficult to capture the structure of the problem by using the desired notation.

Students who are learning software design experience many difficulties, including failure to understand the problem to be solved and not understanding the notation for expressing a solution, use of tools required for creating and executing the notation (e.g., editor, compiler, debuggers, etc.), or using abstract thinking to transform the problem into a solution. Traditionally, novice students are overwhelmed by each of these.

Technology can help in many ways. The goal is to simplify each of the difficulties noted above. Computer-based simulation and/or animation make it easier for students to understand the problem to be solved. Notations for expressing solutions can be tailored to the problem or easily used for solving simple problems. The latter is more traditional in computer science instruction. Computer-based design environments that are created specifically for instructional purposes would make it easier for students to learn how to use these tools.

Teaching students to use abstract thinking in design is perhaps the most difficult aspect. Instruction must be progressive, first teaching the solving of simple problems by using simple notations (suitable for the problem), with easy-to-use design environments. Computer-aided instructional environments, coupled with new visually oriented design notations, would make it much easier for students to learn and to appreciate design in software development activities.

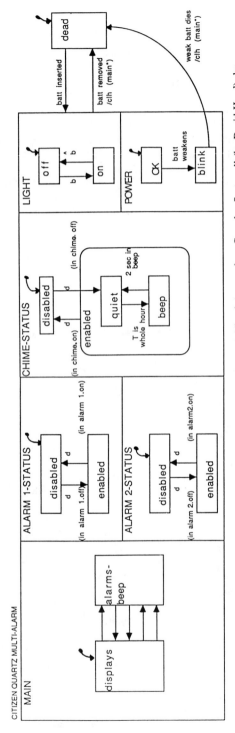

Figure 10 State chart for operation of a digital watch. Reprinted from "Statecharts: A Visual Approach to Complex Systems" (by David Harel), by permission of the author.

REFERENCES

Archer, J., and R. Conway, *"COPE: A Cooperative Programming Environment,"* Technical Report 81-459, Cornell University, Department of Computer Science, Cornell University, Ithaca, NY, May 1981.

Bonar, J., E. Soloway, and K. Ehrlich, "Cognitive strategies and looping constructs," in *Studying the novice programmer,* 191–207, Hillsdale, NJ: Erlbaum, 1989.

Cox, Philip T., and Thomasz Pietrzykowski, "Using a pictorial representation to combine data flow and object orientation in a language-independent programming mechanism," in *Proceedings of the International Computer Science Conference,* 695–704, December 1988.

Dijkstra, E. W., O. J. Dahl, and C. A. R. Hoare, *Structural programming,* New York: Academic Press, 1972.

David Harel, "On visual formalisms," *CACM,* 31(5):514–530, May 1988.

Harper, Robert, David MacQueen, and Robin Milner, "Standard ML," Technical Report ECS-LFCS-86-2, University of Edinburgh, LFCS, Department of Computer Science, University of Edinburgh, The King's Building, Edinburgh EH9 3JZ, March 1986.

Henderson, Peter B., "A computer-aided instructional environment," *Journal of Educational Technology Systems,* 15(3):281–302, January 1987.

Henderson, Peter B., and David L. Ferguson, "A conceptual approach to algorithmic problem solving," in *Proceedings of the Seventh Annual National Educational Computing Conference,* 243–249, June 1986.

Henderson, Peter B., and David L. Ferguson. "The design of algorithms," *Journal of Machine-Mediated Learning,* 2(1):67–82, January 1987.

Henderson, Peter B., and Francisco Romero. "Teaching recursion as a problem-solving tool using Standard ML," *ACM SIGCSE Bulletin,* 20(1):27–30, February 1989.

Henderson, Peter B., "Mathematics and programming: The horse and the cart," in Peter Wegner, (ed.), *Proceedings of the 1990 IFIP Workshop on Informatics Education at the University Level, Journal of Visual Languages and Computing.* New York: Academic Press, in press.

Levine, Marvin, *Principles of effective problem solving,* Englewood Cliffs, NJ: Prentice-Hall, 1988.

Linn, M. C., and M. J. Clancey, "Can experts' explanations help students develop program design skills?" *International Journal of Man-Machine Studies,* in press.

Milner, Robin, "A proposal for Standard ML," in *Proceedings of the ACM Symposium on Lisp and Functional Programming,* August 1984.

Niguidula, David A., and Andries van Dam, *Pascal on the Macintosh: A graphical approach,* Reading, MA: Addison-Wesley, 1987.

Pattis, Richard E., *Karel the robot,* New York: Wiley, 1981.

Shu, N. C., *Visual programming,* New York: Van Nostrand Reinhold, 1988.

Teitlebaum, Tim, and Thomas Reps, "The Cornell program synthesizer: A syntax-directed programming environment," *CACM,* 24:563–573, September 1981.

Wikström, Ake, *Functional programming using ML,* Englewood Cliffs, NJ: Prentice-Hall International, 1987.

Yourdon, Edward, and Larry L. Constantine, *Structured design,* Englewood Cliffs, NJ: Prentice-Hall, 1979.

8

MENDEL: An Intelligent Computer Tutoring System for Genetics Problem Solving, Conjecturing, and Understanding

Michael J. Streibel and Jim Stewart
The University of Wisconsin–Madison

Kenneth Koedinger
Carnegie-Mellon University, Pittsburgh, PA

Angelo Collins
Rutgers University, New Brunswick, NJ

John R. Jungck
Beloit College, Beloit, WI

Abstract This chapter describes an intelligent tutoring system in transmission genetics called MENDEL. MENDEL, like other intelligent computer tutoring systems, computationally models content knowledge of a discipline, problem-solving performance of experts and learners, and tutoring behavior of humans. It is capable of providing students with advice that is tailored to their knowledge of genetics, their problem-solving experience, and their progress toward solving particular transmission genetics problems.

INTRODUCTION

In this chapter, we describe an intelligent tutoring system in transmission genetics called MENDEL. MENDEL, like other intelligent computer tutoring systems (Anderson, Boyle, Farrell, and Reiser, 1984; Clancey, 1983; Schute, Glaser, and Resnick, 1986; Sleeman and Brown, 1982; Wolfe and McDonald, 1984), computationally models content knowledge of a discipline, problem-solving performance of experts and learners, and tutoring behavior of humans. It is capable of providing students with advice that is tailored to their knowledge of genetics, their

An earlier version of this chapter appeared in *Machine-Mediated Learning*, 2(1–2):129–159, 1987.
We acknowledge the support of the IBM Corporation for the support that they are giving to the University of Wisconsin–Madison's Project TROCHOS; the FIPSE (Fund for the Improvement of Postsecondary Education) program of the U.S. Department of Education, Grant #G008301471 and Grant #G0085410.39; and the National Science Foundation, Grant #MDR-8470277.

problem-solving experience, and their progress toward solving particular transmission genetics problems.

We believe that coupling tutoring system research with open-ended problem-solving in science education makes educational sense (National Academy of Science, 1982; Volpe, 1984). A similar set of beliefs can be seen in the pages of *The American Biology Teacher* and *The Science Teacher*, in which various authors describe the effective use of microcomputers in science education. We, therefore, believe that this is an opportune time to bring the theoretical and practical advances in the fields of tutoring systems, psychology, and science education to bear on the design and use of computers in science education. Each of these disciplines has developed enough of a knowledge base so that the intersection of these fields provides fertile ground for a new form of science education. This form treats science education as a design-like, problem-solving activity in which students learn science as they solve open-ended, realistic problems.

Several strands of research within education and psychology have a bearing on this new form of science education, including research on students' alternate conceptions (DiSessa, 1982; Hackling and Treagust, 1984; McClosky, Caramazza, and Green, 1980), expert and novice problem solving (Larkin, McDermott, Simon, and Simon, 1980; Reif, 1983), and teaching for conceptual change (Hewson, 1979; Strike, Posner, Hewson, and Gertzog, 1982). Relevant lines of inquiry within artificial intelligence research deal with knowledge representation schemes (e.g., frames, production rules, and semantic networks), the design of intelligent tutoring systems (Anderson, Boyle, and Reiser, 1985; Brown and Burton, 1978; Clancey, 1983; Sleeman and Brown, 1982; Steels and Campbell, 1985; Wolfe and McDonald, 1984), the instructional potential of intelligent tutoring systems (Lipson, Bunderson, Baillo, Olsen, and Fisher, 1983; Munakata, 1985; Tennyson, 1984), and how problem-solving learning strategies can form the basis for intelligent tutoring systems (Brown, Collins, and Harris, 1978).

The primary objective of the MENDEL project is to provide a computer environment for learning transmission genetics in which students can develop mental models of problem-solving expertise (Stewart, 1983; Stewart and Hafner, 1991) by solving realistic problems and receiving appropriate advice. It is currently being used with high school biology students on a research basis. The development of MENDEL is an experiment that we hope will serve to demonstrate that (a) students can design problem-solving experiments for realistic genetics problems; (b) software designers can integrate geneticists' model-based problem-solving strategies and teachers' tutoring strategies into a computer environment; and (c) students are capable of developing model-based problem-solving when placed in such a simulation and tutoring environment. Specifically, we expect that students who work with MENDEL will accomplish the following:

(1) develop an integrated theoretical and practical knowledge of genetics;
(2) internalize notational systems that:
    (a) connect their knowledge of genetics objects, processes, and states with their knowledge of genetics problem solving;
    (b) connect their knowledge of scientific inquiry with their ability to solve genetics problems; and
    (c) provide a vehicle for solution-justification in model-based terms;
(3) develop a model of inquiry that is transferable to problem solving in other

genetics domains (e.g., microbial genetics). This model of inquiry will include the activities of data redescription, hypothesis generation and testing, consistency checking between causal mechanisms and empirical data, and the final disconfirmation of several alternate hypotheses.

In the remainder of this chapter, we provide a discussion of how our view of science education has driven our development efforts and how educational research has been integrated into the program. These overviews are followed by a detailed description of the MENDEL software.

A VIEW OF SCIENCE EDUCATION

Our view of science education has emerged from several decades of classroom teaching in which we have attempted to help our students learn science and learn about science as an intellectual activity. We have done this by engaging our students in open-ended problem-solving activities that are similar to those of scientists. In other words, we feel that it is important to teach science as science and not as a "rhetoric of conclusions" (Schwab, 1960). Recently, the new form of science education has resulted in a series of genetics simulation programs (Jungck and Calley, 1986) that allow students to act like genetics researchers. From the initial work of Jungck and Calley has grown, in addition to MENDEL, an undergraduate biology curriculum development and revitalization project called BioQUEST. The BioQUEST software and accompanying text material provide students with the opportunity to develop problem-solving skills and long-range research strategies similar to those used by practicing biologists (Peterson and Jungck, 1988; BioQUEST NOTES, 1989a, 1989b, 1990).

The view of science education that we, and BioQUEST authors, developed is described in terms of the 3 Ps of science. These 3 Ps are problem posing, problem solving, and persuasion of peers.

Problem Posing and Problem Solving

Although problem posing is uncommon in science education, it is at the core of science and therefore is a significant experience for students. It is important for students to realize that problems do not come pre-posed. Students could stand in a laboratory or in a field forever, and no textbook-stated problems would come to them. Only if we encourage students to pose problems will they begin to appreciate how posing problems affects both problem solving and the direction that science will take. Sir Peter Medawar (1984) calls this agenda of problem setting and problem posing "the art of the soluble."

We believe that students should have the opportunity to experience the excitement and satisfaction of learning that is both intellectually engaging and satisfying. This can best occur when students are placed in an environment where problem solving is realistic and where the open-ended essence of science is practiced. To do this, the problems must be both posed and solved by the student. In a classroom where posing and solving realistic problems is central, the roles of teachers and students are different than in classrooms where teachers pose problems for students (and normally know the right answer). In the problem-posing classroom, the teacher is a "coach" who alternates between demonstrating for the students as they work jointly on a problem and critiquing the student's solo performance. This view of a teacher is included in MENDEL.

The MENDEL software encourages students to pose problems and ask questions—both critical features of a genuine scientific education. When students begin asking questions, they see that problem posing and problem solving are inseparable and that drawing warranted inferences depends on knowing the assumptions that were made at the time the problem was initially posed.

Experience in posing problems is also important because it helps uncover many of the blatant biases of culture and ideology. Prejudices based on race, gender, ethnicity, class, and religion occur in science, as do prejudices of reductionism, teleology, anthropomorphism, anthropocentricism, and confirmation bias. These biases often creep into the formulation of problems as well as into the strategies for testing hypotheses and persuading peers. These assumptions, if ignored during problem-posing, will be difficult to notice, much less eradicate, at the problem-solving and persuasion states of scientific practice.

Persuasion of Peers

Research is not part of science until members of a research community (colleagues) have been persuaded that the solution to the particular problem is adequate. Colleagues judge if the solution to a research problem is logical and if it is consistent with already accepted related knowledge. In the final analysis, experimentation or data analysis is important because it fits into the context of a theory. This is the central point of English physicist John Ziman's (1968) book, *Public Knowledge*. In it, he asserts the following:

> *A really good experiment, a really novel and exciting one, is connected, in the mind of the experimenter, with the proof of some novel and exciting hypothesis. His communication of the experiment to his colleagues is not merely an exposition of the peculiar events that occurred when he put a piece of litmus paper in the solution; it is an attempt to show that the world behaves as he has conceived it. After the private moment of illumination, there must come the public demonstration, the deliberate process of persuasion. That is why I say that a good experiment is a powerful piece of rhetoric; it has the ability to persuade the most obdurate and skeptical mind to accept a new idea; it makes a positive contribution to public knowledge. (35–36)*

Persuading one's peers is important for students, too, if for no other reason than that by doing so they will better understand the importance of persuasion in science. Angelo Collins (1986) talks about "solutions as hypotheses" that can be used to convince peers. That is, solutions are the result of drawing warranted inferences from well-collected data. No matter how many experiments a student has done, no matter how much data they have collected, no matter how many puzzles they have solved, they have not done science until they have both reported their results and convinced peers that their hypotheses are reasonable.

In the MENDEL system we have drawn on this 3 Ps view of science so that students have the opportunity to pose and solve realistic problems and to persuade both their peers and the MENDEL TUTOR of the adequacy of their solutions.

THE PSYCHOLOGICAL RESEARCH BASE FOR MENDEL

The research that led to the development of the MENDEL software includes studies of expert and novice problem-solving performance, tutoring strategies of genetics teachers, student use of notational tools, and effective advising strategies to help novices understand model-based problem-solving.

More specific research on improving the teaching of genetics at the high school and college levels focuses on an analysis of high school students' knowledge of transmission genetics and how this knowledge influences their problem-solving performance (Stewart, 1983; Stewart and Dale, 1981, 1989; Thomson and Stewart, 1985) as well as on the strategies that novice university students (Albright, 1987), high school students (Slack and Stewart, 1990), and expert geneticists (Collins, 1986; Collins and Stewart, 1987) use to solve realistic genetics problems generated by a microcomputer. This research forms the knowledge base for the MENDEL system described here.

THE MENDEL SYSTEM'S GOALS

The remainder of the chapter describes the MENDEL system in detail and how intelligent advice can be structured to preserve the design approach to science education. The concluding remarks then show how several larger issues are integral to the design approach to science education. These larger issues are (a) problem solving with understanding; (b) problem-based, experiential learning; (c) the integration of rule-based with model-based reasoning; and (d) the role of human collaboration in machine-mediated learning environments.

The primary goals of the MENDEL system are to provide students with tutorial help to develop the following:

(1) an understanding of genetics and genetics problem solving; and
(2) their understanding of scientific research skills such as problem identification, hypothesis generation and testing, data gathering, and long-term inference making.

These two goals are intimately interconnected. They are elaborated throughout the rest of the article.

THE MENDEL SYSTEM'S COMPONENTS

The MENDEL system has the following two primary components:

(1) a problem GENERATOR program that includes:
  (a) a CUSTOMIZE section, and
  (b) a problem-solving environment;
(2) an expert TUTOR program that includes:
  (a) a problem SOLVER,
  (b) a problem-solving ADVISOR,
  (c) a graphics LIBRARIAN, and
  (d) a student MODELER.

These components are summarized in Figure 1.

Each of the MENDEL components has a unique interface structure. The specific interfaces, however, are integrated into an overall visual interface on an IBM computer screen. For example, each component embodies the following functions in a different way (Anderson et al., 1984):

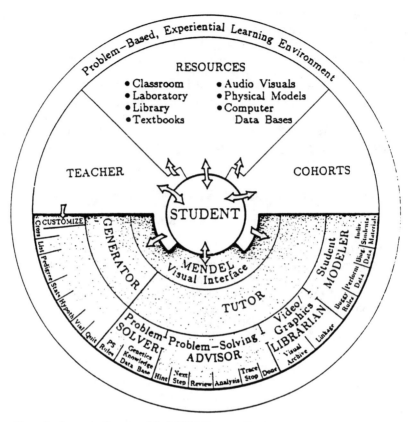

Figure 1 Summary diagram of the MENDEL system's components.

(1) reduce the working-memory load of a student;
(2) aid conceptualization of the genetics content and problem-solving strategies;
(3) decompose the problem into manageable subunits; and
(4) help structure the student's thinking.

The overall visual interface, on the other hand, tries to:

(1) maintain a consistent command structure;
(2) facilitate ease of interaction;
(3) be visually compelling and aesthetically pleasing; and
(4) be pedagogically sound with respect to the project goals.

The GENERATOR Program in the MENDEL System

The GENERATOR program is termed a *strategic simulation* and places students in a computer environment that simulates the problem-solving situations faced by transmission geneticists in a laboratory (Jungck, 1982; Jungck and Calley, 1985). Students who use the GENERATOR program have to pose their own problems from within a predefined class of problems that was customized by a teacher or another user. Students then use their genetics knowledge, their ability to perform genetics crosses, and their ability to use computational tools such as chi-square analysis to work out appropriate solutions. The students' experiences with the GENERATOR program are more realistic than those possible with textbook problems.

There are two parts to the GENERATOR program: a CUSTOMIZE section where teachers or other users create classes of problems (within which cases are randomly generated later by the GENERATOR for students) and a problem-solving environment where users perform genetic crosses to produce data and use data-management tools to manipulate and view the data (see Figure 1).

The CUSTOMIZE Section of the GENERATOR

Within the CUSTOMIZE section, a teacher creates *classes* of problems and defines *sets* of trait and variation names. Classes of problems are created by filling in templates such as the one shown in Figure 2. For example, a teacher can select the number of traits for a genetics problem, a range for the number of progeny from a genetics cross, and a set of *primary inheritance patterns* such as simple dominance, codominance, or multiple alleles. These customizable characteristics permit the program to be used anywhere from junior high school up through graduate-level genetics classes.

Trait and variation names are also defined in the CUSTOMIZE section. A sample bodypart template screen for the Antennae trait of fruit flies is shown in Figure 3. The traits (or bodyparts) that might appear in any problem are selected along with variation names for that trait. In the sample problem discussed below, we use two body parts as traits: Antennae and Wings. The variables chosen in the CUSTOMIZE section of the GENERATOR *define* the problems that the user encounters in the problem-solving section.

The Problem-Solving Environment of the GENERATOR

In the problem-solving section of the GENERATOR program, the student begins with a "field-collected" vial of organisms on the computer screen and then selects one of several functions. Figure 4 below depicts such a vial (i.e., Vial #0) whose contents have been elaborated by the L)ist function. Note that the vials on the computer screen display a shorthand representation of the trait's variation names (e.g., T = Tiny). A user can invoke the L)ist option to see the full names of the traits and their variations. In addition, graphic pedigree diagrams on the computer screen represent a redescription of the Vial #0 data into a form that is appropriate for pedigree analysis. In this example, there are 12 females with tiny antennae (i.e., 2 Tiny/Dumpy, 5 Tiny/Lobed, and 5 Tiny/Short); the second variation names (i.e., Dumpy, Lobed, and Short) refer to the Wings trait.

Figure 4 also shows some of the functions that are available to students:

C)ross—enables a student to cross individuals and obtain offspring;
L)ist—described above;
P)edigree—represents the vial data in a graphic form and is used by the problem solver to analyze the data produced from a cross experiment. The pedigree diagram is a useful, abstract redescription of cross data that makes it easier to see patterns and thus make inferences about genotypes across generations. The

user's hypotheses about genotypes are entered over the question marks (underneath each pedigree box on the screen);

S)tatistics—allows the student to do mathematical calculations and chi-square tests with probabilities;

H)ypotheses—whereas the Pedigree option allows users to make specific hypotheses about parents and offsprings, the Hypotheses command allows users to enter hypotheses about the genetics of the population as a whole;

V)ial-options—helps students store and retrieve vials on the screen (for more space on the screen);

Q)uit—allows the student to abandon the current problem before going on.

CUSTOMIZE Menu Item #1

Enter problem name on the next line:

Simple_Problem_____

Numtraits	2	MinProgeny	20	MaxProgeny	50
Codominance	Y	Maxcodom	1	CodomProb60	
MultAlleles	N	MaxMult	0	MProb	0_
				MaxAlleles	0
Sexlink	N	MaxSexLink	0	SexLinkProb	0_
Linkage	N	HiDistance	0_	LoDistance	0_
Interference	N	HiInt	0_	LoInt	0_
Lethality	N	Maxlethal	0_	LethalProb	0_
Interaction	N	IntProb	0_		
Penetrance	N	Maxpen	0	PProb	0_
HMpen	0_	HTpen	0_		
Pleiotropy	N	PlProb	0_		

Will this be the last menu item? Y

PRESS A KEY: ESC) when done **ARROWS)** to move around **A-Z/0-9)** to fill blanks

Figure 2 Sample menu from the CUSTOMIZE problem-definition screen.

```
┌─────────────────────────────────────────────────────────────────┐
│                                                                   │
│   CUSTOMIZE                                                       │
│                                                                   │
│   Bodypart #6                                                     │
│                                                                   │
│                                                                   │
│   Body Part: Antennae                                             │
│                                                                   │
│   Fill the following blanks with adjectives appropriate to this body part: │
│                                                                   │
│        #1:Straight____    #2:Crinkled___    #3:Thread____         │
│        #4:Stiff_____     #5:Floppy_____    #6:Missing___         │
│        #7:Tiny_____      #8:Aris_pedia_    #9:Stunted____        │
│        #10:Aristaless_     #11:Forked____    #12:Wisp____          │
│        #13:Blunt_____    #14:Crooked___    #15:Bent____          │
│                                                                   │
│                                                                   │
│                                                                   │
│   Is this the last bodypart?   N                                  │
│                                                                   │
│                                                                   │
│  ───────────────────────────────────────────────────────────── │
│   PRESS A KEY:  ESC) when done ARROWS) to move around  A-Z/0-9) to fill blanks │
└─────────────────────────────────────────────────────────────────┘
```

Figure 3   Sample menu from the CUSTOMIZE bodypart-definition screen.

Students who use the GENERATOR program are faced with an open-ended problem: how to explain the genetic mechanisms responsible for the phenotypes of the population of organisms that they see on the screen. Underlying the generation of the field-collected vial and all subsequent offspring vials is a model of the inheritance patterns and modifiers as defined in the CUSTOMIZE component of the GENERATOR.

Within the context of the general problem, students are responsible for posing their own specific problems and for selecting the most appropriate approaches to a solution. This is done by performing crosses on the original set of organisms and/ or successive generations and by doing statistical analyses. Thus, decisions such as whether enough data have been collected or what the results of statistical tests may mean must be made by students as they develop genetics-specific problem-solving strategies as well as more general scientific inquiry skills.

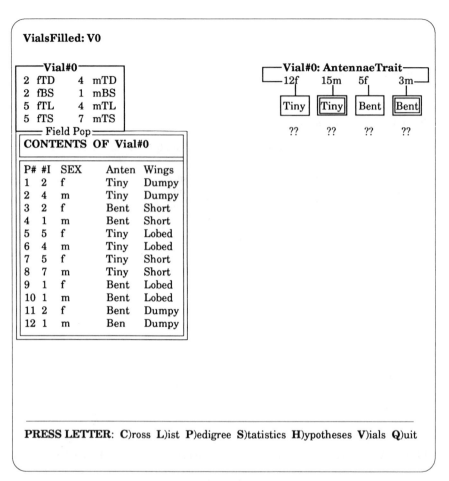

Figure 4   Sample GENERATOR screen of a two-trait problem with the L)ist option for Vial #0 (the parental vial).

As rich as the GENERATOR environment is, it does not completely simulate the genetics laboratory experience. Aside from not having to feed, house, and mate actual organisms, students are also not faced with a critical first step in real genetics problem-solving: how to perceptually divide an organism into discrete, analyzable traits. This is already done by the GENERATOR program. Students therefore bypass the initial abstraction processes (of recognition and identification of traits and variations) involved in confronting data in scientific inquiry. In addition, they do not see many of the complex interactions that an organism's genotype has with its environment (both external and internal). These interactions can lead to a wide variation in the phenotype and are only approximated in the GENERATOR's environment. Nonetheless, GENERATOR-created experiences are far richer than the problem-solving experiences in typical undergraduate courses (Jungck and Calley, 1985).

The TUTOR Program in the MENDEL System

The development of the TUTOR program has emerged from a consideration of the roles and responsibilities of a human tutor who is working with students in the GENERATOR environment. For example, a human tutor must be able to make inferences about the data generated by the student, maintain a history of a student's actions, and make inferences about the reasons for the student's problem-solving actions. Each of these steps is based on a combination of what the student has done and said. Each of these steps also helps the human tutor build a model or representation of each student's or group of students' knowledge of genetics problem solving, such as the following:

(1) comparing the model of a student's knowledge with the tutor's understanding of the problem;
(2) making decisions on the form of tutorial advice and the timing of this advice; and
(3) evaluating whether or not the student has benefited from the advice.

The computer TUTOR adds a few functions that a human tutor cannot provide. For example, the TUTOR provides students with the following:

(1) a set of computational tools for genetics problem solving (Punnett squares, expression charts, etc.);
(2) data-management tools to manipulate the data that they generate (pop-up calculators, data storage and retrieval, etc.);
(3) graphical representation of genetics data and conceptual relations (pedigree and chromosome diagrams); and
(4) multiple windows into the reasoning of the TUTOR.

These last four features are normally *not* available from a human tutor.

The SOLVER Component of the TUTOR

The SOLVER component of the MENDEL system reacts to the same data that the students see on the computer screen and then generates and tests which inheritance patterns best match the available data. It does this in the background without the student's knowledge. The TUTOR does *not* have access to the CUSTOMIZE information that constrains the class of problems. The following discussion begins with the GENERATOR-created screen of a two-trait problem shown in Figure 4. The goal is to infer which inheritance patterns and modifiers account for the distribution of phenotypic data in the population. Several actions can accomplish this goal: (a) generating a hypothesis about a possible inheritance pattern and modifier, (b) generating new data (i.e., invoking the GENERATOR program to perform a cross), (c) checking to see if the data are consistent with the tentative hypothesis, and (d) disconfirming alternate hypotheses. The TUTOR can perform each of these steps on its own because it has a SOLVER component that contains a high-level problem-solving Agenda and specific production rules for solving problems.

1. Redescribe data from initial population for each trait
2. Entertain a hypothesis about inheritance pattern

        [hypothesis generation rules: HGR]
3. Test inheritance pattern hypothesis:
   [Find genotype to phenotype mapping]
   a. Make a cross [cross rules: CR]
   b. Redescribe data from a cross
   c. Explain cross in light of hypothesis
      [cross explanation rules: CER]
   d. Done?
      • If there are no consistent explanations, goto 2
      • If there is more than one explanation, goto 3
      • If there is exactly one explanation, goto 4
      • If there is absolutely no explanation, goto 1
4. Check your result:
   a. Make a prediction to test your hypothesis
   b. Are the crosses already performed consistent?
      [definitive cross rules: DCR]
   c. Disconfirm competing hypothesis
      [disconfirmation rules: DR]

However, only the student actually chooses which crosses to make. Both student and computer then test their hypotheses about the most likely inheritance pattern against the expanded data set in an iterative manner. The SOLVER's Agenda and related rules were extracted from research on how experts solve similar problems (Collins, 1986) and were formalized as condition/action relations (i.e., IF/THEN production rules). Each step in the SOLVER's Agenda is described with the example from Figure 4.

Redescribe Data from Initial Population for Each Trait

The first step in the Agenda directs the SOLVER to go to the GENERATOR-created population of organisms (see Vial #0 in Figure 4), extract key information (e.g., names and numbers of traits and variations), and store this information in the TUTOR's own internal data structures. It also directs the SOLVER to carry out some simple inferences that can be made from the initial population. For example, by focusing on the first trait (i.e., Antennae), the SOLVER can conclude that there are 12 female bugs and 15 male bugs with tiny antennae in the initial population. Another example would be that the Antennae trait had only two variations (i.e., tiny and bent).

Entertain a Hypothesis about Inheritance Pattern

The redescribed data now serve as a set of *conditions* for the Solver's condition/action rules. Hence, the Agenda directs the SOLVER to search through its hypothesis-generating rules (HGR), which in turn "fires" the following rule:

HGR1: **IF**   (1) goal: generate an inheritance pattern hypothesis
                     (2) there are two variations for a trait
          THEN   assume simple dominance is the inheritance pattern for
                     that trait

HGR1 states that after having broken the larger problem into a subproblem (i.e., focusing on one trait at a time), the SOLVER should proceed on the assumption that simple dominance may be the inheritance pattern responsible for the phenotypic data. This accomplishes several things. First, it simplifies the search space of possible underlying mechanisms that might account for the phenotypic data. Second, it makes a best first guess at such a mechanism the way an expert problem solver would do. (Of course, there are several levels of genetics knowledge compiled into HGR1 that would have to be explained to a student who wanted to understand *why* this particular rule was a useful first guess.) Finally, it translates a problem-solving strategy into a specific procedure. The SOLVER now has a way to match the phenotypic-level data against genotypic-level casual relationships.

Test Inheritance Pattern Hypothesis

The Agenda now directs the SOLVER to cross a female and male bug from Vial #0. A cross rule (CR) fires because the appropriate conditions exist in the redescribed data. This rule directs the GENERATOR program to cross unlike variations (i.e., a tiny-antennaed female with a bent-antennaed male) because such a cross produces the most knowledge about the current hypothesis. (As mentioned above for Rule HGR1, cross rules contain several levels of genetics knowledge.) Hence:

> **CR2:** **IF** (1) goal: plan a cross within a trait
> (2) there is a variation, V1, for which you don't have a genotype
> **THEN** cross unlikes: V1 with some other variation

The SOLVER also tells the GENERATOR to randomly choose one of the 12 female tiny-antennaed bugs and one of the 3 male bent-antennaed bugs. The resulting offsprings are placed in Vial #1. Figure 5 shows the computer screen at the end of the problem-solving session. For the time being, we need only focus on Vial #0 and Vial #1.

The data in Vial #1 represent a new set of conditions for the SOLVER's rule to consider. Following the Agenda, the SOLVER first redescribes the new data (Agenda Item 3b) and then applies a series of cross explanation rules (CER; Agenda Item 3c). One rule fires because the appropriate conditions in Vial #0 and Vial #1 exist. Hence:

> **CER6:** **IF** (1) goal: explain a cross within a trait
> (2) assume inheritance pattern is simple dominance for that trait
> (3) parents are of different variations
> (4) offspring are of both variations
> **THEN** (1) one parent and the offspring of the same variation are homozygous recessive
> (2) the other parent and the offspring with this variation are heterozygous dominant

That is, the SOLVER finds that "unlikes" in the parents (tiny-antennaed and bent-antennaed) have produced "unlikes" in the offspring. If simple dominance was in fact the underlying inheritance pattern in our example, the cross could be explained by the abstract genotypic pattern:

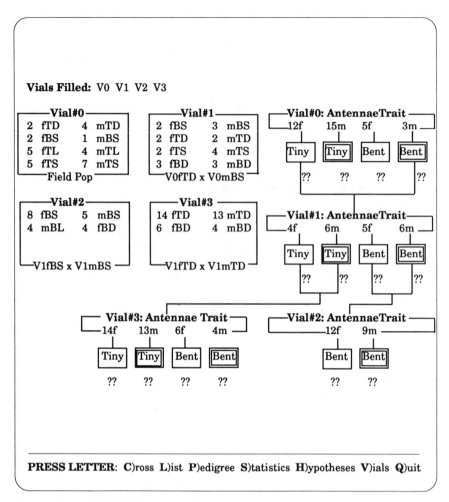

Figure 5 Sample GENERATOR screen of a two-trait problem solved for the Antennae trait.

$$Aa \times aa \rightarrow {}_{1/2}Aa + {}_{1/2}aa.$$

Of course, the SOLVER cannot at this point determine which specific genotype (i.e., *Aa* or *aa*) corresponds with which phenotype (i.e., tiny-antennaed or bent-antennaed) in Vial #1. The SOLVER therefore has to perform more crosses to establish such a correspondence.

A in the genotypic pattern above represents the dominant allele and *a* represents the recessive allele. *Aa* represents a heterozygous allele-pair and *aa* a homozygous recessive allele-pair. Table 1 summarizes all of the possible genotype-to-phenotype matches for the simple dominance case.

At this point, the SOLVER continues to test the current inheritance pattern hypothesis (Agenda Item 3d) because Vial #1 has added new conditions for the original set of cross rules. Hence, the following cross rule fires:

Table 1 Relationship of genotypic to phenotypic data for a simple dominance case of two variations (*V1* and *V2*) of one trait (all possibilities are shown).

Genotypic level*	Phenotypic level**	Cross types	Number of offspring classes
1. $AA \times AA \rightarrow AA$	$V1 \times V1 \rightarrow V1$**	likes	1
2. $aa \times aa \rightarrow aa$	$V1 \times V1 \rightarrow V1$	likes	1
3. $AA \times Aa \rightarrow {}_{1/2}AA + {}_{1/2}Aa$	$V1 \times V1 \rightarrow V1$	likes	1
4. $Aa \times Aa + {}_{1/4}aa \rightarrow {}_{1/4}AA + {}_{1/2}Aa$	$V1 \times V1 \rightarrow {}_{3/4}V1 + {}_{1/4}V2$	likes	2
5. $AA \times aa \rightarrow Aa$	$V1 \times V2 \rightarrow V1$	unlikes	1
6. $Aa \times aa \rightarrow {}_{1/2}Aa + {}_{1/2}aa$	$V1 \times V2 \rightarrow {}_{1/2}V1 + {}_{1/2}V2$	unlikes	2

*A represents the dominant allele, a the recessive allele.
AA represents the homozygous dominant allele-pair.
aa represents the homozygous recessive allele-pair.
Aa represents the heterozygous allele-pair.
**$V1$ represents the first arbitrary variation. Notice that several genotypic patterns can underlie the same phenotypic pattern.

CR16: **IF** (1) goal: identify which of the offspring of an unlike cross are heterozygotes
(2) there are two variations in that offspring;
THEN consider crossing likes from this offspring.

The SOLVER therefore crosses two bugs of the same variation (i.e., bent-antennaed) from Vial #1. The results of the GENERATOR-created data are stored in Vial #2 (see Figure 5). Note that the SOLVER is now reasoning about the data from several generations of data. This strategy was chosen because it approximates optimal problem-solving performance—something that was not always displayed by the experts (Collins, 1986).

The SOLVER now redescribes the data in Vial #2 and tries to explain the data in light of the simple dominance hypothesis. A cross explanation rule fires because the SOLVER has found the correct conditions in both Vial #1 and Vial #2. Hence:

CER7: **IF** (1) goal: explain a cross within a trait
(2) assumed inheritance pattern for that trait is simple dominance
(3) parents have like variations within this trait
(4) parents are either heterozygous or homozygous recessive
(5) offspring have the same variation within this trait as the parents
THEN parents are probably homozygous recessive while offspring are also probably homozygous recessive

CER7 helps the SOLVER conclude that the bent variation of the Antennae trait in Vial #2 is due to a homozygous recessive allele-pair. The reasoning proceeds as follows: The SOLVER has already established from the previous cross that the tiny-antennaed and bent-antennaed variations in Vial #1 are *not* due to a homozygous dominant genotype (i.e., the genotypic pattern $Aa \times aa \rightarrow {}_{1/2}Aa + {}_{1/2}aa$

accounted for the data, thus excluding *AA*). Of the three simple dominance mechanisms that could account for the appearance of a bent-antennaed phenotype data in Vial #2:

$$AA \times AA \rightarrow AA$$
$$AA \times Aa \rightarrow {}_{1/2}AA + {}_{1/2}Aa \text{ (both } appear \text{ the same)}$$
$$aa \times aa \rightarrow aa,$$

the first and second genotype patterns can be eliminated because both involve a homozygous dominant genotype. This leaves the homozygous recessive genotype pattern (i.e., *aa* × *aa* → *aa*) to account for the data in Vial #2. By inference, the SOLVER can also conclude that the tiny-antennaed variation in Vial #0 is due to a heterozygous allele-pair (*Aa*) because that was the only other pair left in Vial #1. (The SOLVER fills in these hypotheses in the pedigree diagram in place of the question marks below the pedigree boxes on the screen for the benefit of the student.)

At this point, the problem seems to be solved. However, there is one more step in the Agenda.

Check Your Result

The SOLVER has accounted for both variations of the Antennae trait in Vial #1 on the assumption that simple dominance was the case. The Agenda therefore directs the SOLVER to carry out one more step: checking the SOLVER's conclusion with an independent cross. Collins (1986) has found that expert geneticists add a definitive cross of two heterozygous individuals at this point in the process. Hence, the SOLVER applies its definitive cross rules (DCR) and fires the following rule:

DCR1:   **IF**   (1)   goal: become more confident in an inheritance pattern for a trait
                             (2)   assumed inheritance pattern is simple dominance with a high degree of confidence
                             (3)   heterozygotes have been identified
        THEN   cross the heterozygous individuals

This rule takes a previously identified heterozygous individual from Vial #1 (i.e., tiny-antennaed), crosses a male and a female with this variation, and places the results in Vial #3 (see Figure 5). Again, because new data have been generated, new conditions exist for the application of the cross application rules. This time, CER8 fires:

CER8:   **IF**   (1)   goal: explain a cross within a trait
                             (2)   assumed inheritance pattern for that trait is simple dominance
                             (3)   parents are heterozygous within this trait
                             (4)   both traits are present within the offspring
                             (5)   test comparing the ratios of offspring variations to 3 : 1 is significant (e.g., probability < .05)

THEN (1) increase confidence in identity of parents as heterozygous

(2) increase confidence in simple dominance as the inheritance pattern

(3) increase confidence that the parent's variation is dominant

This rule confirms that the tiny variation of the Antennae trait could only have come from a heterozygous allele-pair because only one simple dominance rule could account for this data:

$$Aa \times Aa \rightarrow {}_{1/4}AA + {}_{1/2}Aa + {}_{1/4}aa.$$

Notice that both *AA* and *Aa* show up as the same phenotypic variation in the offspring because the allele A is dominant to the recessive allele a. Hence, a 3 : 1 ratio for phenotype characteristics is expected to show up in the offsprings (i.e., ${}_{3/4}A\_\_ + {}_{1/4}aa$).

Notice also that, although we have confirmed the simple dominance hypothesis for this set of data, there still exists the slightest possibility that some other inheritance pattern and/or modifiers could account for the data. Most genetics experts in such a situation eliminate (or disconfirm) these possibilities with some standard disconfirming crosses (Collins, 1986). Hence, the Agenda (Item 4c) directs the SOLVER to try out some final disconfirming rules (DR) such as:

DR1: IF (1) goal: disconfirm alternate hypotheses

(2) inheritance pattern is simple dominance

(3) sex-linkage is modifier under consideration

(4) a cross of a dominant male with a recessive female results in offsprings that are not limited to dominant females and recessive males

THEN sex-linkage modifier is not operating

The example discussed above illustrates the SOLVER's rule-based approach to generating hypotheses about inheritance patterns and to generating crosses within the constraints of these hypotheses. The example shows how rules are used for confirming and disconfirming hypotheses based on the phenotypic data that emerge after each new cross. The SOLVER therefore has the ability to keep track of its own inferences and the ability to build up genetics knowledge appropriate to a given population of organisms. The TUTOR will have access to all of this information and can use it to provide tutorial advice.

Finally, the SOLVER, when solving problems on its own, performs all aspects of problem-solving. However, in the typical case, the SOLVER does not make crosses. Rather, it suggests crosses in light of certain student-chosen hypotheses and makes inferences from student-generated data. In the latter case, the SOLVER works with the crosses that the student has made and then tries to extract as much knowledge as possible from this data in light of hypotheses that the student is entertaining.

The ADVISOR Component of the TUTOR

We now describe the ADVISOR component of the TUTOR along two dimensions: One dimension deals with suggestions about a future action (HINT and NEXT-STEP) or an evaluation of past actions (REVIEW and ANALYSIS); the other dimension deals with specific actions (NEXT-STEP and ANALYSIS) or general strategies (HINT and REVIEW). These relationships are shown in Table 2. This component is under development and only being used in a research setting.

Although we feel it is important for the ADVISOR to have the ability to decide when it is appropriate to offer advice (i.e., to have some TUTOR-initiated intervention strategy), we are currently only focusing on what that advice will be. We have made a deliberate decision to implement the user-initiated advice-giving capabilities of the ADVISOR prior to and independently from a TUTOR-initiated intervention strategy. The former approach has many advantages. First, by having the student decide when he or she would like advice, we can have a workable tutor before actually implementing a TUTOR-initiated intervention strategy. Second, it is easier to add a more sophisticated intervention strategy to an existing advice-giving capability than it is to design both features at the same time. Finally, by implementing these capabilities independently, we can study the effectiveness of alternative intervention strategies (i.e., user-initiated vs. mixed-initiative interventions) before implementing any one.

We will now describe the user-initiated advice-giving capabilities of the ADVISOR.

The HINT Command of the ADVISOR

Students invoke the HINT option when they want a suggestion for what to do next. The ADVISOR then gives them general prompts and, if that advice is not helpful, gives them increasingly specific hints. Even though HINT provides suggestions about future actions, these suggestions may make little sense to a student if there is something seriously wrong with what he or she has already done. In this case, the ADVISOR will comment on the error before providing a hint. If there is nothing seriously wrong, HINTs will be given that are appropriate to one of the following categories of action: performing crosses (through the Cross command); making hypotheses about individual or offspring class genotypes (through the Pedigree command); or making hypotheses about the genetics of the population as a whole (through the Hypotheses command). For example, if the SOLVER determines that it is possible to make a hypothesis about the genetics of the population, then the hints given to the student might proceed from general to specific as follows:

(1) Hints to try to generate a hypothesis. For example:
"Can you make any hypotheses? If so, please enter them."

Table 2 User-requested tutorial options of the ADVISOR component of the TUTOR.

Actions	General advice (series of actions)	Specific advice (single action)
Future (SOLVER data and hypothesis)	HINT	NEXT-STEP
Past (Student data and hypothesis)	REVIEW	ANALYSIS

(2) Global redescription hints to help a student generate an inheritance pattern hypothesis. These include:
"What can you tell me about the initial population?"
"How many traits? What are they?"
"How many variations in each trait? What are they?"
"Have you done other problems with the same number of variations?"
"What does the number of variations suggest to you?"
"What if there were 3 variations instead of 2?"
(3) Hypothesis-generating hints (corresponding to HGR rules).
Students are free to ignore HINTs.

The NEXT-STEP Command of the ADVISOR

The NEXT-STEP command spells out exactly what the TUTOR'S SOLVER would do next in light of the student's current cross data and hypothesis. There are two possible next steps: *Perform a cross* and *State a hypothesis*. When a student receives NEXT-STEP advice, he or she can ask why that advice was given by using the WHY command. In response to WHY, the rule that prompted the specific action is given. If the student seeks further explanation of this rule, the ADVISOR may offer (Clancey, 1983):

(1) strategy explanations, which the student requests by the CLARIFY command; and
(2) support explanations, which the student requests by the JUSTIFY command.

Strategy explanations are designed to clarify the rule by explaining it in terms of more general strategies applicable to many classes of genetics problems. Support explanations use content knowledge and examples to justify the rule by describing or illustrating the genetic mechanisms underlying the rule.

For example, a student may have crossed Vial #0 individuals with the same phenotypes six times while indicating a current hypothesis of simple dominance. If the NEXT-STEP command is now invoked, the ADVISOR would recommend that the student use some of the offspring that have been produced and make a cross of individuals with unlike variations. If the student invokes the WHY command, the ADVISOR would present cross rule 2 (which was used earlier to illustrate the SOLVER's rules). If the student then invoked the CLARIFY command, the ADVISOR would offer a more general strategic explanation (e.g., that crossing unlikes makes it possible for a solver to either construct or identify heterozygous individuals). If the student still was not satisfied, he or she could invoke CLARIFY again and get explanations of a more general nature, such as the following:

(1) To match phenotypes with genotypes requires the identification of heterozygous individuals;
(2) to test inheritance pattern hypotheses requires that all phenotypic variations be matched with genotypes; and
(3) one action in the solving strategy is to Test Inheritance Pattern Hypotheses.

(See Figure 5, Agenda Item 3.) The purpose of CLARIFY is to help the student understand the specific advice provided by the NEXT-STEP command.

The student might also invoke the JUSTIFY command. CR2 relies on the empirical associations of the genotype-to-phenotype relationships illustrated in Table 1. The TUTOR might justify crossing unlikes at this point in the problem-solving process by highlighting relationships 5 and 6: when the variations of the parents are unlike, heterozygous offspring are produced. The next level of explanation would use relationship 4 to illustrate how crossing parents with like variations can be used to match genotypes with phenotypes.

The REVIEW Command of the ADVISOR

The REVIEW command uses data from the student MODELER and possible student errors to look back over the student's performance and make appropriate comments. REVIEW is like ANALYSIS (described below) in that it looks back at student actions. However, REVIEW does a more general evaluation based on the student's behaviors spanning the entire problem solution up to the point when he or she asked for a REVIEW. REVIEW will make general comments about the student's strategy such as "You didn't use offspring as parents very often." Comments like this can be helpful to a student in future problem-solving sessions.

The ANALYSIS Command of the ADVISOR

The ANALYSIS command walks students through the crosses that they made and points out what knowledge the SOLVER can extract from each cross. The ANALYSIS option then debriefs students about the potential significance that each cross had for the problem-solving process and where students may have made one or more of three types of errors: an inconsistent hypothesis, an unwarranted inference, or missed a warranted inference.

The DONE Command of the ADVISOR

The student invokes the DONE command when the problem is finished. The ADVISOR will then do the following:

(1) check the student's solution for consistency and point out inconsistencies;
(2) check the student's solution for completeness and make comments about incompleteness;
(3) allow the student to return to the problem-solving environment if he or she would like to continue working; and
(4) ask the student if they would like a REVIEW or an ANALYSIS.

The Graphics LIBRARIAN Component of the TUTOR

The graphics LIBRARIAN manages computer-generated graphics stored in the computer. Each type of graphics information is accessible to the TUTOR when a decision has been made that a student would benefit from tutorial advice.

The graphics material provides support explanations (e.g., about meiosis events) to accompany tutorial advice. For example, an understanding of the mechanism of meiosis can help a student explain his or her solution to a problem (a desired learning outcome) and recognize trends in the data that may not correspond to a simple independent assortment pattern. Once students recognize such a situation, they can begin to think of how linkage (including variable map distances and/or interference) might help to explain the patterns observed in the data. We have chosen to work with meiosis first because it is so central to understanding genetics problem solving and because students have difficulty understanding mattock processes (Stewart and Dale, 1981, 1989). One of the ways that we have done this is through the development of a module called LINKAGE.

When LINKAGE is invoked by the LIBRARIAN or the student, it helps the students better understand meiosis by providing an opportunity to test various hypotheses that they may have to explain their data. By invoking LINKAGE the students can create customized chromosome/gene models. This is accomplished by allowing the students to do the following:

(1) create chromosome/gene arrangements for two parental organisms;

(2) vary the map distances separating any linked genes and turn interference on or off;

(3) observe the chromosomes that they have created undergo meiosis;

(4) select the number of offspring to result from the crossing of the two parents;

(5) observe the offspring phenotype distribution that results from the cross; and

(6) change any of the above variables and observe how the offspring phenotype data are affected.

Thus, a student working with a three-trait problem might begin with a model in which each individual had three pairs of homologous chromosomes (e.g., where the chromosomes assort independently and therefore are not linked). Two individuals could be identified as parents and the offspring phenotype distributions for a specified number of offspring in that generation could be observed. It would then be possible to construct a single pair of chromosomes so that all three genes are on the same chromosome pair (e.g., linked) and do the exact same thing that was just done for the unlinked situation. The student constructs as many alternative chromosome/gene arrangements as desired, thus having relatively immediate opportunities to observe how multiple chromosome/gene models lead to different patterns in the phenotypic data. The importance of programs like this is not only that they serve a tutorial function but that they provide a student with opportunities to work with multiple models of phenomena—something that is common in science but less so in science instruction.

The Student MODELER Component of the TUTOR

For the TUTOR to intervene in the student's problem-solving process with tutorial advice, it must have access to information about that student. The function of the student MODELER is to gather such information, make inferences from it about the state of the student's knowledge (both strategic and conceptual), and make that information available to the TUTOR.

At the very least, the MODELER must keep a history of student actions such as (a) the vials(s) from which organisms are selected for crosses, (b) the making and checking of hypotheses, (c) the making of inferences about the genotypes of individuals or phenotype classes, and (d) if and when the student does statistical analyses. Some of the information will be directly available from a student's interactions with the basic GENERATOR program (the vials from which parents were taken) or by taking advantage of other GENERATOR functions (statistics or the pedigree chart function). Beyond this, the MODELER will need to recognize patterns in a set of individual actions and to make inferences about some student actions. For example, it is possible to recognize quickly that a student is taking all parental organisms from Vial #0. Although a problem could be solved by doing this, it is not an ideal approach because it does not acknowledge the importance of looking at data from within a lineage of several generations. It is therefore necessary to recognize when a student either misses a warranted inference or makes an unwarranted inference. This could be done directly by noticing when a student fails to enter genotype information on the pedigree chart or enters an unwarranted genotype. To recognize either student action, or lack of action, it is necessary to make comparisons with what action the SOLVER could make in response to the same data.

A student solving problems will execute a set of actions similar to the SOLVER's agenda. These actions can be modeled as problem-solving rules. In addition, there should be conceptual knowledge (more than rules or empirical associations) that underlie the rules. This causal knowledge (e.g., of meiosis) is the basis for problem solving with understanding and model-based reasoning. Both rule-based and model-based reasoning are ultimately important (Koton, 1985). Rule-based reasoning is easier for the MODELER to process, however, so we plan to develop this capability of the MODELER first. The MODELER's ability to infer student conceptual knowledge will be added gradually, bolstered by our research on novice knowledge of genetics and how that knowledge relates to problem-solving actions.

CONCLUDING REMARKS

The MENDEL system described in this chapter is part of an ongoing research and development project. MENDEL both simulates a transmission genetics laboratory and provides computer-generated advice. It is intended to supplement undergraduate genetics education although it is flexible enough to be used in high school biology or graduate courses.

The MENDEL system embodies certain values and commitments to science education that have guided us in our design choices and research questions. Our commitments can be categorized around the following themes:

(1) problem solving with understanding;
(2) problem-based, experiential learning;
(3) integration of rule-based and model-based reasoning; and
(4) collaborative, machine-mediated learning environments that embody the foregoing themes.

Our commitment to the importance of problem solving with understanding (as opposed to efficient problem-solving performance per se) is based on our own experience as science teachers, our research on problem solving, and our critical analysis of the potential dangers of mindless learning in computer-based education.

The importance of problem solving with understanding was driven home in one of our studies with high school genetics students who were using the GENERATOR program. At one point, when a group of these students was having a particularly hard time with one of the computer-generated problems, the instructor inadvertently suggested what our research had shown to be a very powerful problem-solving rule. The students henceforth applied that rule to similar problems without thinking of the underlying genetics mechanisms. We had inadvertently created students who successfully solved problems but who also mindlessly followed rules. This is not to suggest that we are against rules or rule-following.

Rather, we want rules to emerge in the minds (and behaviors) of our learners as a result of experience and understanding. A tutor must therefore do much more than reveal problem-solving rules. This brings up our second commitment.

Problem-based experiential learning is emerging as a alternative approach within medical education (Barrows and Tamblyn, 1980) and business education (Kolb, 1984). We have learned from these traditions as well as from our work on strategic simulations that, in the long-term, inferencing is best learned through a series of experiments and associated problem-solving activities (Jungck, 1982; Jungck and Calley, 1985).

In many ways, problem-based experiential learning is nothing new because most scientists learn to do science in this way. However, most students who take introductory science courses do not become scientists and therefore do not have this experience. At most, they get a simplified, sanitized, rational reconstruction of science from a textbook while sitting in large lecture halls. This is not science but a rhetoric of conclusions.

What we are trying to do is to offer these students some experience at conducting genetics experiments, generating and testing hypotheses, and developing some understanding of genetics problem solving. The MENDEL system is one way to make this feasible. We realize that some aspects of problem-based learning and experiential learning cannot be simulated in our environment. For example, we do not include the initial abstraction stages of identifying traits and variations of organisms. How important perceptual discernment and abstraction are for genetics understanding remains an open research question.

Our version of problem-based experiential learning provides students with significant and realistic transmission genetics problems to solve. Our environment then provides students with computational tools, graphical representation of genetics concepts, and tutorial advice that encourages conceptualization about the underlying genetics mechanisms. It does so by letting students pose questions, make conjectures (i.e., enter hypotheses), and learn from their experience (i.e., perform crosses and use computational tools). Conceptualization here refers to both genetics-specific content and the process of scientific inquiry. This brings us to our next commitment.

As mentioned earlier, students are quite willing to stop at the rule-following level of problem solving. However, we, as educators, have an obligation to help our students reach their full potential. In science education, this means helping students reach a certain level of scientific understanding and scientific inquiry. We try to achieve this within the constraints of the MENDEL system by helping students construct a model of the domain they encounter on the computer and, out of that experience, construct problem-solving rules for future sessions. Rule-based reasoning is aided by the NEXT-STEP command where students are presented with the heuristic problem-solving rules that the SOLVER uses. These commands present rules in the exact problem-solving situation to which they apply. Thus, students can actively engage in applying the rule. Model-based reasoning, on the other hand, is aided by the JUSTIFY command as well as by many of the graphical forms of problem representation that unfold as the computer problem is iteratively solved. For instance, the LINKAGE module of the LIBRARIAN will be used to explain rules for generating and testing linkage hypotheses in model-based terms.

A key aspect of model-based reasoning is that the solution to a problem is actually the hypothesis in the mind of the student throughout the problem-solving process. Students, therefore, have to develop problem-solving strategies that exercise their critical and judgmental faculties and not just their technical (i.e., rule-following) abilities. Students also have to be sensitive to the data that emerge in their experiments. Model-based reasoning becomes the link between theory-directed and data-directed problem solving and becomes the key to understanding the empirical associations of problem-solving rules.

Problem solving with understanding, problem-based experiential learning, and model-based reasoning do not occur in isolation. They are not merely individual psychological processes in the mind of the learner but are inherently social processes. We therefore believe that this type of learning requires collaboration with others. We try to structure our problem-solving environment and our tutorial advice so that collaboration between students and tutors can take place. Furthermore, we have made our simulation of a genetics laboratory complex enough so that robust experimentation takes place (i.e., the GENERATOR is *not* a toy universe) and so that heuristic approaches to solving problems take precedence over algorithmic approaches (e.g., where multiple conceptualizations and mixed data-driven and theory-driven approaches can take place). This is fertile ground for collaboration.

Our final commitment deals with how we believe computers should be used in science education. We believe that computers should be used for strategic simulations in order to supplement science education. Strategic simulations remain a rational reconstruction of scientific experiments, no matter how complex they become. Strategic simulations, therefore, never replace actual experimentation. We also believe that computer tutors should play an advisory rather than a supervisory role. Computer tutoring is a new type of tutoring rather than a substitute for human tutorial engagement. Human tutoring still remains central for science education. Our final commitment, therefore, translates into a vision of the computer as a science teacher's assistant.

ACKNOWLEDGMENTS

We gratefully acknowledge the support of Dean John Palmer and the School of Education, University of Wisconsin–Madison (UW–Madison). We also want to thank the following people who have made significant contributions to the success of our project: Mark Allman, Rich Maclin, and Deborah Servi. Special thanks go to Judith Van Kirk and Gary Price for many helpful comments on earlier drafts of this chapter.

REFERENCES

Albright, W., *Problem-solving strategies used by university students to solve realistic genetics problems*, master's thesis, University of Wisconsin–Madison, 1987.

Anderson, J. R., C. F. Boyle, R. Farrelli and B. J. Reiser, "Cognitive principles in the design of computer tutors," in *Proceedings of the Sixth Annual Conference of the Cognitive Science Society*. Boulder, CO, 1984.

Anderson, J. R., C. F. Boyle, and B. J. Reiser, "Intelligent tutoring systems," *Science*, 228:456–462, 1985.

Barrows, H. S., and R. M. Tamblyn, *Problem-based learning: An approach to medical education*, New York: Springer Publishing, 1980.

BioQUEST NOTES, Vol. 1, No. 1, Beloit College, WI: Department of Biology, 1989a.

BioQUEST NOTES, Vol. 1, No. 2, Beloit College, WI: Department of Biology, 1989b.

BioQUEST NOTES, Vol. 2, No. 1, Beloit College, WI: Department of Biology, 1990.

Brown, J. S., and R. Burton, "Diagnostic models for procedural bugs in basic mathematical skills," *Cognitive Science,* 2(2):155–192, 1978.

Brown, J. S., A. Collins, and G. Harris, "Artificial intelligence and learning strategies," in H. F. O'Neil, Jr. (ed.), *Learning strategies,* New York: Academic Press, 1978.

Clancey, W. J., and R. Letsinger, "NEOMYCIN: Reconfiguring a rule-based expert system for application to teaching," in W. J. Clancey and E. H. Shortliffe (eds.), *Readings in medical artificial intelligence: The first decade,* Reading, MA: Addison-Wesley, 1984.

Collins, A., *Strategic knowledge required for desired performance in solving transmission genetics problems,* Ph.D. dissertation, University of Wisconsin–Madison, 1986.

Collins, A., and J. H. Stewart, "Description of the strategic knowledge of experts solving realistic genetics problems." Project MENDEL, Technical Report #1, 1987.

DiSessa, A. A. "Unlearning Aristotelian physics: A study on knowledge-based learning," *Cognitive Science,* 6(1):37–75, 1982.

Hackling, M., and D. Treagust, "Research data necessary for meaningful review of grade ten high school genetics curricula," *Journal of Research in Science Teaching,* 21:197–209, 1984.

Hewson, P. "A conceptual change approach to learning science," *European Journal of Science Education,* 3:383–396, 1979.

Jungck, J. R., "Strategic simulations: Experiencing research-like problem-solving in computer biology modules," in L. R. Meeth and D. S. Gregory (eds.), *Dunedin, Florida Studies in Higher Education,* 133–134, 1982.

Jungck, J. R., and J. N. Calley, "Strategic simulations and post-Socratic pedagogy: Constructing computer software to develop long-term inference through experimental inquiry," *The American Biology Teacher,* 47(1):11–15, 1985.

Jungck, J. R., and J. N. Calley, *GENETICS: Strategic simulations in Mendelian genetics,* Wentworth, NH: COMpress, 1986.

Kolb, D. A. *Experiential learning,* Englewood Cliffs, NJ: Prentice-Hall, 1984.

Koton, P. A. "Empirical and model-based reasoning in expert systems," in *Proceedings of the 9th International Conference on Artificial Intelligence, Vol. 1,* 297–298, Aug. 18–23, 1985, Los Angeles, CA.

Larkin, J. H., J. McDermott, D. P. Simon, and H. A. Simon, "Expert and novice performance in solving physics problems," *Science,* 208:1335–1342, 1980.

Lipson, J., C. V. Bunderson, B. Baillo, J. B. Olsen, and K. M. Fisher, "Evaluation of an intelligent videodisc for developmental biology instruction," *International Journal of Machine-Mediated Learning,* 1, 1983.

McCloskey, M., A. Caramazza, and B. Green, "Circular motion in the absence of external forces: Naive beliefs about the motion of objects," *Science,* 210(4474):1139–1141, 1980.

Medawar, P. B. *Pluto's Republic: Including the art of the soluble* London, Oxford University Press, 1982.

Munakata, T. "Knowledge-based systems for genetics," *International Journal of Man-Machine Studies,* 23:551–561, 1985.

National Academy of Science and National Academy of Engineering, *Science and mathematics in the schools: A report of a convocation,* Washington, DC: National Academy Press, 1982.

Peterson, N. S., and J. R. Jungck, "Problem-posing, problem-solving and persuasion in biology education," *Academic Computing,* 14–17, 48–50, March/April 1988.

Reif, F. "Understanding and teaching problem-solving in physics," in *Research on physics education: Proceedings of the First International Workshop on Physics Education,* Paris, Editions du Centre Nationale de la Recherche Scientifique, 1983.

Richer, M. H., and W. J. Clancey, "GUIDON-WATCH: A graphic interface for viewing a knowledge-based system," *I.E.E.E. CC&A,* November, 1985.

Schute, V., R. Glaser, and L. Resnick, "Discovering and learning to discover: an intelligent microworld for economics," presented at the annual meeting of the American Educational Research Association, San Francisco, CA, April 1986.

Schwab, J. The teaching of science as enquiry. In J. Schwab and P. Brandwein (eds.), *The teaching of science,* Cambridge, MA: Harvard University Press, 1960.

Slack, S., and J. Stewart, "High school student's problem-solving performance on realistic genetics problems." *Journal of Research in Science Teaching,* 27(1):55–67, 1990.

Sleeman, D., and J. S. Brown (eds.), *Intelligent tutoring systems,* New York: Academic Press, 1982.

Steels, L., and J. A. Campbell, (eds.), *Process in artificial intelligence,* New York: Wiley, 1985.

Stewart, J., "Student problem-solving in high-school genetics," *Science Education*, 67(4):523–540, 1983.

Stewart, J., and M. Dale, "Solutions to genetics problems: Are they the same as correct answers?" *Australian Science Teachers*, 27(3):59–64, 1981.

Stewart, J., and M. Dale, "High school students' understanding of chromosome/gene behavior during meiosis," *Science Education*, 73:501–521, 1989.

Stewart, J., and R. Hafner, "Extending the conception of problem in problem-solving research," *Science Education*, 75(1):105–120, 1991.

Strike, K., G. Posner, P. Hewson, and W. Gertzog, "Accommodation of a scientific conception: Toward a theory of conceptual change," *Science Education*, 66:211–227, 1982.

Tennyson, R. "Artificial intelligence methods in computer-based instructional design," *Journal of Instructional Development*, 7(3):17–22, 1984.

Thompson, N., and J. Stewart, "Secondary school genetics instruction: Making problem-solving explicit and meaningful," *Journal of Biological Education*, 19(1):53–62, 1985.

Volpe, E. P. "The shame of science education," *American Zoologist*, 24:433–443, 1984.

Wolfe, B., and D. D. McDonald, "Building a computer tutor: Design issues." *Computer*, 61–73, Sept., 1984.

Ziman, J. M., *Public knowledge: An essay concerning the social dimension of science*, Cambridge, England: Cambridge University Press, 1968.

Index